Carol Kaplan

THE BEST OF
INTERWEAVE knits

OUR FAVORITE DESIGNS FROM THE FIRST TEN YEARS

edited by ANN BUDD with an introduction by PAM ALLEN

INTERWEAVE PRESS.

Photography, Chris Hartlove, except as noted
Cover and interior design, Paulette Livers

Text © 2007 Interweave Press LLC
Photography © Interweave Press LLC
Illustrations © Interweave Press LLC

Interweave Press LLC
201 East Fourth Street
Loveland, CO 80537-5655 USA
interweave.com

Printed in China by Asia Pacific Offset
Library of Congress Cataloging-in-Publication Data

The best of Interweave knits : our favorite designs from
the first 10 years / Ann Budd, editor.
    p. cm.
 Includes index.
 ISBN-13: 978-1-59668-033-3 (pbk.)
 1. Knitting--Patterns. I. Budd, Ann, 1956- II. Interweave
Press.
 TT820.B588 2007
 746.43'2041--dc22
                        2007015108

10 9 8 7 6 5 4 3 2 1

Joe Coca

For every knitter who has submitted a design for Interweave Knits

contents

introduction

As editor in chief of *Interweave Knits* magazine, I've spent a lot of time poring over design submissions. No matter which projects we finally choose for the magazine, it's a pleasure to see that the creative imagination is always at work in the sketches and swatches that pile up on the table. Whether or not I'm taken with a sweater idea, I'm always interested to see how each designer approaches knitwear design. Sometimes a designer's focal point is a stitch pattern—perhaps it's used all over or only in a particular area of a sweater. Sometimes a designer combines different patterns or adds colors with a happy result—or a not-so-happy result.

A design might use traditional color-work patterns in a fresh way. Or the motifs might be nontraditional: The designer has used the knitted grid to create something entirely new. A design might be based on silhouette or on interesting details—a jacket designed with princess seams or an otherwise plain pullover with a stunning asymmetric collar. Occasionally, a designer has begun with an unusual yarn and found exactly the right style to showcase that yarn's beauty. And from time to time, a designer's combination, though imaginative, doesn't quite come off: Proportions don't work, colors jar, or too many elements compete for attention.

The best moments, however, come when the contents of a submission envelope spill out and elicit a collective "Ahhh!" from the staff. This involuntary response is magical; we gather around and admire the for-the-moment perfect knitted project, one in which all the elements come together in knitted harmony. The stitches, yarn, colors, and proportions simply work!

For *The Best of Interweave Knits*, we've culled as many "Ahhh" projects from past issues as would fit into these pages. We've chosen projects that showcase knitted color work, such as Marta McCall's Weekend Getaway Satchel and Ron Schweitzer's Water Garden Fair Isle pullover; projects that thoughtfully marry stitch pattern to silhouette, such as Norah Gaughan's Cabaret Raglan and Véronik Avery's Threepenny Pullover; breathtaking lace projects, such as Miriam Felton's Icarus Shawl and Faina Letoutchaia's Forest Path Stole; simple sweaters with details that make all the difference, such as Kate Gilbert's Union Square Market Pullover and Barbara Venishnick's Burma Rings—and projects that are just plain good looking and fun to knit, such as Lana Hames's Stripes Go Round T-Top and Debbie Bliss's Simply Marilyn.

We've also added eleven of our regular Beyond the Basics technique columns—to add to your repertoire of knitting skills. We hope that this collection of some of our favorite knitted projects and articles will bring you hours of knitting pleasure.

— *Pam Allen*

Marcel's Sweater

Véronik Avery

The idea for this fitted sweater came to Véronik Avery while her husband, Marcel, an actor, was playing a "voyageur" (a fur trader who traveled by canoe through the Canadian wilderness in the early 1800s) for a Canadian TV program. The arrowhead pattern on the Indian belts typically worn by voyageurs inspired Véronik to use a knitted version in a simple pullover design. Véronik twisted the stitches in the tilting lines to make them more distinct and allowed the arrowheads to form soft points at the neck and sleeve edges. For meticulously neat hems, she used a tubular cast-on and a sewn bind-off.

Finished Size
32½ (36, 39½, 43, 46½, 50)" (82.5 [91.5, 100.5, 109, 118, 127] cm) bust/chest circumference. Sweater shown measures 36" (91.5 cm).

Yarn
DK weight (#3 Light).
Shown here: Jo Sharp Classic DK Wool (100% wool; 107 yd [98 m]/50 g): #009 lilium, 14 (15, 17, 19, 21, 22) balls.

Needles
Size 5 (3.75 mm): straight and set of 4 double-pointed (dpn). Adjust needle size if necessary to obtain the correct gauge.

Notions
Tapestry needle; stitch holders.

Gauge
24 sts and 32 rows = 4" (10 cm) in St st; 31½ sts and 32 rows = 4" (10 cm) in arrowhead pattern, blocked.

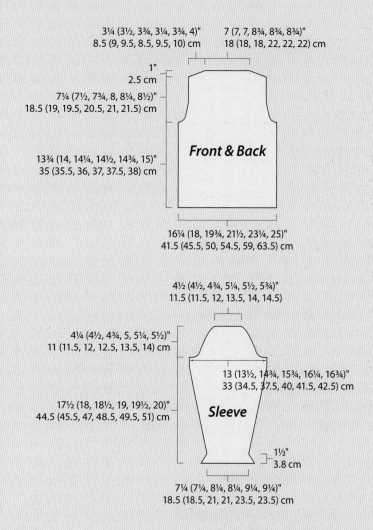

3¼ (3½, 3¾, 3¼, 3¾, 4)"
8.5 (9, 9.5, 8.5, 9.5, 10) cm

7 (7, 7, 8¾, 8¾, 8¾)"
18 (18, 18, 22, 22, 22) cm

1"
2.5 cm

7¼ (7½, 7¾, 8, 8¼, 8½)"
18.5 (19, 19.5, 20.5, 21, 21.5) cm

Front & Back

13¾ (14, 14¼, 14½, 14¾, 15)"
35 (35.5, 36, 37, 37.5, 38) cm

16¼ (18, 19¾, 21½, 23¼, 25)"
41.5 (45.5, 50, 54.5, 59, 63.5) cm

4½ (4½, 4¾, 5¼, 5½, 5¾)"
11.5 (11.5, 12, 13.5, 14, 14.5)

4¼ (4½, 4¾, 5, 5¼, 5½)"
11 (11.5, 12, 12.5, 13.5, 14) cm

13 (13½, 14¾, 15¾, 16¼, 16¾)"
33 (34.5, 37.5, 40, 41.5, 42.5) cm

Sleeve

17½ (18, 18½, 19, 19½, 20)"
44.5 (45.5, 47, 48.5, 49.5, 51) cm

1½"
3.8 cm

7¼ (7¼, 8¼, 8¼, 9¼, 9¼)"
18.5 (18.5, 21, 21, 23.5, 23.5) cm

k tbl on RS; p tbl on WS

p on RS; k on WS

yo

k2tog tbl

ssk: Slip 2 sts individually kwise, replace these sts on left needle, knit them tog through their front loops.

ssp

p2tog

k yo tbl

p yo tbl

no stitch

sl 1 st onto cn and hold in front, p1, k1tbl from cn

sl 1 st onto cn and hold in back, k1tbl, p1 from cn

pattern repeat

Arrowhead A

end body 32½", 39½", 46½"; end sleeve sizes 32½", 36", 46½", 50"

end sleeve sizes 39½", 43" beg, end body sizes 36", 43", 50"

beg sleeve all sizes beg body 32½", 39½", 46½"

Arrowhead B

end body, neckband all sizes; end sleeve sizes 32½", 36", 46½", 50"

end sleeve sizes 39½", 43"

beg body, sleeve, neckband all sizes

Note: For each row where additional collar sts are worked in Arrowhead B patt, work new sts so that a and b sections alternate.

Collar

Cuff

end sleeve sizes 32½", 36", 46½", 50"

end sleeve sizes 39½", 43"

beg sleeve all sizes

Note

- In shaped areas such as sleeve and armhole shapings, when there is not a pair of stitches to cross, work the odd stitch in stockinette.

Back

Using the tubular method (see page 17), CO 128 (142, 156, 170, 184, 198) sts. *Next row:* (RS) K1 (edge st), *k1 through back loop (tbl), sl 1 with yarn in front (wyf); rep from * to last st, k1 (edge st). Rep this row once more on WS. *Next row:* (RS) K1, *k1tbl, p1; rep from * to last st, p1. Work 1 row as established, working the purl sts tbl. Keeping 1 st in St st at each edge, work Rows 1–4 of Arrowhead A chart over center 126 (140, 154, 168, 182, 196) sts until piece measures 13¾ (14, 14¼, 14½, 14¾, 15)" (35 [35.5, 36, 37, 37.5, 38] cm), ending with a WS row.

Shape Armholes

Cont in patt, BO 4 (4, 5, 5, 5, 5) sts at beg of next row, then BO 3 (3, 4, 4, 4, 4) sts at beg of next (WS) row, then BO 4 (4, 5, 5, 5, 5) sts at beg of next 2 rows—113 (127, 137, 151, 165, 179) sts rem. Dec 1 st each end of needle every RS row 2 (4, 6, 8, 10, 12) times, then every 4 rows 2 (5, 6, 8, 9, 11) times—105 (109, 113, 119, 127, 133) sts rem. Cont even in patt until armholes measure about 7¼ (7½, 7¾, 8, 8¼, 8½)" (18.5 [19, 19.5, 20.5, 21, 21.5] cm), ending with Row 4 of chart.

Shape Shoulders and Beg Neck

Row 1: (RS) BO 4 (6, 8, 4, 8, 11) sts (1 st rem on right needle), work 40 (40, 40, 47, 47, 47) more sts as established, work Row 1 of Arrowhead B chart over next 14 sts, work as established to end—101 (103, 105, 115, 119, 122) sts rem.

Row 2: BO 4 (6, 8, 4, 8, 11) sts, work to end as established—97 (97, 97, 111, 111, 111) sts rem.

Row 3: BO 7 sts (1 st rem on right needle), work 26 (26, 26, 33, 33, 33) sts more as established, work Row 3 of Arrowhead B chart over next 28 sts, work as established to end—90 (90, 90, 104, 104, 104) sts rem.

Rows 4 and 6: BO 7 sts, work as established to end—83 (83, 83, 97, 97, 97) sts rem after Row 4; 69 (69, 69, 83, 83, 83) sts rem after Row 6.

Row 5: BO 7 sts (1 st rem on right needle), work 12 (12, 12, 19, 19, 19) sts more as established, work Row 1 of Arrowhead B chart over next 42 sts, work as established to end—76 (76, 76, 90, 90, 90) sts rem.

Row 7: BO 7 sts (1 st rem on right needle), work 0 (0, 0, 5, 5, 5) sts more as established, work Row 3 of Arrowhead B chart over 54 (54, 54, 56, 56, 56) sts (for 3 smallest sizes, slip st rem from BO back to left needle, then beg chart with second st), work as established to end—62 (62, 62, 76, 76, 76) sts rem.

Row 8: BO 7 sts, work as established to end—55 (55, 55, 69, 69, 69) sts rem.

For sizes 32½ (36, 39½)" only

Place rem 55 sts on holder.

For sizes 43 (46½, 50)" only

Work 2 more rows as foll:

Row 9: Beg chart with second st, work Row 1 of Arrowhead B chart across all 69 sts.

Row 10: Work all sts as established. Place sts on holder.

Front

Work as for back until armholes measure about 6¼ (6½, 6¾, 7, 7¼, 7½)" (16 [16.5, 17, 18, 18.5, 19] cm), ending with Row 4 of Arrowhead A chart—105 (109, 113, 119, 127, 133) sts rem.

Shape Neck

K45 (47, 49, 52, 56, 59), work next 14 sts according to Arrowhead B chart, work as established to end. Cont as for back, working 7 more sts on each side of initial 14 sts according to Arrowhead B chart every RS row (last collar patterning row will add only 6 sts at beg of neck and 7 sts at end of neck), until 55 (55, 55, 69, 69, 69) sts have been worked in Arrowhead B patt. *At the same time*, when armholes measure 7¼ (7½, 7¾, 8, 8¼, 8½)" (18.5 [19, 19.5, 20.5, 21, 21.5] cm), work shoulder BO as for back—55 (55, 55, 69, 69, 69) sts rem. Place sts on holder.

Sleeves

Using the tubular method, CO 74 (74, 83, 83, 92, 92) sts. *Next row:* (RS) K1 (1, 0, 0, 1, 1), *k1, sl 1 wyf; rep from * to last st, k1. *Next row:* (WS) K1, *k1, sl 1 wyf; rep from * to last 1 (1, 2, 2, 1, 1) st(s), k1 (1, 2, 2, 1, 1). Keeping 1 edge st in St st at each end of needle, work Rows 1–4 of Cuff chart (working decs as indicated on chart), then work Rows 1–4 of Arrowhead B chart 2 times—58 (58, 65, 65, 72, 72) sts rem. *Set up patt:* Work Row 1 of Arrowhead A chart to last st, M1 kwise (see page 52), k1—59 (59, 66, 66, 73, 73) sts. Work 1 (WS) row even.

Next row: K1, M1 pwise (see page 53), work Row 3 of Arrowhead A chart, k1, M1 pwise, k1—61 (61, 68, 68, 75, 75) sts. Cont in patt, inc 1 st each end of needle in this manner every 8 rows 5 (7, 5, 3, 0, 0) times, then every 6 rows 9 (4, 7, 5, 15, 13) times, then every 4 rows 7 (12, 12, 20, 12, 16) times, working new sts into patt as they become available—103 (107, 116, 124, 129, 133) sts. Cont in patt until piece measures 17½ (18, 18½, 19, 19½, 20)" (44.5 [45.5, 47, 48.5, 49.5, 51] cm) from beg, ending with a WS row.

Shape Cap

BO 8 (8, 10, 10, 10, 10) sts at beg of next 2 rows, then BO 3 sts at beg of next 4 rows, then dec 1 st each end of needle every RS row 8 (10, 11, 11, 13, 14) times—59 (59, 62, 70, 71, 73) sts rem. BO 3 sts at beg of next 8 (8, 8, 4, 4, 4) rows, then BO 4 sts at beg of next 0 (0, 0, 4, 4, 4) rows—35 (35, 38, 42, 43, 45) sts rem. Cont in patt if necessary until cap measures 4¼ (4½, 4¾, 5, 5¼, 5½)" (11 [11.5, 12, 12.5, 13.5, 14] cm). BO all sts.

Finishing

Block pieces to measurements. With yarn threaded on a tapestry needle, sew shoulder seams.

Collar

With dpn, RS facing, and beg at right shoulder seam, k55 (55, 55, 69, 69, 69) held front neck sts, pick up and knit 1 st at left shoulder seam, k55 (55, 55, 69, 69, 69) held back neck sts, pick up and knit 1 st at left shoulder seam—112 (112, 112, 140, 140, 140) sts total. Place marker (pm) and join. Working in the rnd, work Arrowhead B chart (working all rows of chart from right to left and alternating a and b sections as explained in note below chart) for 8 rnds, then work Collar chart for 4 rnds—144 (144, 144, 180, 180, 180) sts. Using the sewn method (see page 30), BO all sts.

Sew sleeve and side seams. Steam-press seams lightly. Weave in loose ends.

Basketweave Pullover

Melissa Leapman

Melissa Leapman enjoys knitting projects that blend beautiful basic yarns with simple, easily memorized stitch patterns. The sweater pieces are worked separately from the bottom up and fitted together with a square (modified drop-shoulder) armhole. The shoulders are slightly angled for a classic fit. Designed for a man, this classic pullover features a basketweave pattern and casual zip-up neck in a soft merino wool. But the clean lines, comfortable fit, and richly textured stitch pattern will appeal to women, too.

Finished Size
44 (48½, 53, 57½)" (112 [123, 134.5, 146] cm) chest circumference. Sweater shown measures 48½" (123 cm).

Yarn
Worsted weight (#4 Medium)
Shown here: Patons Classic Wool (100% wool; 223 yd [204 m]/100 g): #00252 tree bark mix, 10 (10, 11, 12) balls.
Note: This particular yarn has been discontinued.

Needles
Body and sleeves—size 7 (4.5 mm). Ribbing—size 6 (4 mm). Adjust needle size if necessary to obtain the correct gauge.

Notions
Tapestry needle; stitch holder; marker (m); 9" (23 cm) zipper; sharp-pointed sewing needle and matching thread for inserting zipper.

Gauge
22 sts and 29 rows = 4" (10 cm) in basketweave pattern on larger needles.

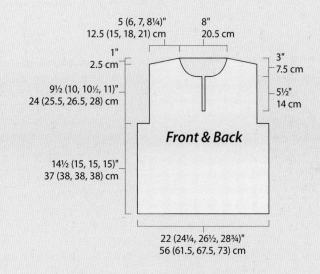

5 (6, 7, 8¼)"
12.5 (15, 18, 21) cm

8"
20.5 cm

1"
2.5 cm

3"
7.5 cm

9½ (10, 10½, 11)"
24 (25.5, 26.5, 28) cm

5½"
14 cm

Front & Back

14½ (15, 15, 15)"
37 (38, 38, 38) cm

22 (24¼, 26½, 28¾)"
56 (61.5, 67.5, 73) cm

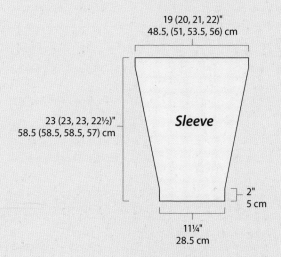

19 (20, 21, 22)"
48.5, (51, 53.5, 56) cm

23 (23, 23, 22½)"
58.5 (58.5, 58.5, 57) cm

Sleeve

2"
5 cm

11¼"
28.5 cm

Back

With smaller needles, CO 122 (134, 146, 158) sts. Work k2, p2 rib (see Stitch Guide) until piece measures 2" (5 cm) from CO, ending with a WS row. Change to larger needles. Beg with Row 1, work basketweave patt (see Stitch Guide) until piece measures about 14½ (15, 15, 15)" (37 [38, 38, 38] cm) from CO, ending with a WS row.

Shape Armholes

BO 12 sts at beg of next 2 rows—98 (110, 122, 134) sts rem. Cont even in patt until armholes measure 9½ (10, 10½, 11)" (24 [25.5, 26.5, 28] cm), ending with a WS row.

Shape Shoulders

BO 7 (8, 10, 11) sts at beg of next 6 rows, then BO 6 (9, 9, 12) sts at beg of foll 2 rows—44 sts rem. BO all sts.

Front

Work as for back until armholes measure 2 (2½, 3, 3½)" (5 [6.5, 7.5, 9] cm), ending with a WS row.

Divide for Zipper

Keeping in patt, work 48 (54, 60, 66) sts, place center 2 sts onto holder, join new yarn and work to end of row—48 (54, 60, 66) sts rem each side. Working each side separately, cont

in patt until armholes measure 7½ (8, 8½, 9)" (19 [20.5, 21.5, 23] cm), ending with a WS row.

Shape Neck

At each neck edge, BO 6 sts once, then BO 4 sts once, then BO 2 sts 2 times—34 (40, 46, 52) sts rem each side. Dec 1 st at each neck edge every row 7 times—27 (33, 39, 45) sts rem each side. Cont even, if necessary, until piece measures same as back to shoulders, ending with a WS row.

Shape Shoulders

At each armhole edge, BO 7 (8, 10, 11) sts 3 times, then BO rem 6 (9, 9, 12) sts.

Sleeves

With smaller needles, CO 62 sts. Work k2, p2 rib until piece measures 2" (5 cm) from beg, ending with a WS row. Change to larger needles. Beg with Row 1, work basketweave patt, and *at the same time* inc 1 st each end of needle every 4th row 0 (7, 13, 24) times, then every 6th row 20 (18, 14, 6) times, then every 8th row 2 (0, 0, 0) times, working new sts into patt—106 (112, 116, 122) sts; piece measures about 20¾ (20¾, 20¾, 20¼)" (52.5 [52.5, 52.5, 51.5] cm) from CO. Cont even in patt until piece measures 23 (23, 23, 22½)" (58.5 [58.5, 58.5, 57] cm) from CO, ending with a WS row. BO all sts.

Finishing

With yarn threaded on tapestry needle, sew shoulder seams.

Neckband

With smaller needles and RS facing, pick up and knit 102 sts around neckline, beg and end at top of zipper opening. Work back and forth in k2, p2 rib until band measures about 3½" (9 cm) from beg. BO all sts in patt.

Zipper Facing

With smaller needles and RS facing, pick up and knit 33 sts along left side of center front opening, k2 held sts, pick up and knit 33 sts along right side of center front opening—68 sts total. *Next row:* BO all sts kwise. Sew zipper to front opening (see Glossary, page 157). Sew sleeves into armholes. Sew sleeve and side seams. Weave in loose ends.

Beyond the Basics: Cast-Ons
based on an article by Ann Budd

All knitting begins with a foundation row of stitches, called the cast-on row. However, there are a variety of ways to cast on, each with its own advantages. Some methods require one needle, others two; some are worked with one end of yarn, others two; some add stitches to the right needle, others to the left. Choosing the right cast-on can greatly enhance the success of the knitted piece, providing such attributes as strength, elasticity, or invisibility, as desired.

Casting on at the Beginning of a Project

For best results, all cast-ons should be worked with firm, even tension. If worked too loosely, the edge will flair and look sloppy. Worked too tightly, the edge will fray and eventually break, especially along sweater cuffs and lower edges.

Long-Tail Cast-On

Also called the Continental method, this cast-on creates a firm, elastic edge that is appropriate for most projects. This method is worked with one needle and two ends of yarn, and it places stitches on the right needle. The resulting edge is smooth on one side (the side facing you as you work) and knotted or bumpy on the other (the side that faces away from you as you work). Most knitters choose to designate the smooth side as the "right" side. This cast-on is specified for the Pearl Buck Swing Jacket (page 134).

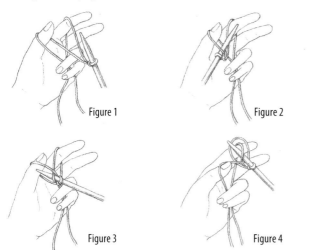

Figure 1   Figure 2

Figure 3   Figure 4

Leaving a long tail (about ½" to 1" [1.3 to 2.5 cm] for each stitch to be cast on), make a slipknot and place it on a needle held in your right hand. Place the thumb and index finger of your left hand between the yarn ends so that the working yarn is around your index finger and the tail is around your thumb, secure the ends with your other three fingers, and twist your wrist so that your palm faces upwards, making a V of yarn around your thumb and index finger (Figure 1). *Bring the needle up through the loop on your thumb (Figure 2), grab the first strand around your index finger with the needle, and bring the needle back down through the loop on your thumb (Figure 3). Drop the loop off your thumb and, placing your thumb back in the V configuration, tighten the resulting stitch on the needle (Figure 4). Repeat from * for the desired number of stitches.

Old Norwegian Cast-On

This method, also called the English cast-on, is similar to the long-tail cast-on but twists the yarn along the base of the needle to form a ropy edge that is both strong and elastic. It is ideal for edges that undergo stress such as waistbands and cuffs. Although it's not specified for any of the projects in this book, the Old Norwegian cast-on is ideal for socks worked from the leg down to the toe.

Leaving a long tail (about ½" to 1" [1.3 to 2.5 cm] for each stitch to be cast on), make a slipknot and place it on a needle held in your right hand. Place the thumb and index finger of your left hand between the yarn ends so that the working yarn is around your index finger and the tail is around your thumb, secure the ends with your other three fingers, and twist your wrist so that your palm faces upwards, making a V of yarn around your thumb and index finger (Figure 1). *Bring the needle in front of your thumb, under both yarns around your thumb, down into the center of the thumb loop, forward again, and over top of the yarn around your index finger (Figure 2), then catch this yarn and bring the needle back down through the thumb loop (Figure 3), turning your thumb slightly to make room for the needle to pass through. Drop the loop off your thumb (Figure 4) and place your thumb back in the V configuration while tightening up the resulting stitch on the needle (Figure 5). Repeat from * for the desired number of stitches.

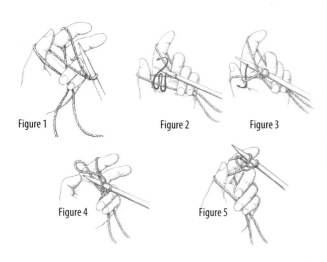

Figure 1   Figure 2   Figure 3

Figure 4   Figure 5

Casting on in the Middle of a Row

There are many occasions when stitches need to be added to those already on the needle, such as when casting on stitches to close a buttonhole or adding stitches to the edge of a piece in progress. Each method shown here can also be used to begin a project, in which case it begins with a slipknot.

Backward-Loop Cast-On

This easy method places a single loop on the right needle. The resulting smooth edge has minimal bulk and looks the same on front and back, but lacks the strength of other methods. Take care to cast on loosely so that it will not be difficult to enter the cast-on loops when you begin knitting.

Place a slipknot on a needle held in your right hand. *Loop the working yarn and place it on the needle backward so that it doesn't unwind. Repeat from * for the desired number of stitches.

Cable Cast-On

This method forms a decorative ropelike edge that is strong and fairly elastic. It adds stitches to the left needle. (To use this method at the beginning of a project, begin with a slipknot followed by a single knitted cast-on stitch.)

*Insert the right needle between first two stitches on the left needle (Figure 1). Wrap the yarn around the needle as if to knit, draw the yarn through (Figure 2), and place the new stitch onto the left needle (Figure 3). Repeat from * for the desired number of stitches, always working between the two stitches closest to the tip of left needle.

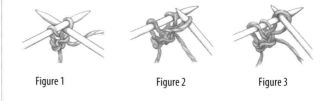

Figure 1   Figure 2   Figure 3

Knitted Cast-On

This method is similar to the cable method and adds stitches to the left needle. The resulting edge tends to be loose and flexible. This is the cast-on used for the Forest Path Stole (page 96) and Threepenny Pullover (page 24).

*With the right needle, knit into the first stitch on left needle (Figure 1) and place the new stitch onto the left needle (Figure 2). Repeat from * for the desired number of stitches, always knitting into the last stitch made.

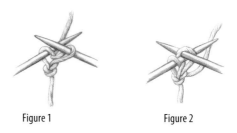

Figure 1   Figure 2

Provisional Cast-Ons

Provisional cast-ons (typically worked with waste yarn) form a secure base that can be removed to expose live stitches that can be worked later in the opposite direction. These methods are good choices when you're unsure of how you want to finish the edge of a project—you can come back later and work the edging after the body is complete. Provisional cast-ons allow two sides of a piece, such as a scarf, to be worked from the center out, so that the stitches on both ends face in the same direction. None of the projects in this book requires a provisional cast-on, but they should be part of every knitter's repertoire.

Crochet Chain Provisional Cast-On

With waste yarn and crochet hook, make a loose crochet chain of about four stitches more than you intend to cast on. With knitting needle, working yarn, and beginning two stitches from end of chain, pick up and knit one stitch through the back loop of each crochet chain stitch (Figure 1) for the desired number of stitches. Work the piece as desired, and when you're ready to work in the opposite direction, pull out the crochet chain to expose live stitches at the base of the knitting (Figure 2).

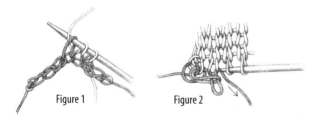

Figure 1   Figure 2

Invisible Provisional Cast-On

Also called the open or twisty-wrap cast-on, this method is worked with both waste yarn and the working yarn.

Make a loose slipknot of working yarn and place it on the right needle. Hold a length of contrasting waste yarn next to the slipknot and around your left thumb; hold the working yarn over your left index finger. *Bring the right needle forward under the waste yarn, over the working yarn, and grab a loop of working yarn (Figure 1), then bring the needle back behind the working yarn and grab a second loop (Figure 2). Repeat from * for the desired number of stitches. When you're ready to work

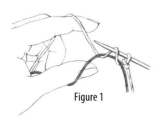 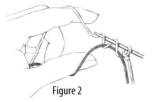

Figure 1   Figure 2

in the opposite direction, place the exposed loops on a knitting needle as you pull out the waste yarn.

Tubular Cast-On

This method, worked with waste yarn that is later removed, is ideal for setting up k1, p1 ribbing. It forms a rounded edge that is both strong and elastic. But be aware that the edge may flair undesirably if worked in bulky yarn. This cast-on is used in Marcel's Sweater (page 8).

With contrasting waste yarn, use the backward-loop method (see page 16) to cast on half the desired number of stitches. Cut off the waste yarn. Continue with the working yarn as follows.

Row 1: K1, *bring yarn to front to form a yarnover, k1 (Figure 1). Repeat from * to end of row.

Rows 2 and 4: K1, *bring yarn to front, slip 1 purlwise, bring yarn to back, k1 (Figure 2). Repeat from * to end of row.

Rows 3 and 5: *Bring yarn to front, slip 1 purlwise, bring yarn to back, k1. Repeat from * to the last stitch, then slip the last stitch.

Continue working k1, p1 rib as desired, removing the waste yarn after a few rows.

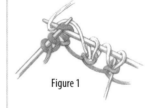 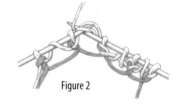

Figure 1   Figure 2

TIPS

✳ If you tend to cast on tightly, use a larger needle than suggested or use two needles held together to open the loops and make the first row easier to knit. Remove the second needle before knitting the first row.

✳ To ensure an elastic cast-on edge when using the long-tail method, stretch the stitches on the needle between cast-on stitches so that there is ⅛–¼" (3–6 mm) between stitches.

✳ To create a firmer edge, cast on stitches with the yarn doubled. You can also use smaller needles or cast on ten to twenty percent fewer stitches for a ribbing, then increase to the required number after the last row of ribbing.

✳ Leave a tail of yarn 12–16" (30.5–40.5 cm) long when casting on pieces to be seamed, then use the tail to sew the seam. To keep the tail out of the way while you're knitting, bundle it up into a butterfly.

✳ To prevent the last cast-on stitch from becoming loose and untidy, pass the tail end of yarn over the working yarn and drop it in back of the work. After working a few stitches, gently pull on the tail to tighten the edge stitch.

Salt Peanuts

Véronik Avery

Music and movies come together in this swingy cardigan, named for a 1941 jazz piece written by Dizzy Gillespie and Kenny Clarke. Véronik Avery based the silhouette on a lingerie jacket from this era, one that a glamour queen might have worn over a slinky satin nightgown. Véronik's version features a lace rib pattern along the cuffs, lower body edge, and wide-set shawl collar. Close the cardigan with an interesting ribbon or find a single spectacular button to secure the fronts together at the base of the collar.

Finished Size
34 (37½, 41½, 45, 49, 53)" (86.5 [95, 105.5, 114.5, 124.5, 134.5] cm) bust/chest circumference, fastened. Sweater shown measures 37½" (95 cm).

Yarn
Worsted weight (#4 Medium).
Shown here: Muench Bergamo (100% wool; 66 yd [60 m]/50 g): #3907 burnt orange, 15 (16, 18, 21, 23, 26) balls.
Note: This particular yarn has been discontinued.

Needles
Size 10½ (6.5 mm): straight. Adjust needle size if necessary to obtain correct gauge.

Notions
Cable needle (cn); marker (m); stitch holders; tapestry needle; about 12" (30.5 cm) ½" (1.3 cm) wide silk ribbon for tie.

Gauge
17 stitches and 25 rows = 4" (10 cm) in stockinette stitch.

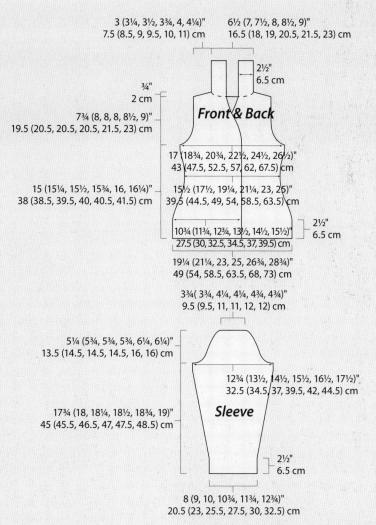

3 (3¼, 3½, 3¾, 4, 4¼)"
7.5 (8.5, 9, 9.5, 10, 11) cm

6½ (7, 7½, 8, 8½, 9)"
16.5 (18, 19, 20.5, 21.5, 23) cm

2½"
6.5 cm

¾"
2 cm

Front & Back

7¾ (8, 8, 8, 8½, 9)"
19.5 (20.5, 20.5, 20.5, 21.5, 23) cm

17 (18¾, 20¾, 22½, 24½, 26½)"
43 (47.5, 52.5, 57, 62, 67.5) cm

15 (15¼, 15½, 15¾, 16, 16¼)"
38 (38.5, 39.5, 40, 40.5, 41.5) cm

15½ (17½, 19¼, 21¼, 23, 25)"
39.5 (44.5, 49, 54, 58.5, 63.5) cm

10¾ (11¾, 12¾, 13½, 14½, 15½)"
27.5 (30, 32.5, 34.5, 37, 39.5) cm

2½"
6.5 cm

19¼ (21¼, 23, 25, 26¾, 28¾)"
49 (54, 58.5, 63.5, 68, 73) cm

3¾ (3¾, 4¼, 4¼, 4¾, 4¾)"
9.5 (9.5, 11, 11, 12, 12) cm

5¼ (5¾, 5¾, 5¾, 6¼, 6¼)"
13.5 (14.5, 14.5, 14.5, 16, 16) cm

12¾ (13½, 14½, 15½, 16½, 17½)"
32.5 (34.5, 37, 39.5, 42, 44.5) cm

Sleeve

17¾ (18, 18¼, 18½, 18¾, 19)"
45 (45.5, 46.5, 47, 47.5, 48.5) cm

2½"
6.5 cm

8 (9, 10, 10¾, 11¾, 12¾)"
20.5 (23, 25.5, 27.5, 30, 32.5) cm

Stitch Guide

K2tog Back Double Decrease
Slip 2 sts onto cn and hold cn parallel to and behind left needle. *Insert right needle into first st on left needle and first st on cn, knit these 2 sts tog; rep from * once—2 sts decreased.

K2tog Front Double Decrease
Slip 2 sts onto cn and hold cable needle parallel to and in front of the left needle. *Insert right needle into first st on cn and first st on left needle, knit these 2 sts tog; rep from * once—2 sts decreased.

Back

CO 82 (90, 98, 106, 114, 122). Work lace rib as foll:

Row 1 and all WS rows: P1, k1, *p2, k2; rep from * to last 4 sts, end p2, k1, p1.

Row 2: K1, p1, *k2tog, yo, p2; rep from * to last 4 sts, end k2tog, yo, p1, k1.

Row 4: K1, p1, *k2, p2; rep from * to last 4 sts, end k2, p1, k1.

Row 6: K1, p1, *yo, ssk, p2; rep from * to last 4 sts, end yo, ssk, p1, k1.

Row 8: Rep Row 4.

Rep Rows 1–8 one more time, then work Row 1 again.

Shape Waist

(RS) K1, ssk, knit to last 3 sts, k2tog, k1—2 sts dec'd. Work 5 rows even in St st. Rep the last 6 rows 7 more times—66 (74, 82, 90, 98, 106) sts rem. Work even until piece measures 11½ (11½, 11¾, 11¾, 12, 12¼)" (29 [29, 30, 30, 30.5, 31] cm) from beg, ending with a WS row. *Next row:* (RS) K2, M1 (see page 52), knit to last 2 sts, M1, k2—2 sts inc'd. Work 7 rows even in St st. Rep the last 8 rows one more time, then work inc row once more—72 (80, 88, 96, 104, 112) sts. Work even until piece measures 15 (15¼, 15½, 15¾, 16, 16¼)" (38 [38.5, 39.5, 40, 40.5, 41.5] cm) from beg, ending with a WS row.

Shape Armholes

BO 2 (4, 5, 5, 6, 6) sts at the beg of next 2 rows, then BO 0 (0, 0, 3, 3, 4, 4) sts at beg of foll 2 rows—68 (72, 72, 80, 84, 92) sts rem. *Next row:* (RS) K2, work k2tog back double dec (see Stitch Guide), knit to last 6 sts, work k2tog front double dec (see Stitch Guide), k2—4 sts dec'd. Work 3 rows even. Rep the last 4 rows 2 (2, 1, 2, 2, 3) more time(s)—56 (60, 64, 68, 72, 76) sts rem.

Shape Shoulders and Neck

Mark center 18 (20, 20, 20, 22, 22) sts. BO 4 (4, 4, 5, 5, 5) sts at beg of row, knit to marked sts and place 14 (15, 17, 18, 19, 21) sts just worked on holder, BO 18 (20, 20, 20, 22, 22) marked center sts, knit to end.

Left Shoulder

Row 1: (WS) BO 4 (4, 4, 5, 5, 5) sts, purl to end—14 (15, 17, 18, 19, 21) sts rem.

Row 2: BO 5 (5, 6, 7, 7, 8) sts (neck edge), knit to end—9 (10, 11, 11, 12, 13) sts rem.

Row 3: BO 4 (4, 5, 5, 5, 6) sts, purl to end—5 (6, 6, 6, 7, 7) sts rem. Knit 1 row. BO rem sts.

Right Shoulder

Place 14 (15, 17, 18, 19, 21) held sts on needle and join yarn with WS facing.

Row 1: (WS) BO 5 (5, 6, 7, 7, 8) sts (neck edge), purl to end—9 (10, 11, 11, 12, 13) sts rem.

Row 2: BO 4 (4, 5, 5, 5, 6) sts, knit to end—5 (6, 6, 6, 7, 7) sts rem. Purl 1 row. BO rem sts.

Left Front

CO 46 (50, 54, 58, 62, 66). Work lace rib as foll:

Row 1 and all WS rows: K2, *p2, k2; rep from * to last 4 sts, end p2, k1, p1.

Row 2: K1, p1, *k2tog, yo, p2; rep from * to last 4 sts, end k2tog, yo, k2.

Row 4: K1, p1, *k2, p2; rep from * to last 4 sts, end k4.

Row 6: K1, p1, *yo, ssk, p2; rep from * to last 4 sts, end yo, ssk, k2.

Row 8: Rep Row 4.

Rep Rows 1–8 once more, then work Row 1 again.

Shape waist

(RS) K1, ssk, knit to last 5 sts, p1, k2tog, yo, k2—45 (49, 53, 57, 61, 65) sts rem. Working last 5 sts in lace rib with 2 garter selvedge sts as established, work body sts in St st, and *at the same time* dec 1 st at beg of RS rows every 6 rows 7 more times—38 (42, 46, 50, 54, 58) sts rem. Work even until piece measures 11½ (11½, 11¾, 11¾, 12, 12¼)" (29 [29, 30, 30, 30.5, 31] cm), ending with a WS row. *Next row:* (RS) K2, M1, work to end—1 st inc'd. Inc 1 st at beg of RS rows in this manner every 8 rows 2 more times—41 (45, 49, 53, 57, 61) sts. Work even until piece measures 15 (15¼, 15½, 15¾, 16, 16¼)" (38 [38.5, 39.5, 40, 40.5, 41.5] cm) from beg, ending with a WS row. *Note:* Armhole shaping, neck shaping, pattern reversal for collar, and short-rows for collar are all worked at the same time; read the following instructions all the way through to the end before proceeding.

Shape Armhole

At armhole edge (beg of RS rows) BO 2 (4, 5, 5, 6, 6) sts once, then BO 0 (0, 3, 3, 4, 4) sts once—39 (41, 41, 45, 47, 51) sts rem. Work 1 WS row even. *Next row:* (RS) K2, work k2tog back double dec, work to end—2 sts dec'd. Work 3 rows even. Rep the last 4 rows 2 (2, 1, 2, 2, 3) more time(s). Work 4 rows even. *Next row:* (RS) K2, k2tog, work to end. *At the same time,* when piece measures 15¾ (16, 16¼, 16½, 16¾, 17)" (40 [40.5, 41.5, 42, 42.5, 43] cm) from beg, ending with a RS row, shape neck as foll.

Shape Neck and Reverse Collar Patt

(WS) K2, p2, k2tog, yo, place marker (pm), work to end. Cont working any required armhole shaping, swap the RS and WS of lace rib at center front so RS of patt will show when collar is folded back, and widen lace rib to 10 sts as foll:

Row 1: (RS) Work to 1 st before m, sl 1 to right needle, remove m, sl 1 back to left needle, pm (7 sts outside m), k1, p2, k4.

Row 2: K2, p2, yo, ssk, p1, remove m, p1, pm (8 sts outside m), work to end.

Row 3: Work to 1 st before m, sl 1 to right needle, remove m, sl 1 back to left needle, pm (9 sts outside m), p1, k2, p2, k4.

Row 4: [K2, p2] 2 times, k1, remove m, k1, pm (10 sts outside m), work to end.

Rows 5, 7, 9, and 11: Work to 2 sts before m, ssk, sl m, p2, k2, p2, k4.

Row 6: K2, p2, k2tog, yo, p2, k2tog, yo, work to end.

Row 8: [K2, p2] 2 times, k2.

Row 10: K2, p2, yo, ssk, p2, yo, ssk, work to end.

Row 12: Rep Row 8.

Cont lace rib patt as for Rows 5–12 on the 10 marked sts at front

edge, and cont to dec before m on RS rows as before every 4 rows 4 (5, 6, 7, 8, 9) times. At the same time, when piece measures 16¾ (17, 17¼, 17½, 17¾, 18)" (42.5 [43, 44, 44.5, 45, 45.5] cm) from beg, insert short-rows (see page 115) into collar as foll:

Short-row 1: (WS) Work 10 lace rib sts as established, turn, yo, work to end.

Short-row 2: Work 10 sts as established, p2tog tbl (the yo and neighboring st), work to end.

Rep these 2 short-rows 5 more times, placing them about

every 4 rows, and, when piece measures 21¼ (21¾, 22, 22¼, 23, 23¾)" (54 [55, 56, 56.5, 58.5, 60.5] cm), rep these 2 short-rows 4 more times, placing them about every other row. When all armhole and neck shaping has been completed, 24 (25, 26, 27, 28, 29) sts rem. Work even in patt until armhole measures 7¾ (8, 8, 8, 8½, 9)" (19.5 [20.5, 20.5, 20.5, 21.5, 23] cm) from beg, ending with a WS row.

Shape Shoulder

At armhole edge (beg of RS rows), BO 4 (4, 4, 5, 5, 5) sts once, then BO 4 (4, 5, 5, 5, 6) sts once, then BO 5 (6, 6, 6, 7, 7) sts once—11 sts rem. Working rem body sts in St st, cont lace rib as established on collar sts until collar measures about 5½" (14 cm) from last shoulder BO. Place sts on holder.

Right Front

CO 46 (50, 54, 58, 62, 66). Work lace rib as foll:
Row 1 and all WS rows: K1, p1, *p2, k2; rep from *.
Row 2: K2, *k2tog, yo, p2; rep from * to last 4 sts, end k2tog, yo, k1, p1.
Row 4: K2, *k2, p2; rep from * to last 4 sts, end k2, p1, k1.
Row 6: K2, *yo, ssk, p2; rep from * to last 4 sts, end yo, ssk, k1, p1.
Row 8: Rep Row 4.
Rep Rows 1–8 once more, then work Row 1 again.

Shape Waist

(RS) K2, k2tog, yo, p1, pm, knit to last 3 sts, k2tog, k1—45 (49, 53, 57, 61, 65) sts rem. Working last 5 sts in lace rib with 2 garter selvedge sts as established, work body sts in St st, and *at the same time* dec 1 st at end of RS rows every 6 rows 7 more times—38 (42, 46, 50, 54, 58) sts rem. Work even until piece measures 11½ (11½, 11¾, 11¾, 12, 12¼)" (29 [29, 30, 30, 30.5, 31] cm) from beg, ending with a WS row. *Next row:* (RS) Work to last 2 sts, M1, k2—1 st inc'd. Inc 1 st at end of RS rows in this manner every 8 rows 2 more times—41 (45, 49, 53, 57, 61) sts. Work even until piece measures 15 (15¼, 15½, 15¾, 16, 16¼)" (38 [38.5, 39.5, 40, 40.5, 41.5] cm) from beg, ending with a RS row. *Note:* Armhole shaping, neck shaping, pattern reversal for collar, and short-rows for collar are worked at the same time; read the following instructions all the way through to the end before proceeding.

Shape Armhole

At armhole edge (beg of WS rows), BO 2 (4, 5, 5, 6, 6) sts once, then BO 0 (0, 3, 3, 4, 4) sts once—39 (41, 41, 45, 47, 51) sts rem. *Next row:* (RS) Work to last 6 sts, work k2tog front double dec, k2—2 sts dec'd. Work 3 rows even. Rep the last 4 rows 2 (2, 1, 2, 2, 3) more time(s). Work 4 rows even. *Next row:* (RS) Work to last 4 sts, ssk, k2. *At the same time,* when piece measures 15¾ (16, 16¼, 16½, 16¾, 17)" (40 [40.5, 41.5, 42, 42.5, 43] cm) from beg, ending with a RS row, shape neck as foll.

Shape Neck and Reverse Collar Patt

(WS) Work to last 6 sts, pm, k2tog, yo, p2, k2. Cont working any required armhole shaping, swap the RS and WS of lace rib at center front so RS of patt will show when collar is folded back, and widen the lace rib to 10 sts as foll:

Row 1: (RS) K4, p2, remove m, k1, pm, work to end (7 sts outside m).
Row 2: Work to 1 st before m, sl 1 to right needle, remove m, sl 1 back to left needle, pm (8 sts outside m), p2, yo, ssk, p2, k2.
Row 3: K4, p2, k2, remove m, p1, pm, work to end (9 sts outside m).
Row 4: Work to 1 st before m, sl 1 to right needle, remove m, sl 1 back to left needle, pm (10 sts outside m), [k2, p2] 2 times, k2.
Rows 5, 7, 9, and 11: K4, p2, k2, p2, sl m, k2tog, work to end.
Row 6: Work to m, [k2tog, yo, p2] 2 times, k2.
Row 8: Work to m, [k2, p2] 2 times, k2.
Row 10: Work to m, [yo, ssk, p2] 2 times, k2.
Row 12: Rep Row 8.

Cont lace rib patt as for Rows 5–12 on the 10 marked sts at front edge, and cont to dec after m on RS rows as before every 4 rows 4 (5, 6, 7, 8, 9) times. *At the same time,* when piece measures 16¾ (17, 17¼, 17½, 17¾, 18)" (42.5 [43, 44, 44.5, 45, 45.5] cm) from beg, insert short-rows into collar as foll:

Short-row 1: (RS) Work 10 lace rib sts as established, turn, yo, work to end.
Short-row 2: Work 10 sts as established, p2tog tbl (the yo and neighboring st), work to end.

Rep these 2 short-rows 5 more times, placing them about every 4 rows, and, when piece measures 21¼ (21¾, 22, 22¼, 23, 23¾)" (54 [55, 56, 56.5, 58.5, 60.5] cm), rep these 2 short-rows 4 more times, placing them about every other row. When all armhole and neck shaping has been completed, 24 (25, 26, 27, 28, 29) sts rem. Work even in patt until armhole measures 7¾ (8, 8, 8, 8½, 9)" (19.5 [20.5, 20.5, 20.5, 21.5, 23] cm) from beg, ending with a RS row.

Shape Shoulder

At armhole edge (beg of WS rows), BO 4 (4, 4, 5, 5, 5) sts once, then BO 4 (4, 5, 5, 5, 6) sts once, then BO 5 (6, 6, 6, 7, 7) sts once—11 sts rem. Working rem body sts in St st, cont lace rib as established on collar sts until collar measures about 5½" (14 cm) from last shoulder BO. Place sts on holder.

Sleeves

CO 34 (38, 42, 46, 50, 54). Work lace rib as for back. Change to St st and inc as foll: K2, M1, knit to last 2 sts, M1, k2—2 sts inc'd. Inc 1 st each end of needle in this manner every 10 rows 9 more times—54 (58, 62, 66, 70, 74) sts. Work even until piece measures 17¾ (18, 18¼, 18½, 18¾, 19)" (45 [45.5, 46.5, 47, 47.5, 48.5] cm) from beg, ending with a WS row.

Shape Cap

BO 2 (4, 5, 5, 6, 6) sts at beg of next 2 rows, then BO 0 (0, 3, 3, 4, 4) sts at beg of foll 2 rows—50 (50, 46, 50, 50, 54) sts rem. *Next row:* (RS) K2, work k2tog back double dec, knit to last 6 sts, work k2tog front double dec, k2—4 sts dec'd. Work 3 rows even. Rep the last 4 rows 3 (3, 1, 1, 0, 0) more time(s)—34 (34, 38, 42, 46, 50) sts rem. *Next row:* K2, k2tog, knit to last 4 sts, ssk, k2—32 (32, 36, 40, 44, 48) sts rem. Work 3 rows even. Rep the last 4 rows 0 (1, 3, 3, 5, 5) more time(s)—32 (30, 30, 34, 34, 38) sts rem. Dec 1 st each end of needle as before every other row 3 (2, 2, 3, 2, 2) times—26 (26, 26, 28, 30, 34) sts rem. Work even if necessary until cap measures 4½ (5, 5, 5, 5½, 5½)" (11.5 [12.5, 12.5, 12.5, 14, 14] cm). BO 3 (3, 2, 3, 2, 3) sts at beg of next 2 rows, then BO 2 (2, 2, 2, 3, 4) sts at beg of foll 2 rows—16 (16, 18, 18, 20, 20) sts rem. BO all sts.

Finishing

Wet-block pieces to measurements and allow to air-dry. With yarn threaded on a tapestry needle, sew shoulder seams. Sew each side of collar to back neck from shoulder to center back neck, so that seam is on the outside. Adjust length of collar edges as necessary by adding or removing rows so the two collar halves meet exactly in the center, then use the three-needle method (see page 29) to BO the two collar halves tog. Sew sleeve caps into armholes. Sew sleeve and side seams. Weave in loose ends. Lightly steam seams. Insert ribbon tie into lace openings at base of collar.

Threepenny Pullover

Véronik Avery

Named for The Threepenny Opera by Kurt Weill, there's a lot to love in this sweater designed by Véronik Avery. In characteristic fashion, Véronik has taken a classic Aran design and has given it dressmaker details by using an assortment of delicate stitches, a curved hem with slide slits, and a rounded neckline edged with extensions knitted onto the tops of the sleeves. The luxurious wool/cashmere yarn is double-stranded to yield a gauge of five stitches to the inch, making this quicker to knit than you might expect.

Finished Size
36 (40, 44, 48, 52)" (91.5 [101.5, 112, 122, 132] cm) bust/chest circumference. Sweater shown measures 36" (91.5 cm).

Yarn
Sportweight (#2 Fine).
Shown here: Lana Gatto VIP (80% wool, 20% cashmere; 218 yd [199 m]/ 50 g): #1291 chocolate brown, 12 (15, 17, 19, 21) balls (used double).

Needles
Body and sleeves—size 8 (5 mm). Edgings—size 7 (4.5 mm). Adjust needle size if necessary to obtain the correct gauge.

Notions
Markers (m); cable needle (cn); stitch holders; tapestry needle.

Gauge
20 stitches and 32 rows = 4" (10 cm) in moss stitch, with yarn doubled.

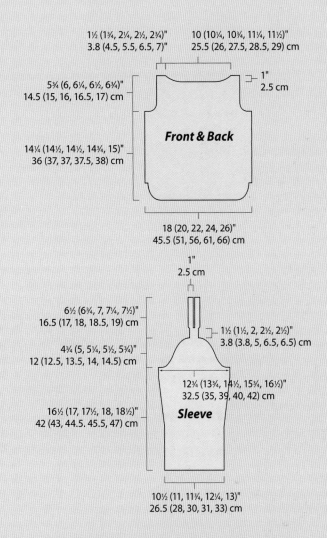

1½ (1¾, 2¼, 2½, 2¾)"
3.8 (4.5, 5.5, 6.5, 7) cm

10 (10¼, 10¾, 11¼, 11½)"
25.5 (26, 27.5, 28.5, 29) cm

5¾ (6, 6¼, 6½, 6¾)"
14.5 (15, 16, 16.5, 17) cm

1"
2.5 cm

Front & Back

14¼ (14½, 14½, 14¾, 15)"
36 (37, 37, 37.5, 38) cm

18 (20, 22, 24, 26)"
45.5 (51, 56, 61, 66) cm

1"
2.5 cm

6½ (6¾, 7, 7¼, 7½)"
16.5 (17, 18, 18.5, 19) cm

1½ (1½, 2, 2½, 2½)"
3.8 (3.8, 5, 6.5, 6.5) cm

4¾ (5, 5¼, 5½, 5¾)"
12 (12.5, 13.5, 14, 14.5) cm

12¾ (13¾, 14½, 15¾, 16½)"
32.5 (35, 39, 40, 42) cm

Sleeve

16½ (17, 17½, 18, 18½)"
42 (43, 44.5, 45.5, 47) cm

10½ (11, 11¾, 12¼, 13)"
26.5 (28, 30, 31, 33) cm

Stitch Guide

Sssk
Slip 3 sts individually as if to knit, return slipped sts to left needle and knit them together through their back loops.

Sssp
Slip 3 sts individually as if to knit, return slipped sts to left needle and purl them together through their back loops.

Cross-Stitch Cable (CSC)
Sl next 4 sts pwise, dropping extra wraps, with left needle tip, pick up the third and fourth sts on right needle, and pass them over the first and second sts, but not off the right needle. Return these 4 sts to left needle and knit them in their new order.

Smock 2
With yarn in back, insert right needle tip from front to back between second and third sts on left needle and draw up a loop, k2, then pass loop over these 2 sts and off the right needle.

Smock 3
With yarn in back, insert right needle tip from front to back between third and fourth sts on left needle and draw up a loop, k3, then pass loop over these 3 sts and off the right needle.

Smock 4
With yarn in back, insert right needle tip from front to back between fourth and fifth sts on left needle and draw up a loop, k4, then pass loop over these 4 sts and off the right needle.

1/2RC
Sl 2 sts onto cable needle and hold in back, k1, k2 from cn.

1/2LC
Sl 1 st onto cable needle and hold in front, k2, k1 from cn.

Moss Stitch (even number of sts)
Rows 1 and 2: *K1, p1; rep from *.
Rows 3 and 4: *P1, k1; rep from *.
Repeat Rows 1–4 for pattern.

Smocked Panel (worked over 22 [24, 26, 28, 30] sts)
Set-up row: (WS) K3 (4, 2, 3, 4), [p4, k2] 3 (3, 4, 4, 4) times, k1 (2, 0, 1, 2).
Row 1: (RS) P3 (4, 2, 3, 4), [smock 4, p2] 3 (3, 4, 4, 4) times, p1 (2, 0, 1, 2).
Row 2: K3 (4, 2, 3, 4), [p4, k2] 3 (3, 4, 4, 4) times, k1 (2, 0, 1, 2).
Row 3: P1, k3 (4, 2, 3, 4), [p2, k4] 2 (3, 3, 3, 4) times, p2 (1, 2, 2, 1), k3 (0, 2, 3, 0), p1 (0, 1, 1, 0).
Rows 4 and 6: K1, p3 (4, 2, 3, 4), [k2, p4] 2 (3, 3, 3, 4) times, k2 (1, 2, 2, 1), p3 (0, 2, 3, 0), k1 (0, 1, 1, 0).
Row 5: P1, smock 3 (4, 2, 3, 4), [p2, smock 4] 2 (2, 3, 3, 4) times, p2 (2, 2, 2, 1), smock 3 (4, 2, 3, 0), p1 (1, 1, 1, 0).
Row 7: P3 (4, 2, 3, 4), [k4, p2] 3 (3, 4, 4, 4) times, p1 (2, 0, 1, 2).
Row 8: Rep Row 2.
Repeat Rows 1–8 for pattern (do not repeat set-up row).

Cable Panel (worked over 22 sts)
Set-up row: (WS) P3, k1, p4, k1, p1, [p1 wrapping yarn twice around needle] 2 times, p1, k1, p4, k1, p3.
Row 1: (RS) Sl 1 wyb (see Notes), k2, p1, k4, p1, CSC (see Stitch Guide), p1, k4, p1, k2, sl 1 wyb.
Row 2: Sl 1 wyf, p2, k1, p1, [p1 wrapping yarn twice around needle] 2 times, p1, k1, p4, k1, p1, [p1 wrapping yarn twice around needle] 2 times, p1, k1, p2, sl 1 wyf.
Row 3: 1/2LC, p1, CSC, p1, k4, p1, CSC, p1, 1/2RC.
Row 4: P3, k1, p4, k1, p1, [p1 wrapping yarn twice around needle] 2 times, p1, k1, p4, k1, p3.
Repeat Rows 1–4 for pattern (do not repeat set-up row).

Notes
- When shaping over moss stitch, work decreases as follows: *Beg of row:* Work 2 sts in established patt; if a knit st foll, k3tog, if a purl st foll, sssp (see Stitch Guide). *End of row:* Work to last 5 sts; if a knit st foll, sssk (see Stitch Guide), if a purl st foll, p3tog; work rem 2 sts in established patt.
- All slipped stitches are slipped as if to purl (pwise) unless otherwise instructed; directions will indicate whether to slip with yarn in back (wyb) or with yarn in front (wyf).

Back
With two strands of yarn held tog and larger needles, CO 66 (68, 70, 72, 74) sts. Establish patts on next row as foll: (WS)

Work set-up row of cable panel over 22 sts, place marker (pm), work set-up row of smocked panel over 22 (24, 26, 28, 30) sts, pm, work set-up row of cable panel over 22 sts. *Next row:* (RS) Using the knitted method (see page 16), CO 4 sts, work CO sts in moss st (see Stitch Guide), pm, work Row 1 of cable panel over 22 sts, slip marker (sl m), work Row 1 of smocked panel over 22 (24, 26, 28, 30) sts, sl m, work Row 1 of cable panel over 22 sts—70 (72, 74, 76, 78) sts. *Next row:* (WS) Using the knitted method, CO 4 sts, work CO sts in moss st, pm, work Row 2 of established patts over center 66 (68, 70, 72, 74) sts, work 4 sts moss st—74 (76, 78, 80, 82) sts. Cont in patts as established, and *at the same time* CO 4 sts at beg of next 6 (8, 10, 12, 14) rows, working CO sts in moss st—98 (108, 118, 128, 138) sts. Work even for 18 rows. CO 4 sts at beg of next 2 rows for top of side slits, working CO sts in moss st—106 (116, 126, 136, 146) sts. Work even until piece measures 14¼ (14½, 14½, 14¾, 15)" (36 [37, 37, 37.5, 38] cm) from beg, ending with a WS row.

Shape Armholes

Cont in patt, BO 6 (7, 7, 8, 8) sts at beg of next 2 rows—94 (102, 112, 120, 130) sts rem. Dec 2 sts in moss st (see Notes) each end of needle every 4th row 2 (3, 4, 5, 6) times, then every 6th row once—82 (86, 92, 96, 102) sts rem. Cont even until armholes measure 4¾ (5, 5¼, 5½, 5¾)" (12 [12.5, 13.5, 14, 14.5] cm), ending with a WS row.

Shape Neck

Work 26 (27, 29, 30, 32) sts in patt, join new yarn, BO 30 (32, 34, 36, 38) sts, work in patt to end—26 (27, 29, 30, 32) sts at each side. Working each side separately, BO 5 sts at each neck edge 3 times, then BO 3 sts once—8 (9, 11, 12, 14) sts rem each side. Work even until armholes measure 5¾ (6, 6¼, 6½, 6¾)" (14.5 [15, 16, 16.5, 17] cm). BO all sts.

Front

Work as for back.

Sleeves

With two strands of yarn held tog and larger needles, CO 55 (57, 61, 63, 67) sts.

Set-up row: (WS) [K1, p1] 12 (12, 13, 14, 15) times, k0 (1, 1, 0, 0), pm, p3, k1, p3, pm, p0 (1, 1, 0, 0), [k1, p1] 12 (12, 13, 14, 15) times.

Row 1: (RS) [K1, p1] 12 (12, 13, 14, 15) times, k0 (1, 1, 0, 0), sl m, k2, sl 1 with yarn in back (wyb), p1, sl 1 wyb, k2, sl m, p0 (1, 1, 0, 0), [k1, p1] 12 (12, 13, 14, 15) times.

Row 2: [P1, k1] 12 (12, 13, 14, 15) times, p0 (1, 1, 0, 0), sl m, p2, sl 1 with yarn in front (wyf), k1, sl 1 wyf, p2, sl m, k0 (1, 1, 0, 0), [p1, k1] 12 (12, 13, 14, 15) times.

Row 3: [P1, k1] 12 (12, 13, 14, 15) times, p0 (1, 1, 0, 0), sl m, 1/2RC, p1, 1/2LC, sl m, k0 (1, 1, 0, 0), [p1, k1] 12 (12, 13, 14, 15) times.

Row 4: [K1, p1] 12 (12, 13, 14, 15) times, k0 (1, 1, 0, 0), sl m, p3, k1, p3, sl m, p0 (1, 1, 0, 0), [k1, p1] 12 (12, 13, 14, 15) times.

Rep the last 4 rows 13 (13, 14, 14, 15) more times—56 (56, 60, 60, 64) patt rows, not including set-up row. Cont in patt, inc 1 st each end of needle on next row, then every foll 14 (10,

10, 8, 8)th row 4 (6, 6, 8, 8) more times, working inc'd sts in moss st—65 (71, 75, 81, 85) sts. Cont even in patt until piece measures 16½ (17, 17½, 18, 18½)" (42 [43, 44.5, 45.5, 47] cm) from beg, ending with a WS row.

Shape Cap

Cont in patt, BO 6 (7, 7, 8, 8) at beg of next 2 rows—53 (57, 61, 65, 69) sts rem. Dec 2 sts in moss st each end of needle

every 4th row 3 (4, 4, 5, 5) times, then every 6th row 3 (2, 3, 2, 3) times, then every 4th row 1 (2, 1, 2, 1) time(s)—25 (25, 29, 29, 33) sts rem. BO 3 (3, 4, 4, 5) sts at beg of next 2 rows, then BO 5 (5, 6, 6, 7) sts at beg of foll 2 rows—9 sts rem; cap measures about 4¾ (5, 5¼, 5½, 5¾)" (12 [12.5, 13.5, 14, 14.5] cm).

Shoulder Strap

Change to smaller needles. Working 1 st at each side in St st, cont center 7 sts in established cable patt until piece measures about 1½ (1½, 2, 2½, 2½)" (3.8 [3.8, 5, 6.5, 6.5] cm) from last sleeve cap BO, ending with a WS row. *Next row:* Work 4 sts in patt, (k1, yo, k1) all in center st, work in patt to end—11 sts. *Next row:* Work 4 sts in patt, k3, work 4 sts in patt. *Next row:* Work 5 sts in patt, knit into the front and back of the next st (k1f&b), work 5 sts in patt—12 sts. Place first 6 sts onto holder to work later for second strap—6 sts rem. Cont even in patt, maintaining established St st selvedge st and working 2 sts at other selvedge in garter st until strap measures about 6½ (6¾, 7, 7¼, 7½)" (16.5 [17, 18, 18.5, 19] cm) from last sleeve cap BO. Place sts on holder. Return held sts for second strap to needle and rejoin yarn with WS facing. Work as for first strap, reversing the placement of the selvedge sts by maintaining the established St st selvedge st, and working the 2 sts at the other selvedge in garter st.

Wrist and Bottom Bands

Wristband Right Half *(make 2)*

With two strands of yarn held tog and smaller needles, CO 6 sts.

Set-up row: (WS) P4, k2.
Row 1: (RS) K2, sl 1 wyb, k3.
Row 2: P3, sl 1 wyf, k2.
Row 3: K2, 1/2LC, k1.
Row 4: P4, k2.
Rep Rows 1–4 until piece measures about 5½ (5¾, 6, 6¼, 6¾)" (14 [14.5, 15, 16, 17] cm) from beg. Place sts on holder and set aside.

Wristband Left Half *(make 2)*

With two strands of yarn held tog and smaller needles, CO 6 sts.

Set-up row: (WS) K2, p4.
Row 1: (RS) K3, sl 1 wyb, k2.
Row 2: K2, sl 1 wyf, p3.

Row 3: K1, 1/2RC, k2.
Row 4: K2, p4.
Rep Rows 1–4 until piece measures same as wristband right half. Place sts on holder and set aside.

Bottom Bands

Make 2 right halves and 2 left halves as for wristbands, making each piece about 12 (13, 14, 15, 16)" (30.5 [33, 35.5, 38, 40.5] cm) long. Place sts on holders and set aside.

Finishing

Block pieces to measurements. Lay one right and one left bottom band horizontally on a table with the sts on holders meeting in the center and the garter st selvedge across the bottom. With a single strand of yarn threaded on a tapestry needle, sew the upper edge (St st selvedge) of one half of band to back, beg at side slit extension and working toward the center. Leave CO edge of band free and ease the band around the shirttail shaping, stopping just before the center back. Rep for other band, working from side slit extension to center again. Adjust band length by adding or removing rows so that bands meet exactly in the center. Using the three-needle method (see page 29), BO bands tog. Sew side seams. Sew CO edges of back bands to sts CO for side slit, centering garter edges on side seams. Attach front bottom bands in the same manner overlapping CO ends of front bands over back bands at the top of the side slits. Apply wrist bands in the same manner with the garter st edges at the bottom and sewing from sides of sleeve toward the center along the St st selvedge of band. Sew sleeve caps to front and back armholes, leaving shoulder extensions free. Sew sleeve seams.

Neckband

With single strand of yarn threaded on a tapestry needle, attach shoulder straps to neckline as for bottom edges, working from the shoulder seams toward the center of the back and front neck and adjusting the length of the bands to meet exactly in the center as before.

Weave in loose ends. Steam seams lightly.

Beyond the Basics: BIND-OFFS

based on an article by Ann Budd

Just like there are different ways to cast on stitches for the beginning of a project, there are a variety of ways to bind them off. The purpose of any bind-off is to secure the final row of knitting while producing an edge that is elastic and flexible. For best results, all bind-offs should be worked with even tension to produce an elastic edge that will stretch with the knitted fabric below it. If worked too loosely, the edge will flair and look sloppy. Worked too tightly, the edge will fray and eventually break, especially along edges that are subject to stretching such as necklines. To prevent an overly tight bind-off, use a needle one (or more) sizes larger than the one used for the body of the project. End by cutting the yarn and pulling the tail through the last stitch.

Standard Bind-Off

This is the most common, and for many knitters, the only method for binding off. Use this method for edges that will be sewn into seams or finished in some way (such as stitches being picked up and knitted).

Knit the first stitch, *knit the next stitch (2 stitches are on the right needle), insert the left needle tip into the first stitch on the right needle (Figure 1) and lift this stitch up and over the second stitch (Figure 2), and off the needle—one stitch remains on the right needle and one stitch has been bound off (Figure 3). Repeat from * for the desired number of stitches.

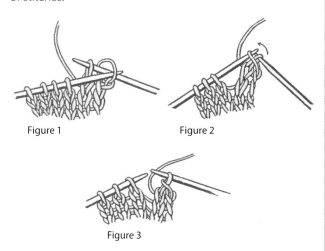

Figure 1   Figure 2

Figure 3

Suspended Bind-Off

This method is similar to the standard bind-off but produces a more elastic edge. Use this method when you want to ensure against a tight bind-off edge.

Slip one stitch, knit one stitch, *insert the left needle tip into the first stitch on the right needle and lift this stitch over the second, keeping the lifted stitch at the end of the left needle (Figure 1). Skipping the lifted stitch, knit the next stitch (Figure 2), then slip both stitches off the left needle—two stitches remain on the right needle and one stitch has been bound off (Figure 3). Repeat from * until no stitches remain on the left needle, then pass the first stitch on the right needle over the second stitch.

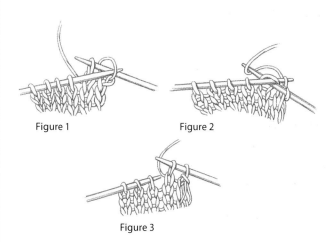

Figure 1   Figure 2

Figure 3

Three-Needle Bind-Off

This popular method joins two pieces together (such as the front and back of a garment at the shoulders) at the same time as the stitches are removed from the needles. This technique was used in the Marseilles Pullover (page 54), Salt Peanuts (page 18), Threepenny Pullover (page 24), VIP Cardigan (page 122), and Water Garden Fair Isle (page 70).

Place the stitches to be joined onto two separate needles and hold the needles parallel to each other so that the right sides of knitting face together. *Insert a third needle into the first stitch on each of the two needles (Figure 1) and knit them together as one stitch (Figure 2). Knit the next stitch on each needle the same way, then use the left needle tip to lift the first stitch over the second and off the needle (Figure 3). Repeat from * until one stitch remains on the third needle. Cut the yarn and pull tail through last stitch to secure.

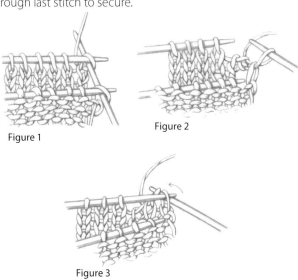

Figure 1

Figure 2

Figure 3

Sewn Bind-Off

This method, popularized by Elizabeth Zimmermann, forms an exceedingly elastic edge that has a ropy appearance, much like a purl row, and was used in the Forest Path Stole (page 96) and Marcel's Sweater (page 8). Work this bind-off with a tapestry needle.

Cut the yarn three times the width of the knitting to be bound off and thread it onto a tapestry needle. Working from right to left, *insert the tapestry needle purlwise (from right to left) through the first two stitches (Figure 1) and pull the yarn through, then bring the needle knitwise (from left to right) through first stitch (Figure 2), pull the yarn through,

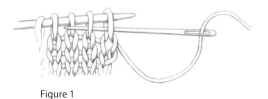

Figure 1

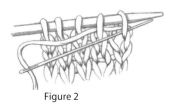

Figure 2

and slip this stitch off the knitting needle. Repeat from * until one stitch remains on the knitting needle, insert the tapestry needle purlwise through the last stitch and pull tight to secure.

Invisible Ribbed Bind-Off

Also called the sewn k1, p1, rib bind-off, this method produces a rounded edge that is extremely elastic. It follows the k1, p1 rib and is ideal for neckbands. Work this bind-off with a tapestry needle.

Cut the yarn three times the width of the knitting to be bound off and thread it onto a tapestry needle. Working from right to left, insert the tapestry needle purlwise (from right to left) through the first (knit) stitch (Figure 1) and pull the yarn through, then bring the tapestry needle behind the knit stitch, insert it knitwise (from left to right) into the second (purl) stitch (Figure 2) and pull the yarn through. *Slip the first knit stitch knitwise off the knitting needle, insert the tapestry needle purlwise into the next knit stitch (Figure 3) and pull the yarn through, then slip the first stitch purlwise off the knitting needle, then bring the tapestry needle behind the knit stitch, insert it knitwise into the next purl stitch (Figure 4), and pull the yarn through. Repeat from * until one stitch remains on the knitting needle, insert the tapestry needle purlwise through the last stitch and pull tight to secure.

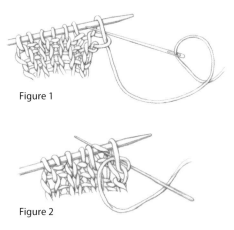

Figure 1

Figure 2

Figure 3

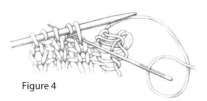

Figure 4

I-Cord Bind-Off

This method, another Zimmermann favorite, forms an I-cord band along the bind-off edge. It's attractive along necklines and the front openings of cardigans.

With right side facing and using the knitted method (see page 16), cast on 3 stitches (for cord) onto the end of the needle holding stitches to be bound off with RS facing, bring working yarn behind work. *K2, k2tog through back loops (the last cord stitch with the first stitch to be bound off; Figure 2), slip these 3 stitches back onto the left needle (Figure 3), and pull the yarn firmly from the back. Repeat from * until 3 stitches remain. Bind off the remaining stitches using the standard method (see page 29).

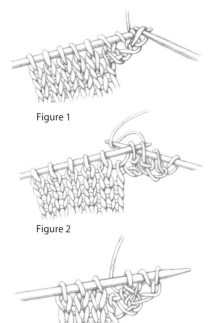

Figure 1

Figure 2

Figure 3

Crochet Bind-Off

This method is worked with a crochet hook. It forms a flexible, nonbinding edge. This bind-off is used in the Ruffle Tank (page 44).

Insert crochet hook into the first stitch on needle as if to knit. Wrap yarn around the hook (Figure 1), pull this loop through the stitch on the needle, and let the stitch drop off the needle. *Insert the hook into next stitch as if to knit, wrap yarn around the hook, and pull the loop through both the stitch on the needle and the first loop on the hook (Figure 2), letting the stitch drop off the needle. Repeat from * for the desired number of stitches.

Figure 1

Figure 2

Lace Peignoir and Simple Shell

Joan McGowan–Michael

Wear this romantic jacket over your nightie when you curl up with a cup of tea or wear it over the accompanying shell when you go out for a special occasion. Either way, the drawstring back provides a shapely silhouette with just a tug of the cord. The main lace stitch is one of the many variations of the ever-popular Old Shale pattern—and is surprisingly simple to knit. The matching shell is gently shaped at the sides for a flattering fit. If you prefer a straight shape, simply omit the side-seam shaping.

Finished Size

Peignoir—34 (39, 44, 49)" (86.5 [99, 112, 124.5] cm) bust circumference, buttoned. Peignoir shown measures 44" (112 cm). Shell—36 (38½, 41, 44, 46, 48, 50)" (91.5 [98, 104, 112, 117, 122, 127] cm) bust circumference. Shell shown measures 36" (91.5 cm).

Yarn

Fingering and worsted weight (#1 Super Fine and #4 Medium).

Shown here: Peignoir—K1C2 Douceur et Soie (70% baby mohair, 30% silk; 225 yd [205 m]/25 g): #8146 cream (MC), 6 (6, 7, 7) balls. GGH Mystik (54% cotton, 46% viscose; 120 yd [110 m]/50 g): #02 cream (CC), 2 balls. Shell—GGH Mystik #02 cream (CC), 5 (6, 6, 7, 7, 8, 8) balls.

Needles

Peignoir body and sleeves—size 8 (4.5 mm): 24" (60 cm) circular (cir). Peignoir collar—size 6 (6, 7, 7) (4 [4, 4.5, 4.5] mm). Shell body—size 6 (4 mm). Shell edging—size 5 (3.75 mm). Adjust needle sizes if necessary to obtain the correct gauge.

Notions

Markers (m); tapestry needle; four ¾" (2 cm) buttons; size G/6 (4 mm) crochet hook.

Gauge

Peignoir—15 stitches and 21 rows = 4" (10 cm) in lace columns pattern on larger needles, after blocking. Shell—20 stitches and 28 rows = 4" (10 cm) in stockinette stitch on larger needles.

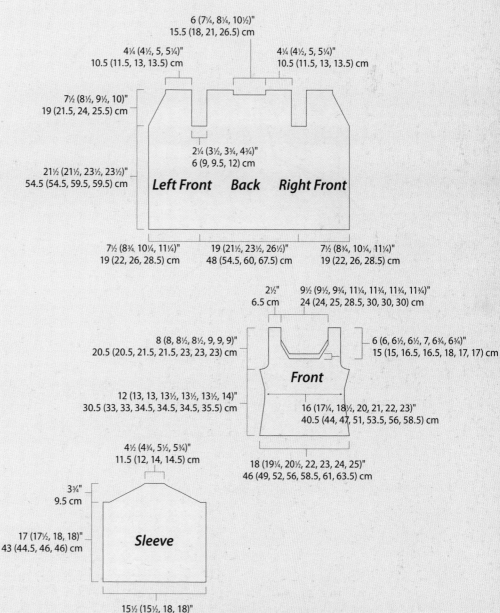

6 (7¼, 8¼, 10½)"
15.5 (18, 21, 26.5) cm

4¼ (4½, 5, 5¼)"
10.5 (11.5, 13, 13.5) cm

4¼ (4½, 5, 5¼)"
10.5 (11.5, 13, 13.5) cm

7½ (8½, 9½, 10)"
19 (21.5, 24, 25.5) cm

2¼ (3½, 3¾, 4¾)"
6 (9, 9.5, 12) cm

21½ (21½, 23½, 23½)"
54.5 (54.5, 59.5, 59.5) cm

Left Front   Back   Right Front

7½ (8¾, 10¼, 11¼)"
19 (22, 26, 28.5) cm

19 (21½, 23½, 26½)"
48 (54.5, 60, 67.5) cm

7½ (8¾, 10¼, 11¼)"
19 (22, 26, 28.5) cm

2½"
6.5 cm

9½ (9½, 9¾, 11¼, 11¾, 11¾, 11¾)"
24 (24, 25, 28.5, 30, 30, 30) cm

8 (8, 8½, 8½, 9, 9, 9)"
20.5 (20.5, 21.5, 21.5, 23, 23, 23) cm

6 (6, 6½, 6½, 7, 6¾, 6¾)"
15 (15, 16.5, 16.5, 18, 17, 17) cm

Front

12 (13, 13, 13½, 13½, 13½, 14)"
30.5 (33, 33, 34.5, 34.5, 34.5, 35.5) cm

16 (17¼, 18½, 20, 21, 22, 23)"
40.5 (44, 47, 51, 53.5, 56, 58.5) cm

18 (19¼, 20½, 22, 23, 24, 25)"
46 (49, 52, 56, 58.5, 61, 63.5) cm

4½ (4¾, 5½, 5¾)"
11.5 (12, 14, 14.5) cm

3¾"
9.5 cm

17 (17½, 18, 18)"
43 (44.5, 46, 46) cm

Sleeve

15½ (15½, 18, 18)"
39 (39, 46, 46) cm

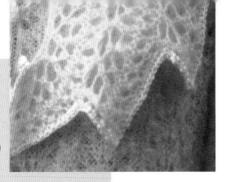

Stitch Guide

yo2

Wrap yarn around needle 2 times. Count the double wrap as 2 sts on following row.

Lace Scallops (multiple of 14 sts + 1)

Row 1: (RS) Knit.

Rows 2 and 4: Purl.

Row 3: *K1, k4tog, [yo, k1] 5 times, yo, k4tog; rep from *, end k1.

Repeat Rows 1–4 for pattern.

Lace Columns (multiple of 8 sts + 9)

Row 1: (RS) K1, yo, ssk, k3, *ssk, yo, k1, yo, k2tog, k3; rep from *, end ssk, yo, k1.

Row 2: Purl.

Repeat Rows 1–2 for pattern.

Peignoir Body

With larger needle and MC, CO 163 (191, 219, 247) sts. Do not join. Work 5 rows garter st (knit every row). *Set-up row:* (RS) K57 (71, 85, 99), place marker (pm), k49, pm, knit to end. Purl 1 row. With RS facing and beg with Row 1 of patterns, work 57 (71, 85, 99) sts in lace scallops patt, 49 sts in lace columns patt, 57 (71, 85, 99) sts in lace scallops patt. Work as established until piece measures 21½ (21½, 23½, 23½)" (54.5 [54.5, 59.5, 59.5] cm) from beg, ending with a WS row.

Shape armholes

(RS) Work 35 (39, 46, 49) sts as established for right front, BO 12 (18, 20, 26) sts for armhole, work 69 (77, 87, 97) sts as established for back, BO 12 (18, 20, 26) sts for other armhole, work rem 35 (39, 46, 49) sts as established for left front. Place sts for back and right front on holders if desired. *Note:* If there are not enough sts at each side to work a complete patt repeat, work any sts outside the patts in St st.

Left Front

Working 35 (39, 46, 49) left front sts only, work patt as established, and *at the same time*, shape neck on RS rows by dec 1 st at end of every other row 6 (7, 13, 15) times, then every 4 rows 6 (7, 5, 5) times—23 (25, 28, 29) sts rem. Cont in patt until armhole measures 7½ (8½, 9½, 10)" (19 [21.5, 24, 25.5] cm). BO all sts.

Right Front

Rejoin yarn to right front sts at armhole edge, ready to work a WS row. Work as for left front, reversing neck shaping by dec at beg of RS rows.

Back

Rejoin yarn to back sts at armhole edge, ready to work a WS row—69 (77, 87, 97) sts. Work even in patt until armholes measure 6½ (7½, 8½, 9)" (16.5 [19, 21.5, 23] cm), ending with a WS row.

Shape Neck

(RS) Work 23 (25, 28, 29) sts as established, join new yarn and firmly BO center 23 (27, 31, 39) sts, work to end as established. Working each side separately, cont in patt until armholes measure same as fronts. BO all sts.

Peignoir Sleeves

With larger needle, CO 85 (85, 99, 99) sts. Work 6 rows garter st. Change to lace scallops patt (see Stitch Guide) and work even in patt until piece measures 17 (17½, 18, 18)" (43 [44.5, 46, 46] cm) from beg, ending with a WS row.

Shape Cap

Cont in patt as established, BO 6 (5, 10, 9) sts at beg of next 2 rows—73 (75, 79, 81) sts rem. Work 6 rows even in patt. BO 4 sts at beg of every row 12 times—25 (27, 31, 33) sts rem. *Next row:* *K1, k2tog; rep from *, end k1 (0, 1, 0)—17 (18, 21, 22) sts rem. BO all sts.

Peignoir Collar *(Make 2)*

With size 6 (6, 7, 7) (4 [4, 4.5, 4.5] cm) needles and MC used double, CO 14 sts. Work 2 rows garter st.

Row 1: K5, [yo2, k2tog] 4 times, k1—18 sts.

Row 2: Yo, k2tog, (k1, p1 in yo2 of previous row), [k1, (k1, p1 in yo2 of previous row)] 3 times, k5.

Row 3: K5, [yo2, k2tog] 6 times, k1—24 sts.

Row 4: Yo, k2tog, (k1, p1 in yo2 of previous row), [k1, (k1, p1 in yo2 of previous row)] 5 times, k5.

Row 5: K5, [yo2, k2tog] 9 times, k1—33 sts.

Row 6: Yo, k2tog, [(k1, p1 in yo2 of previous row), k1] 9 times, k4.

Row 7: Knit.

Rows 8 and 10: Yo, k2tog, k31.

Row 9: K1, [yo, k2tog] 15 times, k2.

Row 11: K5, k2tog, [k2, k2tog] 6 times, k2—26 sts

Row 12: K1, [M1, BO first st by passing it over the M1, k1, BO 1 st as usual] 7 times, [k2tog, k1] 4 times, k2tog, k4—14 sts

Rep Rows 1–12 until a total of 7 points have been made. BO all sts.

Peignoir Finishing

With yarn threaded on a tapestry needle, sew shoulder seams. Sew sleeve seams. Sew sleeves into armholes. Sew the 2 collar pieces tog along their BO edges. With CC and crochet hook, work 1 row single crochet (sc; see Glossary, page 156) around entire front opening and bottom of each sleeve. Mark the beg of neck shaping on each side of front. Sew collar to neck opening bet markers with RS of collar corresponding to WS of body; RS of collar will show when collar is folded back. With CC, work 1 row sc around pointed edge of collar as for front opening. Sew buttons to left front about 2" (5 cm) apart, with the highest 1" (2.5 cm) below collar seam, and placing each button opposite an eyelet on the right front to serve as a buttonhole.

Back Tie

With CC and smaller needles, CO 4 sts. Work back and forth in St st until piece measures 36" (91.5 cm). BO all sts. Thread tie through eyelets on either side of lace column patt in back at waist level. Draw up and tie into a bow at the small of the back.

Shell Back

With larger needles, CO 90 (96, 103, 110, 115, 120, 125) sts. Work even in St st until piece measures 1½" (3.8 cm) from beg.

Shape Waist

Dec 1 st each end of needle every 4 rows 5 times—80 (86, 93, 100, 105, 110, 115) sts rem. Work 14 rows even. Inc 1 st each end of needle on next row, then every 6 rows 5 times total—90 (96, 103, 110, 115, 120, 125) sts. Work even until piece measures 12 (13, 13, 13½, 13½, 13½, 14)" (30.5 [33, 33, 34.5, 34.5, 34.5, 35.5] cm) from beg.

Shape Armholes

BO 5 (5, 7, 7, 7, 8, 9) sts at beg of next 2 rows, then BO 3 (4, 5, 5, 6, 7, 8) sts at beg of foll 2 rows—74 (78, 79, 86, 89, 90, 91) sts rem. Dec 1 st each end of needle every other row 1 (3, 3, 3, 3, 4, 4) time(s)—72 (72, 73, 80, 83, 82, 83) sts rem. Work even for 2" (5 cm) more, ending with a WS row.

Shape Neck

Work 22 sts, join new yarn and BO center 28 (28, 29, 36, 39, 38, 39) sts for neck, work to end—22 sts each side. Working each side separately, dec 1 st at neck edge every other row 10 times—12 sts rem each side. Work even until armholes measure 8 (8, 8½, 8½, 9, 9, 9)" (20.5 [20.5, 21.5, 21.5, 23, 23, 23] cm). BO all sts.

Shell Front

Work as for back until piece measures 1" (2.5 cm) above last row of armhole shaping, ending with WS row.

Shape Neck

Work neck shaping as for back.

Shell Finishing

With yarn threaded on a tapestry needle, sew side and shoulder seams.

Edging

With crochet hook, work 2 rows single crochet (sc; see Glossary, page 156) around neck and arm openings, and around entire lower edge.

Weave in loose ends. Steam lightly with cool iron.

Striped Fringe

Amanda Blair Brown

Stripes are an inexhaustible resource for design innovation, and Amanda Blair Brown has used them to create this imaginative scarf. Amanda worked each stripe in single (knit 1, purl 1) rib and connected them together using the intarsia method of crossing yarns at color changes. She deconstructed her stripe pattern on either end for long, dramatic fringe. The harmonious colors and freed stripes falling in ever-changing configurations turn a simple idea into a fluid and complex garment.

Finished Size
8½" (21.5 cm) wide and an average of 92" (233.5 cm) long, including fringe.

Yarn
Sportweight (#2 Fine).
Shown here: Gems Sport Weight (100% merino; 198 yd [181 m]/100 g): #35 mustard (gold), #43 taupe (gray), #47 terra-cotta, #55 willow (light yellow-green), #52 grape, #50 sage (blue-green) and #02 tobacco (brown), 1 skein each.

Needles
Size 2 (3 mm). Adjust needle size if necessary to obtain the correct gauge.

Notions
Tapestry needle; stitch holders.

Gauge
40 stitches and 31 rows = 4" (10 cm) in k1, p1 rib.

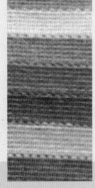

Stitch Guide
K1, P1 Rib (even number of sts)
All rows: Sl 1 pwise with yarn in back, *k1, p1; rep from * until 1 st rem, k1.

Beginning Fringe Strips

With gray, CO 12 sts. Slipping the first st of every row pwise with yarn in back, work k1, p1 rib until piece measures 21" (53.5 cm) from beg. Place sts on holder. Make 12-st fringe strips for each of the rem colors in the lengths indicated, placing each strip on a separate holder when completed: 21½" (54.5 cm) with light yellow-green, 22" (56 cm) with blue-green, 20½" (52 cm) with brown, 21" (53.5 cm) with grape, 20" (51 cm) with gold, and 20½" (52 cm) with terra-cotta.

Center Section

Place held sts onto one needle so they will be worked in the foll order on the first row: gray, light yellow-green, blue-green, brown, grape, gold, terra-cotta—84 sts total. Working sts in colors as established and twisting yarns at each color change to prevent holes, work across all sts as foll: Sl 1 pwise, *k1, p1; rep from * to last st, end k1. Rep this row in colors as established until piece measures 50" (127 cm) from joining row, ending with a row that finishes with a terra-cotta section.

Ending Fringe Strips

On the next row, cont in established rib with terra-cotta on the first 12 sts only until ending fringe strip measures 21½" (54.5 cm) from center section. BO all sts in rib. Work 12-st fringe strips in the same manner for the rem colors in the lengths indicated: 21" (53.5 cm) with gold, 21½" (54.5 cm) with grape, 22" (56 cm) with brown, 21" (53.5 cm) with blue-green, 20½" (52 cm) with light yellow-green, and 21½" (54.5 cm) with gray, respectively.

Finishing

Weave in loose ends. Block lightly if desired.

Beyond the Basics: BLOCKING

based on an article by Ann Budd

When a project comes off the needles, some stitches may look misshapen and the overall appearance may be shabby from all the handling it has endured. To fully reveal its beauty and to give it a polished and finished look, it needs to be blocked. Blocking is the process of adding moisture to a handknit to establish its permanent size and shape. It also evens out individual stitches, smoothes the fabric, and sets the drape and texture. Blocking is absolutely essential to bringing out the texture in lace and openwork patterns.

There are two general methods of blocking—steam-blocking and wet-blocking—and they differ mainly in the amount of moisture added to the fiber. The method to use depends on the fiber content of the yarn, the texture of the knitting, and the overall look you desire. In general, wavy or crimpy fibers such as wool have elastic characteristics that require less moisture than straight fibers such as cotton and linen. Whichever method you choose, you'll need the following supplies.

A **padded surface** at least 1" (2.5 cm) wider in all directions than the piece to be blocked. You can make your own blocking board by covering a piece of porous material (cork is ideal) with a foam pad, absorbent cloth, and a fabric with an even pattern (such as gingham check) that makes measurements easy to see. Some knitters use the top of their beds or a clean sheet or towel placed directly on top of padded carpet on the floor. Whatever surface you select, make sure that it is clean, sufficiently padded to accommodate pins, and out of the way of foot traffic and direct sunlight. Alternatively, you can use manufactured wooden blocking boards (also called wooly boards or blockers) that fit inside socks, gloves, or sweaters; but be aware that, with these, you cannot fine-tune the dimensions of the knitted pieces.

Rustproof pins, preferably T-pins or pins with glass heads that will not melt under the heat of an iron or bleed color onto a damp surface.

Rustproof blocking wires, although not essential, greatly simplify the task of pinning out a piece to measurements. A set of blocking wires includes a number of wires in different lengths and flexibility to accommodate different project sizes and shapes. The wires are inserted along seams of assembled garments or threaded through edge stitches of individual pieces, then pinned in place. The results are perfectly straight edges without the telltale scallops that can result from shaping a piece with pins only.

A **yardstick** to accurately measure widths and lengths. Because tape measures can stretch over time and do not always lay perfectly flat, especially when you're measuring a long distance, a yardstick is preferable.

A **schematic** or list of the desired finished dimensions (usually part of a pattern) so you know what size you're aiming for.

Steam-Blocking

Steam-blocking is the process by which moisture in the form of steam is used to set the fibers in place. It is most effective on wool and wool-blend yarns, which can be stretched and adjusted with even small amounts of moisture. Steam-blocking is most safely done by holding an iron a short distance above the knitted piece. Some sources suggest the alternative of holding the fabric over a pan of boiling water or a teakettle, but this method offers a greater chance of the fabric distorting under its own weight. For best results, use an iron set on the lowest possible steam setting and follow these simple steps. Shape the knitted piece by pinning it wrong side up on a padded surface. Hold the iron ½" to 1" (1.3 to 2.5 cm) above the fabric, allowing the steam to penetrate the fibers. Work from top to bottom of the stitches—working side to side can distort them. Allow the fabric to cool and dry away from direct sun or heat before removing the pins. Steam-blocking is relatively quick, but there are risks—in addition to the obvious danger of burns, the fabric can be scorched.

Wet-Blocking

By definition wet-blocking uses more moisture than steam-blocking and it can be used to stretch and enlarge a knitted piece (although loosely knitted pieces stretch more easily than tightly knitted ones, and any extra inches you gain in width, you may lose in length). There are three degrees of wet-blocking, depending on the amount of moisture added to the knitted fabric.

Spray-Blocking

Spray-blocking is the mildest form of wet-blocking. It works equally well for all fibers—although silks and synthetics require more wetness than wool—and it allows for total control over temperature, dampness, and finished texture because you are not restricted to the temperature and amount of steam that comes out of your iron, and you can gently pat and shape the piece with your hands while you work. Pin the piece to the desired shape right side up on a padded surface placed away from direct sun or heat. Fill a spray bottle with lukewarm tap water and spritz a fine, even mist over the piece. Use your hands to gently pat the moisture into the knitted fabric, if desired, but be careful not to flatten any textured stitches.

Wet-Wrapping

Wet-wrapping imparts moisture deeper into the fibers and is appropriate for all types of yarn, especially cotton and acrylic, which are less resilient than wool and require more moisture penetration to reshape stitches. To wet-wrap, thoroughly soak a large bath towel in water, then run it through the spin cycle of a washing machine to remove excess moisture. Place the knitted piece on top of the towel, then roll the two together jelly-roll fashion. Let the bundle sit until the yarn is completely damp, overnight if necessary. Unroll the towel, remove the knitted piece, and pin it out to the desired measurements on a padded surface away from direct sun or heat.

Immersion Blocking

Immersion imparts moisture thoroughly through the fibers and allows complete reshaping. It is appropriate for all fiber types and particularly ideal for heavily ribbed or cabled fabrics or fabrics that have taken on a biased slant during knitting. It is also the method to use after washing a handknit. Turn the piece inside out and soak it in a basin of lukewarm water for about twenty minutes, or until thoroughly wet, gently squeezing water through the piece if necessary. Drain the water from the basin and gently squeeze excess water out of the knitting (being careful not to twist or wring the fabric). Carry the piece in a bundle to the washing machine and run it through the spin cycle (or roll it in dry towels) to remove additional moisture. Shape the piece right side up on a padded surface, using pins (and blocking wires) as necessary.

TIPS

* Experiment with blocking your gauge swatch before you block an actual project.
* Do not rub, twist, or wring a handknit. Doing so may distort the stitches beyond correction.
* Before blocking, weave in all loose yarn ends—the blocking process will help secure the ends in place.
* It is preferable to block individual pieces before sewing them together. Blocking makes the sewing process easier, and the results of blocking are more consistent when you work with a single layer of fabric. You can block a garment that has been sewed together, but the results may not be as good.
* Many experts warn against blocking ribbing, which will lose its natural elasticity if blocked while stretched open. However, ribbing can be successfully blocked if you squeeze it into its most contracted state (so that all the purl stitches recede behind the knit stitches) before you apply moisture.
* Allow the blocked handknit to air-dry completely before moving it.

Simply Marilyn

Debbie Bliss

The not-so-subtle shaping and shoulder-hugging neckline on this raglan pullover are design elements that hark back to the 1950s when garments called attention to the feminine form. What's new in this sweater is the luxurious loft of the chunky cashmere/merino yarn and the single, oversize, horseshoe cable. The graceful curves of the sweater's silhouette, the wide-neck, fold-over collar (it can artfully slide over the shoulder, if you like), and the buttery soft yarn make an elegant sweater that you can dress up or down.

Finished Size
40 (42½, 45, 48, 50½)" (101.5 [108, 114.5, 122, 128.5] cm) bust/chest circumference. Sweater shown measures 40" (101.5 cm).

Yarn
Chunky weight (#5 Bulky).
  Shown here: Debbie Bliss Cashmerino Super Chunky (55% merino, 33% microfiber, 12% cashmere; 82 yd [75 m]/100 g): #C9 pink, 9 (11, 12, 13, 14) balls.

Needles
Size 10¾ (7.5 mm) and size 10½ (6.5 mm). Adjust needle size if necessary to obtain the correct gauge.

Notions
Cable needle (cn); markers (m); stitch holders; tapestry needle.

Gauge
12 stitches and 19 rows = 4" (10 cm) in stockinette stitch on larger needles; 16-stitch cable panel measures 3¼" (8.5 cm) wide.

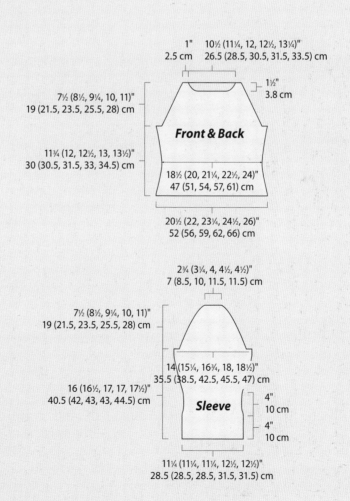

1"   10½ (11¼, 12, 12½, 13¼)"
2.5 cm   26.5 (28.5, 30.5, 31.5, 33.5) cm

7½ (8½, 9¼, 10, 11)"
19 (21.5, 23.5, 25.5, 28) cm

1½"
3.8 cm

Front & Back

11¾ (12, 12½, 13, 13½)"
30 (30.5, 31.5, 33, 34.5) cm

18½ (20, 21¼, 22½, 24)"
47 (51, 54, 57, 61) cm

20½ (22, 23¼, 24½, 26)"
52 (56, 59, 62, 66) cm

2¾ (3¼, 4, 4½, 4½)"
7 (8.5, 10, 11.5, 11.5) cm

7½ (8½, 9¼, 10, 11)"
19 (21.5, 23.5, 25.5, 28) cm

14 (15¼, 16¾, 18, 18½)"
35.5 (38.5, 42.5, 45.5, 47) cm

16 (16½, 17, 17, 17½)"
40.5 (42, 43, 43, 44.5) cm

Sleeve

4"
10 cm

4"
10 cm

11¼ (11¼, 11¼, 12½, 12½)"
28.5 (28.5, 28.5, 31.5, 31.5) cm

Stitch Guide

3/3RC
Sl 3 sts onto cn and hold in back, k3, then k3 from cn.

3/3LC
Sl 3 sts onto cn and hold in front, k3, then k3 from cn.

Cable Panel (worked over 16 sts)
Row 1: (RS) P2, k12, p2.
Row 2 and all WS Rows: K2, p12, k2.
Row 3: P2, 3/3RC, 3/3LC, p2.
Row 5: Rep Row 1.
Row 6: Rep Row 2.
Repeat Rows 1–6 for pattern.

Note

- The seams use up one stitch at each side of every garment piece. The measurements on the schematic show the actual size of the pieces including all stitches. However, the stitches lost in the seams are not counted toward the finished bust/chest size.

Back

With larger needles CO 68 (72, 76, 80, 84) sts. Set up patt as foll: (RS) Work 26 (28, 30, 32, 34) sts in St st, place marker (pm), work Row 1 of cable panel over center 16 sts, pm, work 26 (28, 30, 32, 34) sts in St st. Work 5 more rows as established, maintaining sts outside markers in St st and working center 16 sts according to cable panel patt.

Shape Waist

Keeping in patt, cont as foll: *Dec row:* (RS) K3, sl 1, k1, psso, work in patt to last 5 sts, k2tog, k3—2 sts dec'd. Work 5 rows in patt. Rep the last 6 rows once, then work dec row once more—62 (66, 70, 74, 78) sts rem. Cont even in patt until piece measures 6" (15 cm) from beg, ending with a WS row. *Inc row:* K3, M1 (see page 53), work in patt to last 3 sts, M1, k3—2 sts inc'd. Work 9 rows in patt. Rep the last 10 rows once, then work inc row once more—68 (72, 76, 80, 84) sts. Cont even in patt until piece measures 11¾ (12, 12½ , 13, 13½)" (30 [30.5, 31.5, 33, 34.5] cm) from beg, ending with a WS row.

Shape Armholes

BO 3 sts at beg of next 2 rows—62 (66, 70, 74, 78) sts rem. *Dec row:* (RS) K2, sl 1, k1, psso, work in patt to last 4 sts, k2tog, k2—2 sts dec'd. Work 3 rows even in patt. Rep the last 4 rows 8 (9, 10, 11, 12) more times—44 (46, 48, 50, 52) sts rem. Place sts on holder.

Front

Work as back until a total of 7 (8, 9, 10, 11) dec rows have been completed for armhole—48 (50, 52, 54, 56) sts rem. Work 3 rows even—piece should measure about 6 (7, 7¾, 8½, 9½)" (15 [18, 19.5, 21.5, 24] cm) from beg of armhole.

Shape Neck

Row 1: (RS) K2, sl 1, k1, psso, k7, turn—10 sts on right needle.
Row 2: BO 2 sts, purl to end—8 sts rem.
Row 3: Knit.
Row 4: Rep Row 2—6 sts rem.
Row 5: K2, sl 1, k1, psso, k2—5 sts rem.
Row 6: BO 2 sts, purl to end—3 sts rem.
Place sts on a holder.
With RS facing, place center 26 (28, 30, 32, 34) sts on another holder. Join yarn to rem 11 sts with RS facing and work as foll:
Row 1: (RS) Knit to last 4 sts, k2tog, k2—10 sts rem.
Rows 2, 4, and 6: Purl.
Row 3: BO 2 sts, knit to end—8 sts rem.
Row 5: BO 2 sts, knit to last 4 sts, k2tog, k2—5 sts rem.
Row 7: BO 2 sts, knit to end—3 sts rem.
Place sts on a holder.

Sleeves

With larger needles CO 34 (34, 34, 38, 38) sts. Establish k2, p2 rib as foll: (RS) K2, *p2, k2; rep from *. Work in patt as established (work all sts as they appear) until piece measures 4" (10 cm) from beg, ending with a WS row. Change to smaller needles. Work rib as established for 4" (10 cm) more, ending with a WS row. Change to larger needles. Beg with a RS row, work St st for 2 rows. *Inc row:* (RS) K3, M1, knit to last 3 sts, M1, k3—2 sts inc'd. Work 5 (5, 3, 3, 3) rows even in St st. Rep the last 6 (6, 4, 4, 4) rows 3 (5, 7, 7, 8) more times—42 (46, 50, 54, 56) sts rem. Cont even until piece measures 16 (16½, 17, 17, 17½)" (40.5 [42, 43, 43, 44.5] cm) from beg, ending with a WS row.

Shape Raglan

BO 3 sts at beg of next 2 rows—36 (40, 44, 48, 50) sts rem. *Dec row:* (RS) K2, sl 1, k1, psso, knit to last 4 sts, k2tog, k2—2 sts dec'd. Work 3 rows even. Dec 1 st each end of needle in

this manner every 4 rows 3 (4, 5, 6, 7) more times—28 (30, 32, 34, 34) sts rem. Dec 1 st each end of needle every other row 10 times, ending with a WS row—8 (10, 12, 14, 14) sts rem. Place sts on holder.

Finishing

With yarn threaded on a tapestry needle, sew sleeve front raglan edges to front and sew right back raglan seam.

Collar

With smaller needles and RS facing, join yarn to beg of left sleeve sts. Work left sleeve sts as k6 (8, 10, 12, 12), k2tog; work sts on first front holder as k2tog, k1; pick up and knit 8 (10, 9, 10, 9) sts along left side front neck; work held center front sts as k7 (8, 9, 9, 10), k2tog, k8 (8, 8, 10, 10), k2tog, k7 (8, 9, 9, 10); pick up and knit 8 (10, 9, 9, 9) sts along right side front neck; work sts on last front holder as k1, k2tog; work right sleeve sts as k2tog, k4 (6, 8, 10, 10), k2tog; work held back neck sts as k2tog, k14 (15, 16, 17, 18), [k2tog] 8 times,

k12 (13, 14, 15, 16)—92 (104, 110, 119, 122) sts total. *Next row:* (WS) P2, *k1, p2; rep from *. *Next row:* K2, *p1, k2; rep from *. Rep the last 2 rows until collar measures 2" (5 cm) from pick-up row, ending with a WS row. *Inc row:* (RS) K2, *p1, M1, k2; rep from *—122 (138, 146, 158, 162) sts. *Next row:* P2, *k2, p2; rep from *. *Next row:* K2, *p2, k2; rep from *. Cont in rib as established until collar measures 7" (18 cm) from first row of ribbing, ending with a WS row. BO all sts pwise on next RS row (knit side of BO will show when collar is folded down). With yarn threaded on a tapestry needle, sew left back raglan and collar seam, reversing seam allowance on rib section of collar so RS of seam will show when collar is folded down.

Sew side and sleeve seams, reversing seam allowance on lower 5" (12.5 cm) of sleeve so RS of seams will show when cuffs are folded up, if desired. Weave in loose ends.

Ruffle Tank

Leigh Radford

Inspired by an article on knitted ruffles by Pam Allen in the Summer 2002 issue of *Interweave Knits*, Leigh Radford designed a flirty linen tank with ruffle details. The front and back are worked in a slimming rib pattern. After the font is knitted, stitches are picked up for a series of ruffles along the wide center front panel. For a simple edge that doesn't distract from the ruffles, Leigh worked narrow I-cord around the neckline and added a keyhole opening with button closure at the back.

Finished Size

37½ (40½, 43½, 47, 50)" (95 [103, 110.5, 119.5, 127] cm) bust/chest circumference. Sweater shown measures 37½" (95 cm).

Yarn

Sportweight (#2 Fine).

Shown here: Euroflax Sport Weight (100% linen; 270 yd/100 g): #354 mustard, 3 (4, 4, 5, 5) skeins.

Needles

Size 4 (3.5 mm): 24" (60 cm) circular (cir) and set of 2 double-pointed (dpn). Adjust needle size if necessary to obtain the correct gauge.

Notions

Markers (m); tapestry needle; one ½" (1.3 cm) button; contrasting waste yarn.

Gauge

24½ stitches and 32 rows = 4" (10 cm) in stockinette stitch.

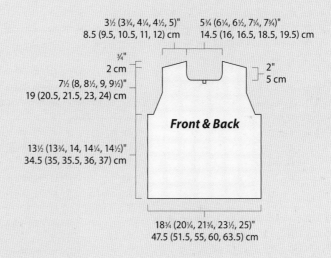

3½ (3¾, 4¼, 4½, 5)"
8.5 (9.5, 10.5, 11, 12) cm

5¾ (6¼, 6½, 7¼, 7¾)"
14.5 (16, 16.5, 18.5, 19.5) cm

¾"
2 cm

2"
5 cm

7½ (8, 8½, 9, 9½)"
19 (20.5, 21.5, 23, 24) cm

Front & Back

13½ (13¾, 14, 14¼, 14½)"
34.5 (35, 35.5, 36, 37) cm

18¾ (20¼, 21¾, 23½, 25)"
47.5 (51.5, 55, 60, 63.5) cm

Front

With cir needle, CO 115 (124, 133, 144, 153) sts. Do not join.

Row 1: Sl 1 kwise, p6 (6, 6, 7, 7), [k2, p9 (10, 11, 12, 13)] 3 times, place marker (pm), k35 (38, 41, 44, 47), pm, [p9 (10, 11, 12, 13), k2] 3 times, p6 (6, 6, 7, 7), sl 1 kwise.

Row 2: P2, k5 (5, 5, 6, 6), [p2, k9 (10, 11, 12, 13)] 3 times, sl m, p35 (38, 41, 44, 47), sl m, [k9 (10, 11, 12, 13), p2] 3 times, k5 (5, 5, 6, 6), p2.

Rep Rows 1 and 2 until piece measures 13½ (13¾, 14, 14¼, 14½)" (34.5 [35, 35.5, 36, 37] cm) from beg, ending with a WS row. Cont as for back until armholes measure 5½ (6, 6½, 7, 7½)" (14 [15, 16.5, 18, 19] cm)—77 (84, 91, 98, 105) sts rem.

Shape Neck

Cont in patt, work 23 (25, 27, 29, 31) sts, join new yarn and BO next 31 (34, 37, 40, 43) sts, work to end—23 (25, 27, 29, 31) sts each side. Working each side separately, dec 1 st at each neck edge every other row 2 times—21 (23, 25, 27, 29) sts rem each side. Cont even until armholes measure 7½ (8, 8½, 9, 9½)" (19 [20.5, 21.5, 23, 24] cm).

Shape Shoulders

Work as for back.

Back

With cir needle, CO 115 (124, 133, 144, 153) sts. Do not join.

Row 1: (RS) Sl 1 kwise, p6 (6, 6, 7, 7), *k2, p9 (10, 11, 12, 13); rep from *, end last rep p6 (6, 6, 7, 7), sl 1 kwise.

Row 2: P2, k5 (5, 5, 6, 6), *p2, k9 (10, 11, 12, 13); rep from *, end last rep k5 (5, 5, 6, 6), p2.

Rep Rows 1 and 2 until piece measures 13½ (13¾, 14, 14¼, 14½)" (34.5 [35, 35.5, 36, 37] cm) from beg, ending with a WS row.

Shape Armholes

BO 7 (7, 7, 8, 8) sts at beg of next 2 rows—101 (110, 119, 128, 137) sts rem. Dec 1 st each end of needle on next row as foll: Sl 1, p1, p2tog, work in patt to last 4 sts, p2tog, p1, sl 1—99 (108, 117, 126, 135) sts rem. *Next row:* (WS) P1, work as established to last st, p1. Dec 1 st each end of needle in this manner every other row 11 (12, 13, 14, 15) more times—77 (84, 91, 98, 105) sts rem. Cont even until armholes measure 5 (5½, 6, 6½, 7)" (12.5 [14, 15, 16.5, 18] cm), ending with a WS row.

Shape Neck

Cont in patt, work 37 (40, 44, 47, 51) sts, join new yarn and BO next 3 (4, 3, 4, 3) sts, work to end—37 (40, 44, 47, 51) sts each side. Working each side separately, cont even until armholes measure 6½ (7, 7½, 8, 8½)" (16.5 [18, 19, 20.5, 21.5] cm). On next row, BO 14 (15, 17, 18, 20) sts at each neck edge—23 (25, 27, 29, 31) sts rem each side. Dec 1 st at each neck edge every row 2 times—21 (23, 25, 27, 29) sts rem each side. Cont even until armholes measure 7½ (8, 8½, 9, 9½)" (19 [20.5, 21.5, 23, 24] cm).

Shape Shoulders

At each armhole edge, BO 7 (7, 9, 9, 10) sts once, then BO 7 (8, 8, 9, 10) sts once—7 (8, 8, 9, 9) sts rem. BO all sts.

Finishing

Weave in loose ends. Block pieces to measurements. With yarn threaded on a tapestry needle, sew shoulder seams. Sew side seams, leaving lower 2½" (6.5 cm) open.

Neckband

With dpn, CO 2 sts. With WS facing and beg at left shoulder, work attached I-cord as foll: *K1, sl 1, pick up and knit 1 st from neck edge, psso, slide sts to right tip of needle; rep

from *. Cont in this manner around neckline, picking up and knitting about 1 st for every 2 rows. At right back corner, turn as foll: K2 (do not pick up st along neck edge), slide sts to right tip of needle, k1, sl 1, pick up and knit 1 st from corner, psso, slide sts to right tip of needle, k2 (do not pick up st along neck edge)—3 rows of I-cord worked; 1 neck corner st joined. Turn left back neck corner as foll: Work attached I-cord to 3 rows below left back corner, work 3 rows of I-cord without joining to form button loop, k1, sl 1, pick up and knit 1 st from corner, psso, slide sts to right tip of needle, k2 (do not pick up along neck edge), cont working attached I-cord to end.

Sew button to back opposite loop.

Ruffles

With contrasting waste yarn, mark position of 4 ruffles along center front St st panel as foll (counting sts from right to left): along the 7 (8, 9, 10, 11)th, 14 (15, 17, 18, 20)th, 22 (24, 25, 27, 28)th, and 29 (31, 33, 35, 37)th sts. With cir needle, working yarn, RS facing, and beg at neck edge for the 2 ruffles on the left and beg at the lower body edge for the 2 ruffles on the right, pick up and knit 3 sts for every 4 rows—114 (118, 124, 128, 132) sts.

Rows 1 and 3: (WS) Purl.

Row 2: K1f&b in every st—228 (236, 248, 256, 264) sts.

Row 4: *K1, k1f&b; rep from *—342 (354, 372, 384, 396) sts.

Using the crochet method (see page 31), BO all sts.

Stripes Go Round

Lana Hames

Hemp yarn is both comfortable to wear and easy to care for. Lana Hames has used four shades of sportweight hemp for this simple, lightweight top. Worked in the round from the bottom up with circular yoke shaping, the stripes are uninterrupted from hem to neck. Lana twists two stitches at each side of the body to produce "phony" seams that define the boundaries between the back and front. The lower body, sleeves, and neck are edged with narrow bands of garter stitch.

Finished Size
31 (32½, 36, 40, 45, 49½)" (78.5 [82.5, 91.5, 101.5, 114.5, 125.5] cm) bust/chest circumference. Top shown measures 31" (78.5 cm).

Yarn
Sportweight (#2 Fine).
Shown here: Hemp for Knitting All Hemp Hemp3 (100% hemp; 150 yd [137 m]/40 g): brick (MC), 3 (3, 4, 4, 5, 6) skeins; pumpkin (orange), 2 (2, 2, 2, 3, 3) skeins; avocado and Dijon (gold), 1 (1, 1, 1, 2, 2) skein(s) each.

Needles
Body and sleeves—size 3 (3.25 mm): 24" (60 cm) circular (cir) and set of 4 double-pointed (dpn). Edging—size 2 (2.75 mm): 24" (60 cm) cir and set of 4 dpn. Adjust needle size if necessary to obtain the correct gauge.

Notions
Marker (m); stitch holders; tapestry needle.

Gauge
27 stitches and 32 rounds = 4" (10 cm) in stockinette stitch worked in the round on larger needles.

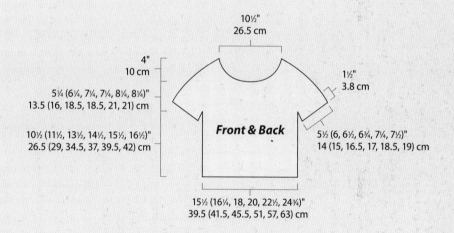

10½"
26.5 cm

4"
10 cm

5¼ (6¼, 7¼, 7¼, 8¼, 8¼)"
13.5 (16, 18.5, 18.5, 21, 21) cm

10½ (11½, 13½, 14½, 15½, 16½)"
26.5 (29, 34.5, 37, 39.5, 42) cm

1½"
3.8 cm

Front & Back

5½ (6, 6½, 6¾, 7¼, 7½)"
14 (15, 16.5, 17, 18.5, 19) cm

15½ (16¼, 18, 20, 22½, 24¾)"
39.5 (41.5, 45.5, 51, 57, 63) cm

Body

With MC and smaller cir needle, CO 198 (210, 232, 256, 288, 318) sts. Place marker (pm) and join, being careful not to twist sts. Work garter st (knit 1 rnd, purl 1 rnd) for 4 rnds. *Next rnd:* Change to larger cir needle and knit, inc 10 (10, 12, 12, 16, 16) sts evenly spaced—208 (220, 244, 268, 304, 334) sts. Change to avocado and work the first row of the stripe sequence, placing another marker after the first 104 (110, 122, 134, 152, 167) sts to indicate position of other side "seam." Cont in stripe sequence, working twists to indicate fake seams as foll: Work LT (see Stitch Guide) over first 2 sts, knit to next marker (m), work RT over next 2 sts, knit to end of rnd, then work 2 rnds even in stripe patt. Rep the last 3 rnds for fake seams. Cont in stripe sequence until piece measures about 10½ (11½, 13½, 14½, 15½, 16½)" (26.5 [29, 34.5, 37, 39.5, 42] cm) from beg, ending with 1 rnd of avocado.

Shape Armholes

With orange, k8 (9, 10, 10, 11, 11) and place these sts on holder for left underarm, k88 (92, 102, 114, 130, 145) for front, knit next 16 (18, 20, 20, 22, 22) sts and place these 16 (18, 20, 20, 22, 22) sts on another holder for right underarm, k88 (92, 102, 114, 130, 145) for back, place rem 8 (9, 10, 10, 11, 11) sts on first holder for left underarm. Set aside.

Sleeves

With MC and dpn, CO 70 (74, 78, 80, 84, 86) sts. Place m and join, being careful not to twist sts. Work garter st for 4 rnds as for body. *Next rnd:* Change to larger dpn and knit, inc 6 (8, 10, 11, 12, 13) sts evenly spaced—76 (82, 88, 91, 96, 99) sts. Change to avocado and work stripe sequence for 10 rnds, ending with the first rnd of orange of stripe sequence. Place first and last 8 (9, 10, 10, 11, 11) sts on holder for underarm—60 (64, 68, 71, 74, 77) sts rem. Set aside. Make another sleeve to match.

Yoke

With orange, k88 (92, 102, 114, 130, 145) back sts, pm, k60 (64, 68, 71, 74, 77) left sleeve sts, pm, k88 (92, 102, 114, 130, 145) front sts, pm, k60 (64, 68, 71, 74, 77) right sleeve sts, pm, and join—296 (312, 340, 370, 408, 444) sts total. Cont working color sequence as established, knit 9 rnds. *Dec Rnd 1:* *K6 (6, 8, 8, 10, 10), k2tog; rep from *—259 (273, 306, 333, 374, 407) sts rem. Work 9 rnds in patt. *Dec Rnd 2:* *K5 (5, 7, 7, 9, 9), k2tog; rep from *—222 (234, 272, 296, 340, 370) sts rem. Work 9 rnds in patt. *Dec Rnd 3:* *K4 (4, 6, 6, 8, 8), k2tog; rep from *—185 (195, 238, 259, 306, 333) sts rem. Work 9 rnds in patt.

Size 31" only

Skip to All sizes.

Sizes 32½", 36", 40", 45", and 49½" only

*K(37, 5, 5, 7, 7), k2tog; rep from *—(190, 204, 222, 272, 296) sts rem. Work 7 rnds in patt.

Size 32½" only

Skip to All Sizes.

Sizes 36", 40", 45", and 49½" only

*K(15, 4, 6, 6), k2tog; rep from *—(192, 185, 238, 259) sts. Work 5 rnds in patt.

Sizes 36" and 40" only

Skip to All Sizes.

Sizes 45" and 49½" only

*K(5, 5), k2tog; rep from *—(204, 222) sts. Work 5 rnds in patt. *Next rnd:* *K(15, 4), k2tog; rep from *—(192, 185) sts.

All sizes

185 (190, 192, 185, 192, 185) sts rem when all decs have been worked. Work 2 (2, 4, 4, 5, 5) more rnds, dec 0 (5, 7, 0, 7, 0) sts evenly in first rnd, and ending with 1 rnd gold—185 sts rem for all sizes; yoke measures about 5¼ (6¼, 7¼, 7¼, 8¼, 8¼)" (13.5 [16, 18.5, 18.5, 21, 21] cm) from joining rnd.

Neckband

With smaller cir needles and MC, knit 1 rnd, dec 6 sts evenly spaced—179 sts rem. Purl 1 rnd. Rep the last 2 rnds once more—173 sts rem. BO all sts as foll: *K2tog through back loop (tbl), return st on right needle to left needle; rep from * until 1 st rem. Cut yarn and fasten off last st.

Finishing

Place underarm sts on dpn. With matching color threaded on a tapestry needle, use Kitchener st (see page 152) to graft sts tog. Weave in loose ends, matching colors on WS. Wash gently in mild detergent and block to measurements while wet.

Beyond the Basics: INCREASES

based on an article by Ann Budd

Most knitting patterns specify that stitches be increased at some point to add width to a piece and/or give an angled shape to an edge. Over the centuries, knitters have devised a number of ways to accomplish this goal. Some methods create decorative holes, others are nearly invisible; some create stitches that slant to the right, others to the left. Knitting patterns don't always specify a particular type of increase but instead leave it up to the knitter to decide how to perform this task. Often, knitters choose to use the same type of increase (usually the type first learned) all the time. However, knitters who have a repertoire of methods, and understand the subtleties of each, can choose the method that is best suited for the project at hand and thereby obtain a more refined, finished look.

When increases are used to add width to a piece, several are generally worked at even intervals across a single row, such as at the top of a ribbed waist or cuff or at the boundary between stitch patterns that have different gauges. In these cases, a single type of increase is repeated the specified number of times. A number of increase methods are equally suitable here, and whether the increase slants to the left or right is of little consequence. However, when the purpose of the increases is to form an angled edge (such as along the edges of a sleeve that is knitted from the cuff to the armhole or around the upper body of a sweater that is knitted from the neck down), care should be taken to choose a method that follows the direction of the slant. Many increase methods can be worked with left or right slants for just this purpose. Moreover, these directional increases can be paired around a center stitch or group of stitches to give a symmetrical appearance.

Yarnover Increase

The simplest of increase methods, the yarnover increase is usually specified for openwork patterns. This decorative increase produces a visible hole that is the basis for knitted lace. Many knitters mistakenly wrap the yarn in the wrong direction, especially when they're working a yarnover between a knit and purl stitch. Although the visual difference is slight, incorrect yarnovers can produce different-size holes. To make all yarnovers consistent, it is important that you work the motion separately from the next stitch and that your motion always brings the yarn from below the needle in front, around and over the top of the needle, ending below the needle in the back, at which point the yarn is positioned for the next stitch. On the following row, work the yarnover as a normal stitch (unless otherwise directed).

Between Two Knit Stitches

Wrap the yarn around the needle from front to back (Figure 1).

Figure 1

After a Knit Stitch and Before a Purl Stitch

Bring the yarn to the front under the needle, around the top of the needle to the back, and then under the needle to the front (Figure 2).

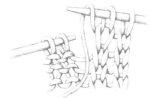

Figure 2

Between Two Purl Stitches

Bring the yarn over the top of the needle (front to back), then around the bottom of the needle and to the front again (Figure 3).

Figure 3

After a Purl Stitch and Before a Knit Stitch

Bring the yarn over the top of the needle (again, from front to back), then around to the back of the needle (Figure 4).

Figure 4

Bar Increase

Unlike the yarnover method, a bar increase does not produce a hole. When worked in stockinette stitch, it forms a visible horizontal bar (that looks much like a purl stitch) to the left of the increased stitch. However, this increase can be quite invisible when used correctly in ribbing—worked in a knit stitch immediately before a purl stitch. The bar will fall after the knit stitch and recede into the ribbing with the purl stitch, and, therefore, is far less visible than most other increases worked in ribbing.

The advantage to this method is that the visible horizontal bar can be used to count and keep track of the number of increases that have been worked, such as when working sleeve increases. Do not use this method in color-work patterns if the increased stitches are different colors (the horizontal bar will interrupt the color change). To get a symmetrical appearance, work the bar increase one stitch farther in from the left edge than the right edge.

Knit Stitch

Knit into a stitch but leave the stitch on the left needle (Figure 1), then knit through the back loop of the same stitch (Figure 2) and slip the original stitch off the needle (Figure 3).

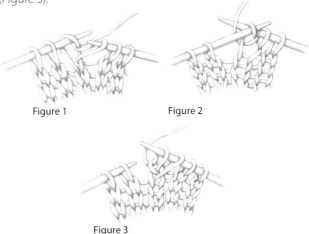

Figure 1   Figure 2

Figure 3

Purl Stitch (P1f&b)

Purl into a stitch but leave the stitch on the left needle (Figure 1), then purl through the back loop of the same stitch (Figure 2) and slip the original stitch off the needle.

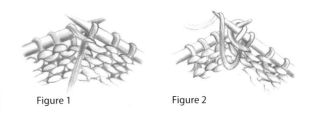

Figure 1   Figure 2

Raised Increase

Also called "make 1," this invisible increase is worked into the horizontal strand that lies between two stitches. The horizontal strand is lifted onto the left needle, then knitted in such a way as to twist it and thereby prevent a hole. Depending on the way that the horizontal strand is lifted and knitted, the increased stitch can slant to the left or the right. This type of increase is typically specified for color work or other patterns in which it's important that the increase not affect the stitches already on the needles.

Left Slant (M1L)

Note: Use the left slant if no direction of slant is specified. With the left needle tip, lift the strand between the last knitted stitch and the first stitch on the left needle from front to back (Figure 1), then knit the lifted loop through the back (Figure 2).

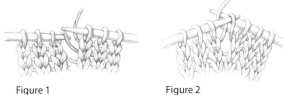

Figure 1   Figure 2

Right Slant (M1R)

With the left needle tip, lift the strand between the last knitted stitch and the first stitch on the left needle from back to front (Figure 1), then knit the lifted loop through the front (Figure 2).

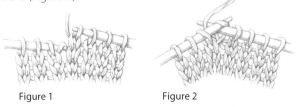

Figure 1   Figure 2

Purlwise (M1 pwise)

With the left needle tip, lift the strand between the last knitted stitch and the first stitch on the left needle from back to front (Figure 1), then purl the lifted loop through the front (Figure 2).

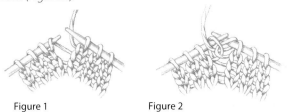

Figure 1   Figure 2

Lifted Increase

Another type of invisible increase, the lifted increase, is performed by working into the stitch in the row below the stitch that's on the needle, then working the stitch on the needle as usual. This type of increase is ideal for increasing stitches in the middle of a piece where you want the increase to be as inconspicuous as possible. If the increases are to be stacked one on top of another in the same location, as down the front of a skirt worked from waist to hem, space lifted increases at least three rows apart. Otherwise, there is a good chance that the stacked increases will pull up the work and distort the overall appearance.

Left Slant

Insert the left needle tip into the back of the stitch below the stitch just knitted (Figure 1), then knit this stitch (Figure 2) and slip it off the needle.

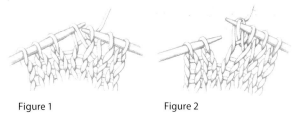

Figure 1   Figure 2

Right Slant

Note: If no slant direction is specified, use the right slant. Knit into the back of the stitch (in the "purl bump") in the row directly below the stitch on the needle (Figure 1), then knit the stitch on the needle (Figure 2), and slip the original stitch off the needle.

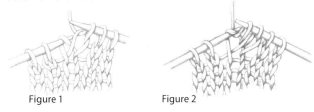

Figure 1   Figure 2

TIPS

✳ Work increases one or two stitches in from the edge of a knitted piece to make seaming easier.

✳ To get the least conspicuous result, choose an increase that twists the stitch to avoid holes.

✳ When increasing within a ribbed pattern, work double increases to maintain the continuity of the pattern (increase on either side of a purl stitch and work the purl stitch as a knit stitch) or position bar increases in knit stitches that are immediately followed by purl stitches.

✳ When working increases along the edge to shape a piece, work the new stitches into the pattern as they become available—when there are enough stitches to work in the pattern repeat, do so. Otherwise, simply knit or purl the new stitches until there are enough.

Marseilles Pullover

Kathy Zimmerman

In this slim cabled pullover, Kathy Zimmerman combined trellis-like diamonds with garter-stitch interiors and crisscrossing ribs to reflect the layout of hedgerows and plantings in a formal summer garden. Kathy chose a simple boatneck (the back and front are identical), narrow garter-stitch edgings, and plain ribbed sleeves to keep the focus on the interplay of textures. Worked in baby alpaca, the sweater is comfortable and soft next to the skin.

Finished Size
34 (38, 42, 46, 50)" (86.5 [96.5, 106.5, 117, 127] cm) bust/chest circumference. Sweater shown measures 38" (96.5 cm).

Yarn
Worsted weight (#4 Medium).
Shown here: Goddess Yarns Phoebe (100% alpaca; 73 yd [67 m]/50 g): #C734 daylily melon (coral), 14 (15, 17, 19, 20) skeins.

Needles
Body—sizes 8 (5 mm) and 7 (4.5 mm).
Sleeves—size 8 (5 mm) straight and spare needle for three-needle BO. Adjust needle size if necessary to obtain the correct gauge.

Notions
Cable needle (cn); markers (m; optional); 4 stitch holders; tapestry needle.

Gauge
20 sts and 25½ rows = 4" (10 cm) in k1, p4 rib patt on larger needles after blocking; 70 center sts of cable chart = 12" (30.5 cm) wide after blocking.

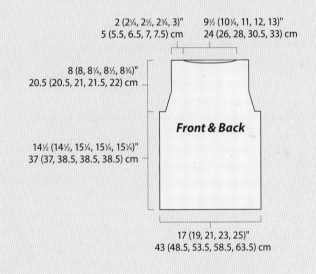

2 (2¼, 2½, 2¾, 3)"
5 (5.5, 6.5, 7, 7.5) cm

9½ (10¼, 11, 12, 13)"
24 (26, 28, 30.5, 33) cm

8 (8, 8¼, 8½, 8¾)"
20.5 (20.5, 21, 21.5, 22) cm

Front & Back

14½ (14½, 15¼, 15¼, 15¼)"
37 (37, 38.5, 38.5, 38.5) cm

17 (19, 21, 23, 25)"
43 (48.5, 53.5, 58.5, 63.5) cm

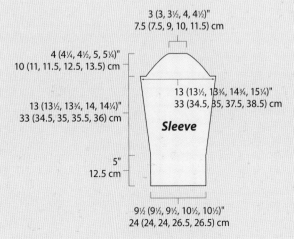

3 (3, 3½, 4, 4½)"
7.5 (7.5, 9, 10, 11.5) cm

4 (4¼, 4½, 5, 5¼)"
10 (11, 11.5, 12.5, 13.5) cm

13 (13½, 13¾, 14¾, 15¼)"
33 (34.5, 35, 37.5, 38.5) cm

13 (13½, 13¾, 14, 14¼)"
33 (34.5, 35, 35.5, 36) cm

Sleeve

5"
12.5 cm

9½ (9½, 9½, 10½, 10½)"
24 (24, 24, 26.5, 26.5) cm

Note

- Work all increases and decreases inside garter edge stitches.

Back

With larger needles, CO 96 (106, 116, 126, 136) sts. *Next row:* (WS) Work Set-up row of Cable chart across all sts. Work Rib Rows 1–8, then work Rib Rows 1–4 (0, 0, 1, 1, 1) more time(s)—9 (9, 13, 13, 13) rows completed, including Set-up row; piece measures about 1¼ (1¼, 2, 2, 2)" (3.2 [3.2, 5, 5, 5] cm) from CO. Work Rows 1–24 of main patt a total of 3 times, then work Rows 1–12 once more—84 rows of main patt completed; piece measures about 14½ (14½, 15¼, 15¼, 15¼)" (37 [37, 38.5, 38.5, 38.5] cm) from CO.

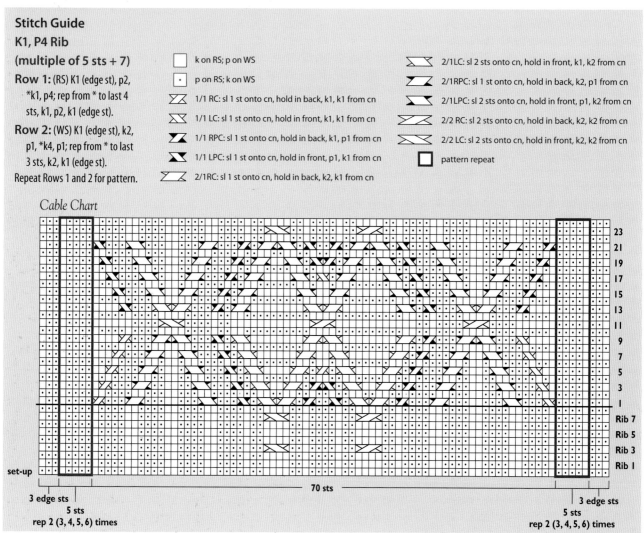

Stitch Guide

K1, P4 Rib

(multiple of 5 sts + 7)

Row 1: (RS) K1 (edge st), p2, *k1, p4; rep from * to last 4 sts, k1, p2, k1 (edge st).

Row 2: (WS) K1 (edge st), k2, p1, *k4, p1; rep from * to last 3 sts, k2, k1 (edge st).

Repeat Rows 1 and 2 for pattern.

☐ k on RS; p on WS

· p on RS; k on WS

⧄ 1/1 RC: sl 1 st onto cn, hold in back, k1, k1 from cn

⧄ 1/1 LC: sl 1 st onto cn, hold in front, k1, k1 from cn

⧄ 1/1 RPC: sl 1 st onto cn, hold in back, k1, p1 from cn

⧄ 1/1 LPC: sl 1 st onto cn, hold in front, p1, k1 from cn

⧄ 2/1RC: sl 1 st onto cn, hold in back, k2, k1 from cn

⧄ 2/1LC: sl 2 sts onto cn, hold in front, k1, k2 from cn

⧄ 2/1RPC: sl 1 st onto cn, hold in back, k2, p1 from cn

⧄ 2/1LPC: sl 2 sts onto cn, hold in front, p1, k2 from cn

⧄ 2/2 RC: sl 2 sts onto cn, hold in back, k2, k2 from cn

⧄ 2/2 LC: sl 2 sts onto cn, hold in front, k2, k2 from cn

☐ pattern repeat

Cable Chart

3 edge sts
5 sts
rep 2 (3, 4, 5, 6) times

70 sts

3 edge sts
5 sts
rep 2 (3, 4, 5, 6) times

Shape Armholes

Cont in patt, BO 4 (5, 5, 6, 7) sts at beg of next 2 rows—88 (96, 106, 114, 122) sts rem. Dec 1 st each end of needle on RS rows 5 (5, 6, 6, 6) times—78 (86, 94, 102, 110) sts rem. Work even in patt until armholes measure about 7½" (19 cm), ending with Row 12 of chart—48 patt rows completed from beg of armhole shaping.

Neckband

Change to smaller needles and work in garter st (knit every row) for 5 (5, 7, 9, 11) rows, break yarn—armholes measure 8 (8, 8¼, 8½, 8¾)" (20.5 [20.5, 21, 21.5, 22] cm). With WS facing, place first 11 (13, 15, 16, 17) sts on holder, join new yarn and BO center 56 (60, 64, 70, 76) sts for neck, place rem sts on separate holder—11 (13, 15, 16, 17) sts rem for each shoulder.

Front

Work same as for back.

Sleeves

With larger needles, CO 47 (47, 47, 52, 52) sts. Beg and ending with WS Row 2, work even in k1, p4 rib patt (see Stitch Guide) for 5" (12.5 cm). Cont in patt, and beg on the next RS row, inc 1 st each end of needle inside edge sts (see Notes) every 6 rows 1 (4, 7, 4, 7) time(s), then every 8 rows 8 (6, 4, 7, 5) times, working new sts into k1, p4 rib patt—65 (67, 69, 74, 76) sts. Work even in patt until piece measures 18 (18½, 18¾, 19, 19¼)" (45.5 [47, 47.5, 48.5, 49] cm) from CO, ending with a WS row.

Shape Cap

Cont in patt, BO 4 (5, 5, 6, 7) sts at beg of next 2 rows—57 (57, 59, 62, 62) sts rem. Dec 1 st each end of needle on RS rows 7 (8, 9, 10, 12) times, then work 1 WS row even—43 (41, 41, 42, 38) sts rem. BO 2 sts at beg of next 0 (2, 2, 4, 4) rows, then BO 3 sts at beg of next 4 (2, 4, 2, 0) rows, then BO 4 sts at beg of next 4 (4, 2, 2, 2) rows—15 (15, 17, 20, 22) sts rem. Work 1 WS row even in patt. BO all sts loosely.

Finishing

Place held shoulder sts on larger needles with RS touching. Use the three-needle method (see page 29) to BO shoulder sts tog. With yarn threaded on a tapestry needle, sew sleeve caps into armholes. Sew sleeve and side seams. Weave in loose ends. Block lightly to measurements.

Kristin's Favorite Carry-All

Kristin Nicholas

Inspired by a woven wool bag from Ecuador that she used as a knitting bag, then overnight bag, then diaper bag, Kristin Nicholas designed this generous knitted alternative. She drew upon the motifs in Turkish carpets and Scandinavian Fair Isles for extra inspiration. Kristin worked this bag in the round, cutting it to form a front and a back, then used a "gusset" strip to join the two pieces along the sides and bottom. She purposely chose a two-color motif with small repeats that would be easy to knit, then added a dash of chartreuse with duplicate stitch.

Finished Size
About 16" (40.5 cm) wide, 18" (46 cm) long excluding handle, and 2" (5 cm) deep.

Yarn
Worsted weight (#4 Medium).
Shown here: Classic Elite Montera (50% llama, 50% wool; 127 yd [116 m]/100 g): #3876 pacha mama brown and #3868 ancient orange, 3 skeins each; #3835 lima green, 1 skein.

Needles
Size 9 (5.5 mm). Adjust needle size if necessary to obtain the correct gauge.

Notions
Tapestry needle; small amount of strongly plied yarn for seaming; one 1¼" (3.2 cm) button; ⅝ yd (60 cm) lining fabric.

Gauge
18 stitches and 20 rows = 4" (10 cm) in color pattern.

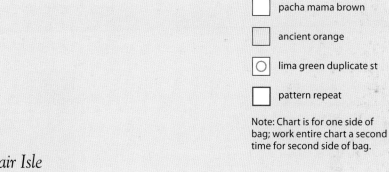

☐ pacha mama brown

☐ ancient orange

◯ lima green duplicate st

☐ pattern repeat

Note: Chart is for one side of bag; work entire chart a second time for second side of bag.

Fair Isle

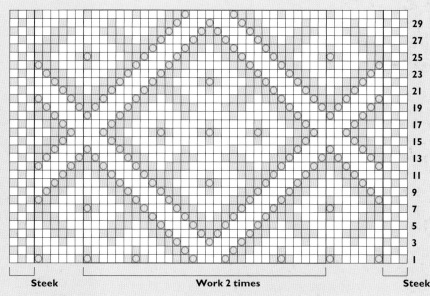

29 27 25 23 21 19 17 15 13 11 9 7 5 3 1

Steek   Work 2 times   Steek

Body

With brown, CO 158 sts. Place marker (pm) and join, being careful not to twist sts. Join orange and beg with Row 1, work through Row 30 of Fair Isle chart 2 times (noting that only one side of the bag is charted), then work Rows 1–28 once more—piece should measure 18" (46 cm) from beg. BO all sts.

Cut Steeks

Machine-zigzag down each side of the center 2 sts of each 6-st dot (steek) patt. Then machine-stitch just inside (in the ditch) of the large pattern at each side of the dot patts. Cut between the zigzag sts.

Upper Edge

With green, pick up and knit 73 sts along top edge of each piece. Knit 3 rows. BO knitwise.

Gusset

With brown, CO 13 sts. Work stripe patt as foll:
Row 1: (RS) With brown, knit.
Rows 2 and 4: With brown, knit.
Row 3: With brown, purl.
Rows 5 and 6: With orange, knit.
Row 7: With orange, purl.
Row 8: With orange, knit.
Rep Rows 1–8 until piece measures 49" (124.5 cm) from CO. BO all sts.

Finishing
Handle

With brown, CO 13 sts. Work stripe patt as foll:
Rows 1 and 2: With brown, knit.
Rows 3 and 4: With orange, knit.
Rep Rows 1–4 until piece measures about 30" (76 cm) or desired length, keeping in mind that the knitted strip will stretch when the bag is weighted.

Button Flap

With brown, CO 11 sts. Work stripe patt as foll:
Rows 1 and 2: With brown, knit.
Rows 3 and 4: With green, knit.
Rep Rows 1–4 until piece measures 5½" (14 cm) from beg. On next row, work buttonhole as foll: K3, BO 5 sts, knit to end. On next row, CO 3 sts over the BO sts. Cont in stripe patt until piece measures 6½" (16.5 cm) from beg. BO all sts.

Duplicate Stitch

With green, work duplicate st (see Glossary, page 157) as indicated on chart.

With seaming yarn threaded on tapestry needle, sew gusset to one side of bag by stitching down one side, around bottom, and up the other side, working seam so that the 6-st dot patts do not show. Attach gusset to other side of bag in the same manner. Sew CO and BO edges of handle to tops of gusset. Sew button flap to center top of one side. Sew on button opposite buttonhole.

Lining

Measure bag width and length. Cut lining fabric 1" (2.5 cm) wider and 1" (2.5 cm) longer than these measurements. Fold in half with RS facing and machine-stitch along open side and across bottom. Turn under top edge. Pin to inside of bag. Hand stitch in place.

Beyond the Basics: DECREASES

based on an article by Ann Budd

Most knitting patterns require that stitches be reduced at some point—to shape the armhole or neck of a sweater; the heel, gusset, and toe of a sock; the top of a hat or mitten. As with all knitting techniques, there are several ways to decrease stitches, and the one to choose depends on the project in hand and the effect you want to achieve. The main difference between the methods is in the direction that the top (and most visible) stitch lies, which dictates the overall appearance of the decrease. When worked to create a shaped edge, most (but not all) knitting patterns specify decreases in which the top stitch is aligned with the shaped edge.

Decreases are most often worked one at a time to reduce the width of the knitting by one stitch in a particular area. Such decreases can be scattered throughout the entire width of knitting, as when shaping the crown of a hat, or concentrated in specific areas, as when shaping the armholes or neck of a sweater. For shaping armholes or necks, single decreases are typically paired—left-slanting decreases are worked on the right edge (at the beginning of right-side rows) and right-slanting decreases are worked on the left edge (at the end of right-side rows). If the decreases are lined up a few stitches in from the edge, as for an armhole or neck edge, the decrease line becomes pronounced and the resulting shaping is called "full-fashioned." If you prefer to minimize the appearance of the decreases, work them on the edge stitches, which will be hidden in the seam.

Left-Slant Single Decreases

Viewed from a right-side row, the top stitch in a left-slanting decrease leans toward the left. To emphasize the decrease line on armholes or necks, work left-slanting decreases at the beginning of right-side rows and at the end of wrong-side rows.

Knit 2 Together Through Back Loops

This is the simplest way to achieve a left-slanting decrease on a right-side row. The same effect is achieved on wrong-side rows by purling two stitches together through their back loops. Note that this maneuver causes both stitches to twist, a subtle inconsistency that may or may not be acceptable for your project.

Knit two stitches together through their back loops.

Slip 1, Knit 1, Pass Slipped Stitch Over (sl 1, k1, psso)

This technique is similar to binding off a single stitch.

Slip one stitch knitwise onto the right needle, knit the next stitch (Figure 1), then use the left needle tip to lift the slipped stitch over the knitted stitch and off the needle (Figure 2).

Figure 1   Figure 2

Slip, Slip, Knit (ssk)

This technique has essentially the same look as sl 1, k1, psso but is slightly quicker to execute.

Slip two stitches individually knitwise onto the right needle (Figure 1), insert the left needle tip into the front of these two slipped stitches, and use the right needle to knit them together through their back loops (Figure 2). *Note:* To make the decrease line slightly more pronounced, slip the second stitch purlwise.

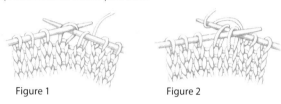

Figure 1   Figure 2

Slip, Slip, Purl (Ssp)

This maneuver is equivalent to the ssk decrease but is worked on wrong-side rows.

Holding the yarn in front, slip two stitches individually knitwise onto the right needle (Figure 1), insert the left needle tip into the front of these two slipped stitches and slip them back onto the left needle in their twisted orientation, then insert the right needle tip through the back loops of these stitches (going through the second first, then the first), and purl them together through their back loops (Figure 2).

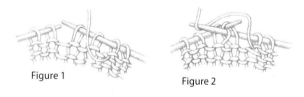

Figure 1   Figure 2

Right-Slant Single Decreases

As the name implies, the top stitch in a right-slanting decrease leans to the right on right-side rows. To emphasize the decrease line, work this type of decrease at the end of right-side (knit) rows and at the beginning of wrong-side (purl) rows.

Knit 2 Together (k2tog)

This, the simplest of all decreases, is generally worked on right-side rows.

Knit two stitches together as if they were a single stitch.

Purl 2 Together (p2tog)

This decrease is the same as k2tog but is generally worked on wrong-side rows.

Purl two stitches together as if they were a single stitch.

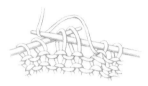

Double Decreases

Double decreases eliminate two of three adjacent stitches at once. Double decreases are less common for armhole and neck shaping than single decreases but are necessary when a large number of stitches needs to be eliminated in a few rows. Depending on the method you choose, the decrease can lean to the left, lean to the right, or it can appear vertically aligned.

Slip 1, Knit 2 Together, Pass Slipped Stitch Over (sl 1, k2tog, psso)

This left-slanting double decrease is generally worked on right-side rows.

Slip one stitch knitwise onto right needle, knit the next two stitches together (Figure 1), then use the tip of the left needle to lift slipped stitch up and over the knitted stitches (Figure 2), then off the needle.

To get the same result on a wrong-side row, purl two stitches together, place the resulting decreased stitch back onto the left needle, pass the second stitch on the left needle over decreased stitch and off needle, then return decreased stitch to right needle.

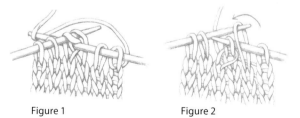

Figure 1   Figure 2

Slip, Slip, Slip, Knit (sssk)

For a more pronounced left slant, work a modification of the ssk decrease.

Slip three stitches individually knitwise (Figure 1), insert the left needle tip in to the front of these three slipped stitches, and use the right needle to knit them together through their back loops (Figure 2).

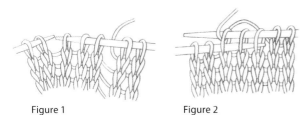

Figure 1   Figure 2

Slip 1, Knit 1, Pass Slipped Stitch Over, Return to Left Needle, Pass Second Stitch Over

This double decrease slants to the right.

Slip one stitch knitwise to the right needle, knit one stitch, pass the slipped stitch over the knited stitch (Figure 1), return this decreased stitch to the left needle and pass the second stitch on the left needle over this decreased stitch (Figure 2), then return this decreased stitch to the right needle (Figure 3).

An alternate method that has a more pronounced right slant is to simply knit three stitches together (abbreviated k3tog).

To get the same result on a wrong-side row, slip one stitch purlwise, purl the next two stitches together, then pass slipped stitch over purled stitches and off the needle.

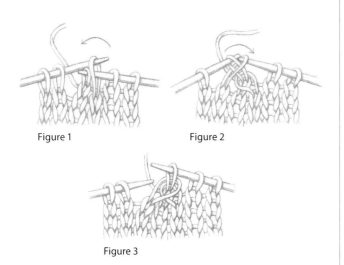

Figure 1   Figure 2

Figure 3

Centered Double Decrease

This decrease is worked on right-side rows and forms a prominent vertical line.

Slip two stitches together knitwise onto the right needle (Figure 1), knit the next stitch (Figure 2), then pass the two slipped stitches over the knitted stitch (Figure 3) and off the needle.

To get a similar effect on wrong-side rows, slip two stitches individually knitwise onto the right needle, then place these two twisted stitches onto the left needle, insert right needle through the back loops of the second then first slipped stitch, and slip them together onto the right needle, then purl one and pass the two slipped stitches over the purled stitch.

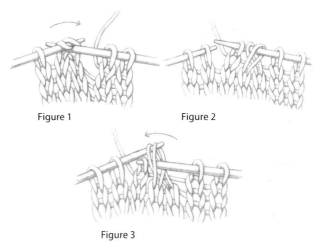

Figure 1   Figure 2

Figure 3

Tips

* Work decreases two to three stitches in from the edge of a knitted piece to make seaming easier.
* When working decreases to shape the edge of a piece (such as an armhole or neck), work the established stitches in the pattern stitch until they are reduced by the decreases. The decreases will form a distinct visual line that will truncate the stitch pattern nicely.
* Use the same type of decrease for the same purpose throughout a pattern, i.e., along the neck or armhole of a sweater.

Millennium Argyle Vest

Nancy Marchant

For this contemporary vest, Nancy Marchant has taken a basic argyle pattern and "broken the rules" by enlarging the diamonds from their traditional smaller size and using a different color for each diagonal line of stitches. To speed up the knitting and add an element of surprise, she worked the back in simple stripes. Nancy provided two colorways—one predominantly gold, the other predominantly plum—but feel free to play around and come up with your own color mix.

Finished Size
39½ (42, 44½)" (100 [107, 113] cm) bust/
   chest circumference. Vest shown measures
   42" (107 cm).

Yarn
DK weight (#3 Light).
   Shown here: Jo Sharp Classic DK Wool
   (100% wool; 107 yd [98 m]/50 g). Shown
   in two colorways (gold /plum): #320
   gold/#505 plum (MC), 2 (3, 3) balls; #312
   Renaissance (blue)/#902 ebony, #506
   chestnut/#002 pistachio (green), and #319
   violet/#312 Renaissance, 1 (1, 2) ball(s)
   each; #902 ebony/#003 tangerine, #333
   brick/#319 violet, and #002 pistachio/#322
   ginger, 1 ball each.

Needles
Size 6 (4 mm). Adjust needle size if necessary
   to obtain the correct gauge.

Notions
Stitch holder; tapestry needle.

Gauge
19 sts and 24½ rows = 4" (10 cm) in
   stockinette stitch.

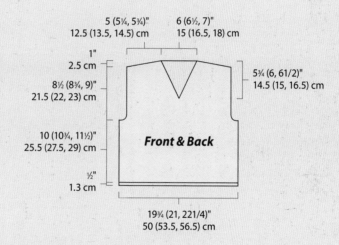

Stitch Guide

Stripe Pattern for Gold Vest Back

In St st, work [2 rows Renaissance, 2 rows pistachio] 2 times, 2 rows violet, 2 rows pistachio, [2 rows violet, 2 rows brick] 2 times, 2 rows ebony, 2 rows brick, 2 rows ebony, 2 rows chestnut, 2 rows ebony, 2 rows chestnut, 2 rows gold, 2 rows chestnut, 2 rows gold, 2 rows Renaissance, 2 rows gold. Repeat these 42 rows for pattern.

Stripe Pattern for Plum Vest Back

In St st, work 4 rows each in Renaissance, ginger, violet, pistachio, tangerine, ebony, plum. Repeat these 28 rows for pattern.

☐ gold/plum

+ diamond color

● diagonal line color

▬▬▬ size 39½" repeat and diamond outline

▬▬▬ size 42" repeat and diamond outline

▬▬▬ size 44½" repeat and diamond outline

See illustrations on page 67 for diamond and diagonal line color placement.

Argyle

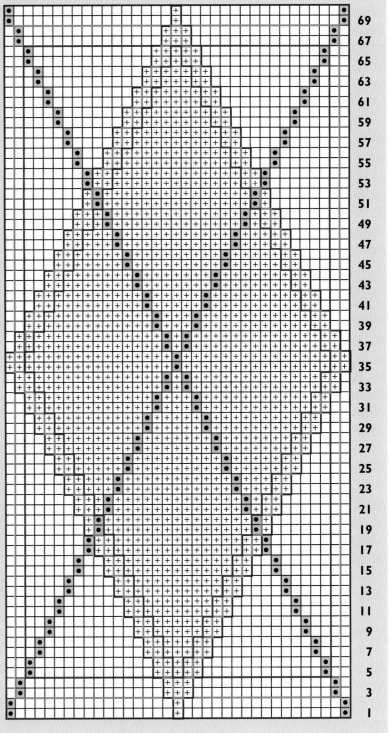

Joe Coca

Gold Colorway

Plum Colorway

violet   ebony   brick   pistachio   ebony   Renaissance

ginger   pistachio   ebony   Renaissance   pistachio   tangerine

■ brick	tangerine	Renaissance
plum	gold	violet

ebony	ginger
chestnut	pistachio

Joe Coca

Gold Colorway

Plum Colorway

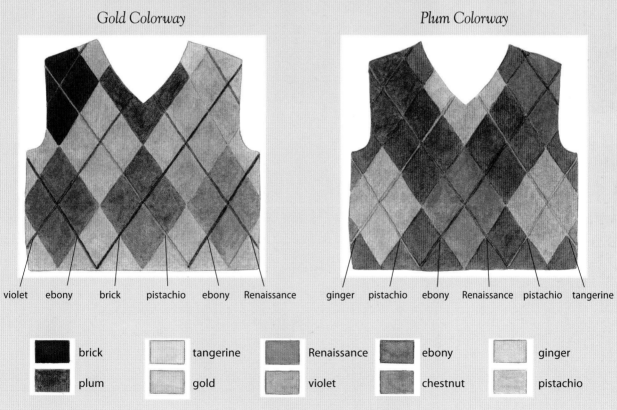

violet   ebony   brick   pistachio   ebony   Renaissance

ginger   pistachio   ebony   Renaissance   pistachio   tangerine

| brick | | tangerine | | Renaissance | | ebony | | ginger |
| plum | | gold | | violet | | chestnut | | pistachio |

Notes

- When two colors are given, separated by a backslash (/), the first color refers to the gold colorway and the second refers to the plum colorway.
- The vest front is worked in intarsia throughout, with a separate strand of yarn for each diamond and diagonal line.

Back

With gold/plum, CO 95 (101, 107) sts. Purl 1 row. Work 3 rows in St st, ending with a RS row. Knit 1 WS row for fold line. Work stripe patt for your colorway for 62 (66, 70) rows, ending with a WS row—piece should measure about 10 (10¾, 11½)" (25.5 [27.5, 29] cm) from fold line.

Shape Armholes

Cont in stripe patt, BO 4 (5, 5) sts beg of next 2 rows, then BO 2 sts beg of foll 2 rows—83 (87, 93) sts rem. Dec 1 st each end of needle every other row 3 times—77 (81, 87) sts rem. Work even until a total of 114 (120, 126) rows of stripe patt have been worked, ending with a WS row— armholes should measure about 8½ (8¾, 9)" (21.5 [22, 23] cm).

Shape Shoulders

BO 8 (9, 9) sts at beg of next 2 rows, then BO 8 (8, 9) sts at beg of foll 4 rows—29 (31, 33) sts rem. BO all sts.

Front

With gold/plum, CO 95 (101, 107) sts. Purl 1 row. Work 3 rows in St st, ending with a RS row. Knit 1 WS row for fold line. Working a gold/plum selvedge st in St st at each end of needle, rep Argyle chart according to your colorway and size 3 times over center 93 (99, 105) sts. Work as charted until a total of 62 (66, 70) rows have been

worked and piece measures same as back to armhole, ending with a WS row.

Shape Armholes

Cont in patt, BO 4 (5, 5) sts at beg of next 2 rows, then BO 2 sts beg of foll 2 rows— 83 (87, 93) sts rem. Dec 1 st each end of needle every other row 3 times—77 (81, 87) sts rem. Work even until a total of 84 (88, 92) rows have been worked from fold line, ending with a WS row—armholes measure about 3¾ (3¾, 3½)" (9.5 [9.5, 9] cm).

Shape Neck

(RS) K38 (40, 43), place next st on a holder, join ebony/pistachio and work in patt to end—38 (40, 43) sts each side. Working each side separately, dec 1 st at neck edge every other row 14 (15, 16) times—24 (25, 27) sts rem each side; 114 (120, 126) rows total; armholes measure 8½ (8¾, 9)" (21.5 [22, 23] cm).

Shape Shoulders

At armhole edge, BO 8 (9, 9) sts once, then BO 8 (8, 9) sts 2 times.

Finishing

Block pieces to measurements. With yarn threaded on a tapestry needle, sew left shoulder seam.

Neckband

With gold/plum and RS facing, pick up and knit 29 (31, 33) sts across back neck, 33 (35, 37) sts along left neck to center front, knit held center front st, pick up and knit 34 (36, 38) sts along right neck—97 (103, 109) sts total.

Row 1: (WS) Purl, working p3tog dec at center front—95 (101, 107) sts rem.

Row 2: Knit, working k3tog dec at center front—93 (99, 105) sts rem.

Row 3: Change to chestnut/violet and knit (to make foldline).

Row 4: Knit, inc 1 st each side of center front st—95 (101, 107) sts.

Row 5: Purl, inc 1 st on each side of center front st—97 (103, 109) sts.

BO all sts.

Armbands

With gold/plum, RS facing, and beg at underarm, pick up and knit 45 (46, 47) sts along armhole edge to shoulder, then pick up and knit 45 (46, 47) sts back down to underarm—90 (92, 94) sts total. Work 2 rows St st. Change to Renaissance/tangerine (for left armhole) or violet/ginger (for right armhole) and knit 1 WS row. Work St st for 2 more rows. BO all sts.

Sew right shoulder seam, including neckband. Sew side seams, including armbands. Fold neckband, armbands, and lower edge hem to inside along fold lines and sew in place to WS of garment. Weave in loose ends. (*Note:* To eliminate flare in the hems, run a thread through the finished hem along the fold line and pull the thread to gather the edge slightly, lightly steam-block, then remove the thread.)

Water Garden Fair Isle

Ron Schweitzer

Ron Schweitzer got the idea for this unisex pullover while viewing a friend's photograph of a residential water garden in Calcutta. A low wall behind the garden had been masterfully designed using small tiles mirroring the colors and shapes of the water plants and their reflections, perfectly complementing the light and shadow of the water garden. This sweater is constructed in the round in the traditional Fair Isle style, with drop shoulders, only two colors per round, and steeks at the armholes and neck opening.

Finished Size
44 (46¾, 49½)" (112 [118.5, 125.5] cm) bust/chest circumference. Sweater shown measures 49½" (125.5 cm).

Yarn
Fingering weight (#1 Super Fine).

Shown here: Yarns International Shetland 2000 (100% wool; 190 yd [174 m]/50 g): moorit (dark brown) and Shetland black, 4 (4, 5) skeins each; shaela (gray), 3 (4, 4) skeins; Shetland white and mooskit (tan), 2 (3, 3) skeins each.

Needles
Ribbing—size 3 (3.25 mm): 24" (60 cm) circular (cir) and set of 4 double-pointed (dpn). Body and sleeves—size 4 (3.5 mm): 32" (80 cm) cir and set of 4 dpn. Adjust needle sizes if necessary to obtain the correct gauge.

Notions
Markers (m); stitch holders; tapestry needle.

Gauge
32 stitches and 32 rows = 4" (10 cm) in body pattern on larger needles.

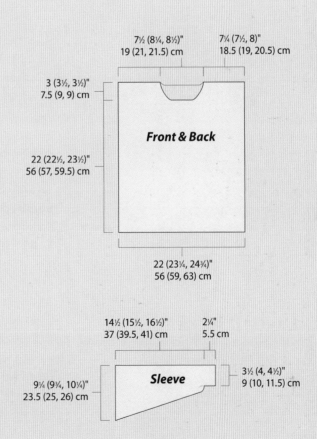

Legend

- O — Shetland white
- ◣ — Mooskit (tan)
- ‖ — shaela (gray)
- + — moorit (dark brown)
- ◆ — Shetland black
- ☐ — purl with appropriate color

Body

beg S sleeve   beg L sleeve   beg M sleeve

25
23
21 beg M sleeve
19
17
15
13 beg S sleeve
11
9
7
5
3 beg L sleeve
1

beg M body   beg S, L body

Ribbing

19
17
15
13
11
9
7
5
3
1

Body

With black and smaller needle, CO 150 (160, 170) sts for front, place marker (pm), CO 150 (160, 170) sts for back—300 (320, 340) sts total. Place m and join, being careful not to twist sts. Work Rows 1–19 of Ribbing chart, purling sts as indicated. With black, knit 1 rnd then purl 1 rnd. With black, inc on next rnd as foll:

Size Small only

*K6, [M1, k5, M1, k6] 12 times, [M1, k6] 2 times; rep from *—352 patt sts.

Size Medium only

*K9, [M1, k5, M1, k6] 13 times, M1, k8; rep from *—374 patt sts.

Size Large only

*K4, [M1, k6] 27 times, M1, k4; rep from *—396 patt sts.

All sizes

Change to larger needle. Beg as specified for your size, work Body chart until piece measures 15½ (16, 16½)" (39.5 [40.5, 41] cm) from CO.

Armhole Steeks

Set up and work steeks as described in the box on page 73.

Sizes Small and Large only

Place first st of front on holder, set first armhole steek, work all front sts, place first st of back on holder, set second armhole steek, work to end of rnd.

Size Medium only

Place last st of back and first st of front on holder, set first armhole steek, work to last st of front, place last st of front and first st of back on holder, set second armhole steek, work to end of rnd—350 (370, 394) body sts rem.

All sizes

Cont as charted until piece measures 22 (22½, 23½)" (56 [57, 59.5] cm) from CO.

Front Neck Steek

Work 71 (75, 80) front sts, place next 33 (35, 37) sts on holder for front neck, set front neck steek, work rem 71 (75, 80) front sts, work to end. Dec 1 st each side of front neck steek every rnd 6 (7, 7) times. *Work 1 rnd even. On next rnd, dec 1 st each side of front neck steek. Rep from * 7 (7, 8) more times—57 (60, 64) sts rem each side. Cont even until piece measures 24 (25, 26)" (61 [63.5, 66] cm) from beg.

Back Neck Steek

Cont in patt, work across all front sts, work 60 (63, 67) back sts, place next 55 (59, 63) sts on holder, set back neck steek, work to end of rnd. On next and foll alternate rnds, dec 1 st each side of back neck steek 3 times—57 (60, 64) patt sts rem each side. Cont in patt until piece measures 25 (26, 27)" (63.5 [66, 68.5] cm). On next rnd, BO sts for all steek sts. Using the three-needle method (see page 29), BO front and tog at shoulders.

Sleeves

Cut armhole steek between center sts. With dark brown (dark brown, black), larger dpn, and beg at underarm, pick up and knit 74 (78, 82) sts to shoulder join, pick up and knit 73 (77, 81) sts from shoulder to underarm—147 (155, 163) sts total. Pick up and knit 1 (2, 1) held underarm st(s) and for size medium only, knit these 2 tog to make 1 st. This underarm st marks the "seam" line and is not included in the st count; it will be eliminated in the dec rnd before the sleeve border. Join into a rnd. *First patt rnd:* Work Body chart in the opposite direction (from top to bottom) and read from left to right. Beg with Row 12 (20, 2) as indicated for your size, work to right edge of chart, work 22-st rep 6 (7, 7) times, work rem 7 (0, 4) sts. Work 1 (3, 3) rnd(s) even. On next rnd (Row 10 [16, 24] of chart) and every foll 3 (4, 4) rnds, dec 1 st each side of underarm st 37 (9, 20) times, then dec 1 st each side every 3 rnds 0 (27, 15) times—71 (81, 91) patt sts. Work 0 (2, 2) rnds even, ending with Row 1 of chart (all sizes). With smaller dpn and black, knit 1 rnd, then purl 1 rnd. On next rnd, dec as foll:

Size Small only
K2 [k2tog, k4] 11 times, k2tog, k2—60 sts rem.
Size Medium only
K2, [k2tog, k5] 11 times, k2tog, k1—70 sts rem.
For Size Large only
K1, [k2tog, k6] 11 times, k2tog, k1—80 sts rem.

Cuff

Working Ribbing chart in the opposite direction (from top to bottom), work Row 19 through Row 1. With black, BO all sts in patt.

Finishing
Neckband

Cut front and back neck steek sts bet center sts. With smaller dpn and dark brown, k55 (59, 63) held back neck sts, pick up and knit 26 (28, 30) sts to front neck, k33 (35, 37) held front neck sts, pick up and knit 26 (28, 30) sts to back neck—140 (150, 160) patt sts. Place marker (pm) and join. Purl 1 rnd. Work Rows 10 through 19 of Ribbing chart. With black, BO all sts in patt. Trim all steeks and sew in place as shown below. Weave in loose ends. Wash and block to finished measurements.

Working Steeks

To maintain knitting in the round, set steeks at armholes and neck "openings" by casting on 10 extra stitches (using the backward-loop method; see page 16), alternating the two colors used in that row. Keeping the first and last of those 10 stitches (the edge stitches) in the background color, alternate colors on the center 8 stitches to form a checkerboard pattern. After the knitting is complete, cut the piece between the fifth and sixth steek stitches (there is no need to baste before cutting because Shetland wools designed for Fair Isle knitting cling to each other and will not ravel). Pick up and knit stitches for the sleeves or neckband from the edge steek stitches (the ones worked in the background color every round). To finish, trim the steeks to 3 stitches in width and, with yarn threaded on a tapestry needle, use a cross-stitch as shown below to tack in place.

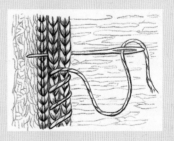

Beyond the Basics: WORKING WITH TWO YARNS

based on an article by Beth Brown-Reinsel

In Fair Isle (also called color-stranding) knitting, the stitches alternate colors based on a charted pattern. Most patterns involve just two colors per row and both yarns travel across the entire row, taking turns being used. The nonworking yarn trails, or strands, behind the stitches of the working yarn. The nonworking color may strand for a single stitch or several stitches, depending on the pattern; then the yarns trade places and the first yarn is stranded while the other color is worked. Knitters who hold just one yarn at a time must drop the old yarn and pick up and tension the new yarn at every color change, a process that can be slow and tedious. However, knitters who can hold and tension both yarns at the same time can work this type of color pattern quickly and easily.

There are two predominant styles of knitting: English, in which the working yarn is carried in the right hand, and Continental, in which the working yarn is carried in the left hand. Each style can be used with two strands of yarn, or you can combine styles and hold one yarn in each hand. Keep in mind that just as there is no "right way" to knit or purl, there is no "right way" to work with two yarns: Each method has its advantages.

Holding Both Yarns in the Right Hand

Most Americans learn to knit the English method, holding the yarn in their right hand. For these knitters, it is a relatively easy step to add another yarn to the same hand. Starting by placing both balls of yarn on your right side, bring the working end from each ball to the palm of your right hand, and insert your index finger down between the two yarns so that one yarn (the back yarn) is behind your index finger and the other yarn (the front yarn) is in front of your index finger (Figure 1). Tighten your other fingers around the two yarns for tension. (If necessary, wind the two yarns around your little finger for more tension.) Keep your hands relaxed and close to the needles.

Right-Side Rows
To Knit with the Front Yarn
Holding both yarns in back of the work, use the right needle to enter the stitch knitwise (from front to back), twist your wrist so that your palm faces you, wrap the yarn that's in front of your index finger counterclockwise around the needle (Figure 2), untwist your wrist, then bring the new stitch through the old, pulling the old stitch off the needle as you do so.

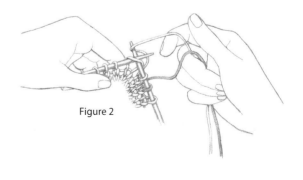

Figure 2

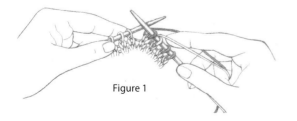

Figure 1

To Knit with the Back Yarn

Holding both yarns in back of the work, use the right needle to enter the stitch knitwise (from front to back), twist your wrist so that your palm faces away from you, wrap the yarn that's behind your index finger counterclockwise around the needle (Figure 3), untwist your wrist, then bring the new stitch through the old, pulling the old stitch off the needle as you do so.

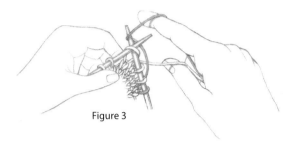

Figure 3

Wrong-Side Rows
To Purl with the Front Yarn

Holding both yarns in front of the work, use the right needle to enter the stitch purlwise (from back to front), twist your wrist so your palm faces you, wrap the yarn that's in front of your index finger counterclockwise around the needle (Figure 4), untwist your wrist, then bring the new stitch through the old, pulling the old stitch off the needle as you do so.

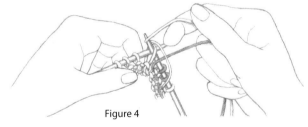

Figure 4

To Purl with the Back Yarn

Holding both yarns in front of the work, use the right needle to enter the stitch purlwise (from back to front), twist your wrist so that your palm faces away from you, wrap the yarn

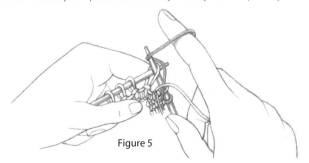

Figure 5

that's behind your index finger counterclockwise around the needle (Figure 5), untwist your wrist, then bring the new yarn through the old, pulling the old stitch off the needle as you do so.

Holding Both Yarns in the Left Hand

Most Europeans learn to knit the Continental method, holding the yarn in their left hand. Like the English method, two colors are worked by holding a second yarn in the same hand. Knitters who hold both yarns in their left hand have an advantage when they work with double-pointed needles—the tension on both yarns can be maintained as the work progresses from one needle to the next.

Start by placing both balls of yarn on your left side, bring the working end from each ball to the palm of your left hand and over your left index finger. Insert your middle finger between the two yarns so that one yarn (the front yarn) is under this finger and closest to your wrist, and the other yarn (the back yarn) is over the middle finger and closest to your fingertips (Figure 1). Tighten your other fingers around the two yarns for tension. (If necessary, wind the two yarns around your little finger for more tension.) Keep your hands relaxed and close to the needles and work the stitches close to the needle tips. Practice keeping the yarns on different areas of your two fingers, such as on either side of your first index knuckle so the yarns are separated and easier to work individually.

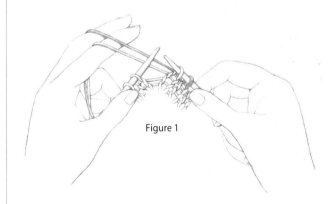

Figure 1

Right-Side Rows
To Knit with the Front Yarn

Holding both yarns in back of the work, use the right needle to enter the stitch knitwise (from front to back) and scoop the yarn that's nearest to you (the one that's on your index finger only) in a counterclockwise motion (Figure 2), then bring the new stitch through the old, pulling the old stitch off the needle as you do so.

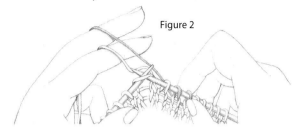
Figure 2

To Knit with the Back Yarn

Holding both yarns in back of the work, use the right needle to enter the stitch knitwise (from front to back), reach over the nearest yarn on your index finger (the front yarn) and scoop the farthest yarn (the one on your middle finger) in a counterclockwise motion (Figure 3), then bring the new stitch through the old, pulling the old stitch off the needle as you do so.

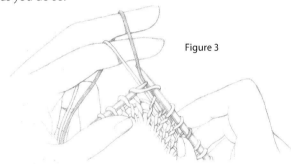
Figure 3

Wrong-Side Rows
To Purl with the Front Yarn

Holding both yarns in front of the work, bring the right needle behind both yarns and enter the stitch purlwise (from back to front), rotate the needle counterclockwise to catch the front yarn, and complete the stitch by bringing the needle forward through the stitch as if the back yarn were not there (Figure 4), pulling the old stitch off the needle as you do so.

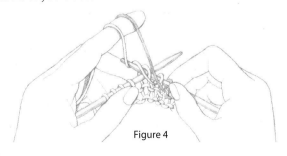
Figure 4

To Purl with the Back Yarn

Holding both yarns in front of the work, bring the right needle behind both yarns and enter the stitch purlwise (from back to front), rotate the needle counterclockwise to reach over the front yarn and catch the back yarn, and complete the stitch by bringing the needle forward and out of the stitch (Figure 5), pulling the old stitch off the needle as you do so.

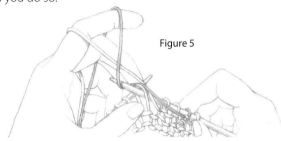
Figure 5

Holding One Yarn in Each Hand

The method of holding one yarn in each hand involves both the English and Continental methods of knitting. If you're not already familiar with both methods, holding one yarn in each hand can be slow going at first, but once you master the technique, knitting is rapid and there is little chance of confusing the two yarns. Hold one yarn in the right hand as for the English method and one yarn in the left hand as for the Continental method (Figure 1).

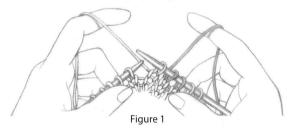
Figure 1

Right-Side Rows
To Knit with the Yarn in the Right Hand

Holding both yarns in back of the work, enter the stitch knitwise (from front to back), use your right index finger to wrap the yarn counterclockwise around the needle (Figure 2), then bring the new stitch through the old, pulling the old stitch off the needle as you do so.

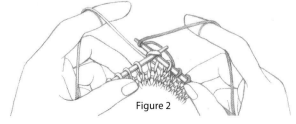
Figure 2

To Knit with the Yarn in the Left Hand

Holding both yarns in back of the work, enter the stitch knitwise (from front to back), use the right needle to scoop the yarn in a counterclockwise motion (Figure 3), then bring the new stitch through the old, pulling the old stitch off the needle as you do so.

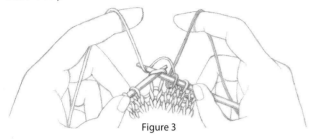

Figure 3

Wrong-Side Rows
To Purl with the Yarn in the Right Hand

Holding both yarns in front of the work, bring the right needle behind the left yarn (to prevent it from stranding on the right side of the work) and enter the stitch purlwise (from back to front); use your right index finger to wrap the right yarn counterclockwise around the needle (Figure 4), then bring the new stitch through the old, pulling the old stitch off the needle as you do so.

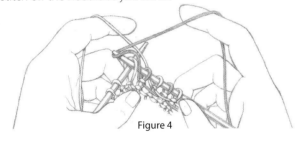

Figure 4

To Purl with the Yarn in the Left Hand

Holding both yarns in front of the work, enter the stitch purlwise (from back to front); use the right needle to scoop the yarn in a counterclockwise motion (Figure 5), then bring the new stitch through the old, pulling the old stitch off the needle as you do so.

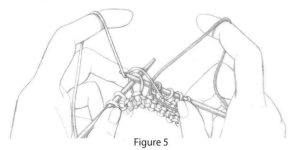

Figure 5

Yarn Dominance

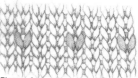

Figure 1

The way that two yarns relate to each other within a row is called yarn dominance. In her book *The Art of Fair Isle Knitting* (Interweave Press, 1996), Ann Feitelson demonstrates how the yarn that comes from beneath the other will appear more prominently in a design. This yarn will make a slightly larger stitch than that formed by the yarn that travels over (Figure 1). The dominant color is typically designated the "pattern" color and the other color is designated the "background" color. No matter how you hold your two yarns, you can consciously choose to make one yarn dominant simply by being consistent in the way that you pick up the new yarn at each color change.

When you're working right-side rows with two yarns in the right hand, hold the pattern color behind your index finger (designated the back yarn) and always pick it up from beneath the background yarn held in front of your index finger (designated the front yarn), so that the back yarn always strands under the front yarn. The background yarn is held in front of the index finger and is always stranded over the pattern color. When you're purling wrong-side rows, switch how you hold the two yarns so that the front yarn is the pattern yarn, and strand it under the background yarn (the back yarn).

When you're working right-side rows with two yarns in the left hand, hold the pattern yarn closer to you (the front yarn) on your index finger and pick it up from beneath the background yarn held on your middle finger (the back yarn). When you're purling wrong-side rows, place the pattern yarn in the back position, further away on your index finger, treat the back yarn as the pattern yarn, and pick it up from underneath the front yarn.

When you're working right-side rows with one yarn in each hand, hold the pattern yarn in your left hand; it will naturally strand under the background yarn. Hold the background yarn in your right hand; it will naturally strand over the pattern yarn. When you're purling wrong-side rows, treat the yarn in the right hand as the pattern yarn—it will strand underneath the background yarn.

If all these variations seem too overwhelming, just look at your yarns as you work; all you need to remember is that the yarn that is picked up from underneath will be more visible.

Cabaret Raglan

Norah Gaughan

Norah Gaughan used eyelets and two-stitch cables (also called traveling stitches) to give definition to the angled lines of the raglan armholes and decorate the front yoke of this otherwise simple pullover. She worked just a few garter ridges to prevent the cuffs, lower body, and broad neck from rolling and give the sweater a casual look. The yarn used here—a worsted-weight cotton tape named Cabaret—makes the sweater comfortable and surprisingly lightweight.

Finished Size
About 36½ (40½, 44, 48, 52)" (92.5 [103, 112, 122, 132] cm) bust/chest circumference. Sweater shown measures 40½" (103 cm).

Yarn
Worsted weight (#4 Medium).
Shown here: Reynolds Cabaret (100% cotton; 78 yd [71 m]/50 g): #158 rose, 10 (11, 12, 14, 15) balls (also shown in burgundy on page 80).
Note: This particular yarn has been discontinued.

Needles
Size 7 (4.5 mm) and 9 (5.5 mm). Adjust needle size if necessary to obtain the correct gauge.

Notions
Stitch holders; markers (m); cable needle (cn); tapestry needle.

Gauge
17 stitches and 24 rows = 4" (10 cm) in stockinette stitch on larger needles.

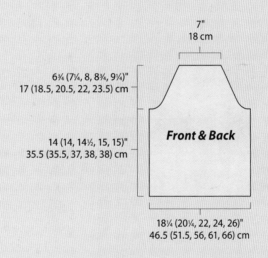

7"
18 cm

6¾ (7¼, 8, 8¾, 9¼)"
17 (18.5, 20.5, 22, 23.5) cm

14 (14, 14½, 15, 15)"
35.5 (35.5, 37, 38, 38) cm

Front & Back

18¼ (20¼, 22, 24, 26)"
46.5 (51.5, 56, 61, 66) cm

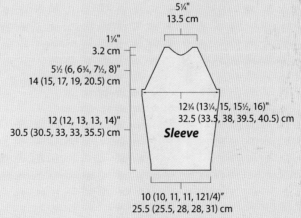

5¼"
13.5 cm

1¼"
3.2 cm

5½ (6, 6¾, 7½, 8)"
14 (15, 17, 19, 20.5) cm

12 (12, 13, 13, 14)"
30.5 (30.5, 33, 33, 35.5) cm

12¾ (13¼, 15, 15½, 16)"
32.5 (33.5, 38, 39.5, 40.5) cm

Sleeve

10 (10, 11, 11, 121/4)"
25.5 (25.5, 28, 28, 31) cm

Back

With smaller needles CO 78 (86, 94, 102, 110) sts. Knit 3 rows. Purl 1 row. Knit 2 rows. Change to larger needles. Beg with a knit row (RS), work St st until piece measures 14 (14, 14½, 15, 15)" (35.5 [35.5, 37, 38, 38] cm) from beg, ending with a WS row.

Shape Raglan

BO 3 sts at beg of next 2 rows—72 (80, 88, 96, 104) sts rem. *RS Dec Row:* K1, ssk, yo, ssk, knit to last 5 sts, k2tog, yo, k2tog, k1—2 sts dec'd. *WS Dec Row:* P3, p2tog, purl to last 5 sts, ssp (see page 62), p3—2 sts dec'd. Rep the last 2 rows 0 (2, 4, 6, 8) more times—68 sts rem. Work RS Dec Row

once more—2 sts dec'd. Purl next row (WS) even. Rep the last 2 rows 18 more times—30 sts rem; armhole measures about 6¾ (7¼, 8, 8¾, 9¼)" (17 [18.5, 20.5, 22, 23.5] cm). Place sts on holder.

Front

Work as for back to raglan shaping.

Shape Raglan

BO 3 sts at beg of next 2 rows—72 (80, 88, 96, 104) sts rem.

Size 36½" only

Skip to All Sizes.

Sizes (40½, 44, 48, 52)" only

Dec as foll:

RS Dec Row: K1, ssk, yo, ssk, knit to last 5 sts, k2tog, yo, k2tog, k1—2 sts dec'd. *WS Dec Row:* P3, p2tog, purl to last 5 sts, ssp, p3—2 sts dec'd. Rep the last 2 rows (1, 3, 5, 7) more time(s)—72 sts.

All sizes

Work Rows 1–40 of Front Yoke chart—30 sts rem; armhole measures about 6¾ (7¼, 8, 8¾, 9¼)" (17 [18.5, 20.5, 22, 23.5] cm). Place sts on holder.

Sleeves

With smaller needles CO 42 (42, 46, 46, 52) sts. Knit 3 rows. Purl 1 row. Knit 2 rows. Change to larger needles. Beg with a knit row (RS), work in St st for 4 rows, ending with a WS row. *Inc row:* (RS) K2, M1 (see page 52), knit to last 2 sts, M1, k2—2 sts inc'd. Work 9 (7, 5, 5, 7) rows even. Rep the last 10 (8, 6, 6, 8) rows 5 (6, 8, 9, 7) more times—54 (56, 64, 66, 68) sts. Cont even until piece measures 12 (12, 13, 13, 14)" (30.5 [30.5, 33, 33, 35.5] cm) from beg, ending with a WS row.

Shape Raglan

BO 3 sts at beg of next 2 rows—48 (50, 58, 60, 62) sts rem. *Dec row:* (RS) K1, ssk, knit to last 3 sts, k2tog, k1—2 sts dec'd. Work next row (WS) even. Rep the last 2 rows 1 (1, 7, 7, 7) more time(s)—44 (46, 42, 44, 46) sts rem. Work Dec row once more—2 sts dec'd. Work 3 rows even. Rep the last 4 rows 6 (7, 5, 6, 7) more times—30 sts; armhole measures about 5½ (6, 6¾, 7½, 8)" (14 [15, 17, 19, 20.5] cm).

Divide for Sleeve Notch

(RS) K1, ssk, k10, k2tog, join new yarn, ssk, knit to last 3 sts, k2tog, k1—13 sts each side. Working each side separately, cont as foll:

Row 1: (WS) For first section, purl to last 2 sts, ssp; for second section, p2tog, purl to end—1 st dec'd each section.

Row 2: For first section, k1, ssk, knit to last 2 sts, k2tog; for second section, ssk, knit to last 3 sts, k2tog, k1—2 sts dec'd each section.

Rep Rows 1 and 2 two more times—4 sts rem in each section. Work Row 1 once more—3 sts in each section; raglan measures about 6¾ (7¼, 8, 8¾, 9¼)" (17 [18.5, 20.5, 22, 23.5] cm). With RS facing, BO all sts kwise.

Finishing

With yarn threaded on a tapestry needle, sew both front raglan seams and sew right back raglan seam.

Neckband

With smaller needles, RS facing, and beg at left back raglan, pick up and knit 100 sts around neck opening as foll: 10 sts from top of left sleeve to center of notch, 10 sts from notch to top of left sleeve, 30 sts from front holder, 10 sts from top of right sleeve to center of notch, 10 sts from notch to top of right sleeve, 30 sts from back holder. Knit 2 rows. With WS facing, BO all sts kwise.

Sew rem raglan seam. Sew sleeve and side seams. Weave in loose ends. Block to measurements.

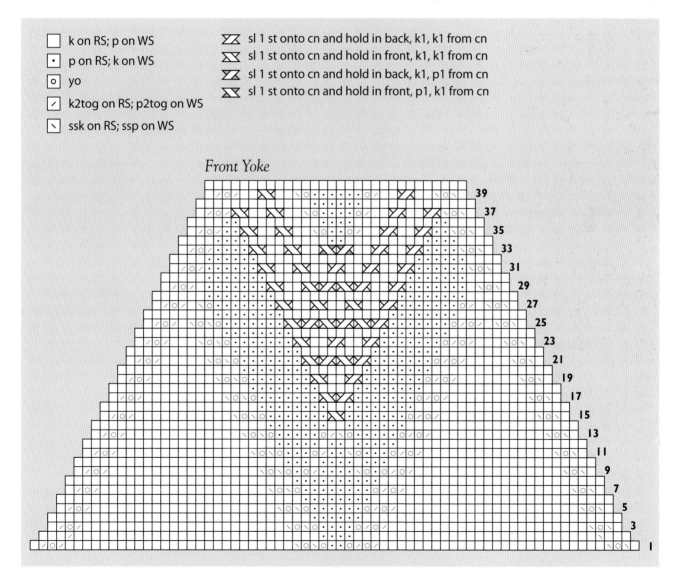

□ k on RS; p on WS
· p on RS; k on WS
o yo
∕ k2tog on RS; p2tog on WS
∖ ssk on RS; ssp on WS

sl 1 st onto cn and hold in back, k1, k1 from cn
sl 1 st onto cn and hold in front, k1, k1 from cn
sl 1 st onto cn and hold in back, k1, p1 from cn
sl 1 st onto cn and hold in front, p1, k1 from cn

Front Yoke

Lotus Blossom Tank

Sharon Shoji

This little top, worked in bamboo yarn, combines a delicate repeating lace pattern with a square neckline and unusual shoulder detail. To avoid side seams, the body is worked in the round to the armhole. From there, the front and back are worked separately back and forth in stockinette stitch. A smooth shoulder line and interesting bodice detail are created by extending the back over the shoulders and then sewing the straps, at a slight angle. The seams form a decorative detail on the front.

Finished Size
33¾ (39, 44, 48)" (85.5 [99, 112, 122] cm) bust
 circumference. Tank shown measures 33¾"
 (85.5 cm).

Yarn
DK weight (#3 Light).
 Shown here: South West Trading Company
 Bamboo (100% bamboo; 250 yd [229 m]/100 g):
 turquoise green, 2 (3, 4, 4) balls.

Needles
Body—sizes 6 (4 mm) and 5 (3.75 mm): 24"
 circular (cir). Neckband—size 5 (3.75 mm): 16"
 cir. Adjust needle size if necessary to obtain the
 correct gauge.

Notions
Markers (m); stitch holders; removable markers
 or safety pins; tapestry needle.

Gauge
22 stitches and 36 rounds = 4" (10 cm) in
 stockinette stitch on smaller needle; 23 stitches
 and 35 rounds = 4" (10 cm) in lace pattern on
 smaller needle after blocking.

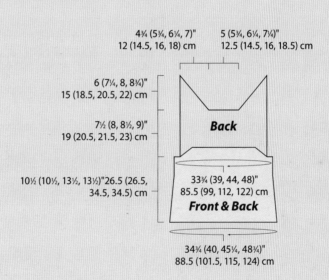

4¾ (5¾, 6¼, 7)"
12 (14.5, 16, 18) cm

5 (5¾, 6¼, 7¼)"
12.5 (14.5, 16, 18.5) cm

6 (7¼, 8, 8¾)"
15 (18.5, 20.5, 22) cm

7½ (8, 8½, 9)"
19 (20.5, 21.5, 23) cm

Back

10½ (10½, 13½, 13½)"26.5 (26.5, 34.5, 34.5) cm

33¾ (39, 44, 48)"
85.5 (99, 112, 122) cm

Front & Back

34¾ (40, 45¼, 48¾)"
88.5 (101.5, 115, 124) cm

S2kp2

Sl 2 sts as if to k2tog, k1, pass 2 slipped sts over knitted st.

Sk2p

Sl 1 st kwise, k2tog, pass slipped st over.

Lotus Lace (multiple of 10 sts)

Rnds 1, 3, and 5: Knit.

Rnds 2 and 4: Purl.

Rnd 6: *Yo, k3, s2kp2 (see above), k3, yo, k1; rep from * to end of rnd.

Rnd 7: K1, *yo, k2, s2kp2, k2, yo, k3; rep from *, end last rep k2 instead of k3.

Rnd 8: K2, *yo, k1, s2kp2, k1, yo, k5; rep from *, end last rep k3.

Rnd 9: K3, *yo, s2kp2, yo, k7; rep from *, end last rep k4.

Rnd 10: K1, *p2, k3; rep from *, end last rep k2.

Rnd 11: *Yo, ssk, p1, yo, s2kp2, yo, p1, k2tog, yo, k1; rep from * to end of rnd.

Rnd 12: K2, *p1, k3, p1, k5; rep from *, end last rep k3.

Rnd 13: K1, *yo, ssk, yo, s2kp2, yo, k2tog, yo, k3; rep from *, end last rep k2.

Rnd 14: K1, *p1, k5, p1, k3; rep from *, end last rep k2.

Rnd 15: K1, *p1, k1, yo, s2kp2, yo, k1, p1, k3; rep from *, end last rep k2.

Rnd 16: Rep Rnd 14.

Repeat Rnds 1–16 for pattern.

Decrease pattern

Row 1: (RS) K2, ssk, knit to last 4 sts, k2tog, k2—2 sts dec'd.

Row 2: (WS) Purl.

Row 3: K2, sk2p (see above), knit to last 5 sts, k3tog, k2—4 sts dec'd.

Row 4: Purl.

Note

- The first 9 rounds of lace pattern are worked on larger needle to keep the hem from pulling in; all successive rounds are worked on smaller needle.

Body

With larger cir needle, CO 200 (230, 260, 280) sts. Place marker (pm) and join for working in the rnd, being careful not to twist sts. Work Rnds 1–9 of lotus lace (see Stitch Guide). Change to smaller cir needle and cont in patt until 4 (4, 5, 5) patt repeats are complete; piece measures about 7 (7, 9, 9)" (18 [18, 23, 23] cm) from CO. Knit 1 rnd, dec 14 (16, 18, 16) sts evenly spaced—186 (214, 242, 264) sts rem. Place removable m on needle at halfway point. Slip m every rnd and work Rnds 1–4 of lotus lace. Discontinue lace patt and work in St st (knit every rnd) for 3 (3, 4, 4)"—piece measures about 10½ (10½, 13½, 13½)" (26.5 [26.5, 34.5, 34.5] cm) from CO.

Shape Front

Note: Front is worked back and forth in rows across first 93 (107, 121, 132) sts; you may want to place back sts on holder to facilitate working the front. Remove m at beg of rnd and BO 5 (5, 6, 6) sts, knit to next m. Remove second m and turn work, BO 5 (5, 6, 6) sts and purl to last 2 sts, p2tog—82 (96, 108, 119) sts rem for front. *Next row:* (RS) Ssk, knit to last 2 sts, k2tog—80 (94, 106, 117) sts rem. *Next row:* (WS) P2tog, purl to end—79 (93, 105, 116) sts rem. Attach safety pins or removable markers onto first and last st to mark beg of angle seam. Work Rows 1–4 of decrease patt (see Stitch Guide) 4 (4, 5, 5) times—55 (69, 75, 86) sts rem. Knit 3 rows. BO all sts kwise.

Shape Back

(RS) Join yarn and BO 5 (5, 6, 6) sts, knit to end of back sts. Turn work, BO 5 (5, 6, 6) sts and purl to last 2 sts, p2tog—82 (96, 108, 119) sts rem. *Next row:* (RS) Ssk, knit to last 2 sts, k2tog—80 (94, 106, 117) sts rem. *Next row:* (WS) P2tog, purl to end—79 (93, 105, 116) sts rem. Work even in St st (knit RS rows, purl WS rows) until armholes measure 7½ (8, 8½, 9)", ending with a WS row.

Shape Shoulders

Work short-rows as foll:

Row 1: (RS) K66 (78, 88, 97), turn.

Row 2: (WS) Place a safety pin or removable marker on (not through) working yarn and sl next st, p52 (62, 70, 77), turn.

Row 3: Place a safety pin on (not through) working yarn and sl next st, k45 (54, 61, 67), turn.

Row 4: Place a safety pin on working yarn and slip next st, p38 (46, 52, 57), turn.

Row 5: Place a safety pin on working yarn and sl next st, knit to first gap (safety pin will be hanging on a loop of yarn under right-hand needle), *lift pin and place loop on left-hand needle with the right "leg" of loop in front, knit loop tog with next st and remove pin*, knit to next gap and rep from * to * once, knit to end of row.

Row 6: Purl to first gap (safety pin will be hanging on a loop of yarn under right-hand needle), *sl first st on left-hand needle pwise onto right-hand needle, lift pin and place loop on left-hand needle with right "leg" of loop in front, sl first st back onto left-hand needle, purl loop tog with next st and remove pin*, purl to next gap and rep from * to * once, purl to end of row.

Shape Neck

(RS) K26 (31, 35, 38) for right shoulder, place rem sts on a holder. With 26 (31, 35, 38) sts on needle, work 3 rows even in St st, ending with a WS row. *Dec row:* (RS) Knit to last 2 sts, k2tog—1 st dec'd. *Next row:* (WS) Purl. Rep last 2 rows until 1 st rem. Fasten off last st. Leaving center 27 (31, 35, 40) sts on holder, sl 26 (31, 35, 38) left shoulder sts to smaller cir needle. With RS facing, join yarn and work 4 rows in St st. *Dec row:* (RS) Ssk, knit to end—1 st dec'd. *Next row:* (WS) Purl. Rep last 2 rows until 1 st rem. Fasten off last st.

Finishing

Block pieces lightly to measurements with cool iron and pressing cloth. Mark 3 (3, 3¾, 3¾)" (7.5 [7.5, 9.5, 9.5] cm) from pointed end of shoulder piece. Match point of shoulder piece to safety pin at beg of angle seam, and match mark to end of decrease patt (end of angle). With tapestry needle, sew angled seam, beg at the safety pin. Sew second angled seam in same manner. With 16" (40 cm) smaller cir needle and RS facing, pick up and knit 96 (102, 108, 114) sts around armhole. Purl 1 rnd, knit 1 rnd. BO all sts pwise. Rep for second armhole.

Neckband

With 16" cir needle and RS facing, pick up and knit 33 (39, 43, 47) sts along front right side, k27 (31, 35, 40) neck sts from holder, pick up and knit 33 (39, 43, 47) sts along front left side. Knit 2 rows. BO all sts kwise on WS. With yarn threaded on a tapestry needle, weave in loose ends. Block armholes and neckband if needed.

Lite Lopi Pullover

Norah Gaughan

Norah Gaughan looked to traditional Bohus knitting for the color and stitch patterns on her round-yoke sweater where the signature purl stitches in Bohus designs create a subtle "pop" effect—small dots of color and texture in an otherwise straightforward Fair Isle pattern. The sweater is seamless; the body and sleeves are knitted separately in the round, transferred to a single circular needle, then the yoke is worked to the neck in pattern. The soft mellow colors and rustic yarn combine to make this an all-around comfort sweater, the kind of garment you toss on a chair, ready to throw on morning, noon, and night.

Finished Size

36 (39, 42, 45, 48, 51)" (91.5 [99, 106.5, 114.5, 122, 129.5] cm) bust/chest circumference. Sweater shown measures 39" (99 cm).

Yarn

Worsted weight (#4 Medium).

Shown here: Reynolds Lite Lopi (100% wool; 109 yd [100 m]/50 g): #418 light blue heather (MC), 7 (7, 8, 9, 10, 11) balls; #421 celery heather and #427 rust heather, 1 (1, 1, 2, 2, 2) ball(s) each; #417 cordovan and #432 grape heather, 1 ball each.

Needles

Body and sleeves—size 8 (5 mm): 16" and 24" (40 and 60 cm) circular (cir) and set of 4 (or 5) double-pointed (dpn). Neckband—size 6 (4 mm): 16" (40 cm) cir. Adjust needle sizes if necessary to obtain the correct gauge.

Notions

Marker (m); stitch holders or waste yarn; tapestry needle.

Gauge

16 stitches and 24 rounds = 4" (10 cm) in stockinette stitch on larger needles, worked in the round.

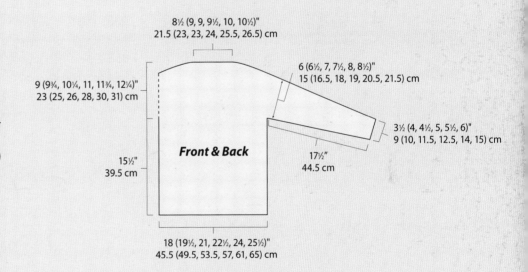

8½ (9, 9, 9½, 10, 10½)"
21.5 (23, 23, 24, 25.5, 26.5) cm

6 (6½, 7, 7½, 8, 8½)"
15 (16.5, 18, 19, 20.5, 21.5) cm

9 (9¾, 10¼, 11, 11¾, 12¼)"
23 (25, 26, 28, 30, 31) cm

3½ (4, 4½, 5, 5½, 6)"
9 (10, 11.5, 12.5, 14, 15) cm

Front & Back

15½"
39.5 cm

17½"
44.5 cm

18 (19½, 21, 22½, 24, 25½)"
45.5 (49.5, 53.5, 57, 61, 65) cm

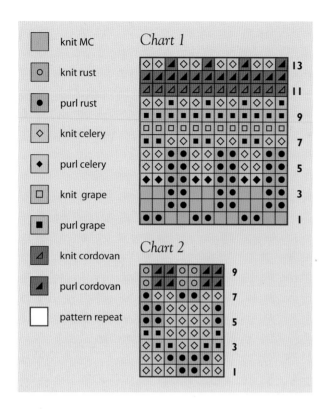

Chart 1

Chart 2

Legend:
- knit MC
- o — knit rust
- • — purl rust
- ◇ — knit celery
- ◆ — purl celery
- □ — knit grape
- ■ — purl grape
- ◿ — knit cordovan
- ◢ — purl cordovan
- pattern repeat

Body

With longer cir needle and MC, CO 144 (156, 168, 180, 192, 204) sts. Place marker (pm) and join, being careful not to twist sts. Work even in St st until piece measures 15½" (39.5 cm) from beg, ending 6 sts before marker on last rnd.

Divide for Front and Back

BO 12 sts (1 st on right needle), k59 (65, 71, 77, 83, 89) for front, BO 12 sts, knit to end for back—60 (66, 72, 78, 84, 90) sts each for front and back. Do not break yarn. Set aside.

Sleeves

With dpn and MC, CO 28 (32, 36, 40, 44, 48) sts. Place m and join, being careful not to twist sts. Work even in St st until piece measures 1" (2.5 cm) from beg. *Inc rnd:* K1, M1 (see page 52), knit to last st, M1, k1—2 sts inc'd. Inc 1 st each side of m in this manner every 10 rnds 9 more times—48 (52, 56, 60, 64, 68) sts. Cont even until piece measures 17½" (44.5 cm) from beg, ending 6 sts before m on last rnd.

Bind Off for Armholes

BO 12 sts, knit to end—36 (40, 44, 48, 52, 56) sts rem. Place sts on holder or waste yarn.

Yoke

Note: Change to shorter needle when necessary. Return sts for first sleeve to dpn, and using yarn and needles from body, k36 (40, 44, 48, 52, 56) sleeve sts, pm, k60 (66, 72, 78, 84, 90) front sts, pm, return sts for second sleeve to dpn and k36 (40, 44, 48, 52, 56) sleeve sts, pm, k60 (66, 72, 78, 84, 90) back sts—192 (212, 232, 252, 272, 292) sts total. Place m for beg of rnd and join. Knit 4 rnds. *Dec rnd:* *K1, k2tog, knit to 3 sts before next m, ssk, k1, slip m; rep from * 3 times more—8 sts dec'd. Dec in this manner every 4 rnds 2 (3, 4, 5, 6, 7) more times—168 (180, 192, 204, 216, 228) sts rem. Knit 4 rnds. Work Rnds 1–13 of Chart 1. With celery, knit 1 rnd. *Next rnd:* With celery, knit 1 rnd, and *at the same time* dec 14 (19, 24, 22, 27, 32) sts evenly spaced—154 (161, 168, 182, 189, 196) sts rem. Work Rnds 1–9 of Chart 2. With rust, knit 1 rnd. *Next rnd:* With rust, knit 1 rnd, and *at the same time* dec 28 (29, 36, 44, 45, 46) sts evenly spaced—126 (132, 132, 138, 144, 150) sts rem. Work 9 rnds as foll:

Rnds 1 and 2: *P1 with celery, k2 with rust; rep from *.
Rnd 3: Knit with grape.
Rnd 4: Purl with grape.
Rnd 5: Knit with rust.
Rnd 6: Knit with cordovan, and *at the same time* dec 31 (33, 33, 34, 35, 36) sts evenly spaced—95 (99, 99, 104, 109, 114) sts rem.
Rnd 7: Purl with rust.
Rnd 8: Knit with rust.
Rnd 9: Knit with rust, and *at the same time* dec 25 (25, 25, 26, 27, 28) sts evenly spaced—70 (74, 74, 78, 82, 86) sts rem. Change to smaller cir needle and with rust, knit 1 rnd, dec 2 sts evenly spaced—68 (72, 72, 76, 80, 84) sts rem.

Neckband

Work k2, p2 rib as foll: 2 rnds rust, 2 rnds celery, 1 rnd grape—5 rnds total. With cordovan, BO all sts in rib.

Finishing

With MC threaded on a tapestry needle, sew underarm seams. Weave in loose ends. Block lightly.

Beyond the Basics: READING CHARTS

based on an article by Ann Budd

Many beginning knitters pale at the sight of a charted knitting pattern, temporarily paralyzed by the seemingly complicated abbreviations and symbols (k2tog, ssk, brackets, parentheses, asterisks). But symbol language is actually quite simple; rather than an unbreakable code, it is truly useful shorthand. Curiously, however, many knitters never make the jump to following charted patterns, failing to understand how logical and, yes, easy to follow, they really are.

Charts have several advantages over row-by-row knitting instructions written out in words: They let you see at a glance what's to be done and what the pattern will look like knitted; they help you recognize how the stitches relate to one another; and they take up less space than written instructions. To save space, more and more stitch patterns are charted instead of written out row-by-row, and that means it is more important than ever to learn how to read them.

The Anatomy of a Chart

Charts are a visual representation of a knitted fabric viewed from the right side. Charts are plotted on graph paper so that one square represents one stitch and one horizontal row represents one row of knitting. The symbols or colors in the squares indicate how to work each stitch. For color-work charts, the colors represent yarn colors—see the Water Garden Fair Isle (page 70) and Weekend Gateway Satchel (page 140) for examples. For texture work, the symbols represent stitch manipulations—see the Marseilles Pullover (page 54), Cabaret Raglan (page 78), and VIP Cardigan (page 122). Some charts include symbols for color as well as stitch manipulations—see the Lite Lopi Pullover (page 86). Unless otherwise specified, charts are read from the bottom to the top; right to left for right-side rows and left to right for wrong-side rows. When knitting in the round (where the right side of the knitting is always facing out), all rows are read from right to left.

The charts in this book are plotted on a square grid. Because knitted stitches tend to be wider than they are tall, motifs worked from these charts will appear somewhat squattier in the actual knitting than they appear on the grid. To avoid this discrepancy when designing your own project, use proportional knitter's graph paper (available at many knitting stores).

Symbols

Though not all publications use exactly the same symbols (for example, some use a horizontal dash to denote a purl stitch, others use a dot), for the most part, the symbols represent what the stitches look like when viewed from the right side of the fabric. Symbols that slant to the left represent left-slanting stitches. Symbols that slant to the right represent right-slanting stitches. Notice how the symbols in the charts on page 90 mimic the stitches in the knitted fabrics. Think of a knitting chart as a shorthand cartoon representation of the knitted fabric. Each square represents one stitch. The shapes and slants of the symbols imitate the shapes and slants of the knitted stitches.

Because charts are presented as viewed from the right side only, most symbols represent two different maneuvers—one for right-side rows and another for wrong-side rows. For example, for stockinette stitch, you knit the stitches on right-side rows and purl them on wrong-side rows. However, charted stockinette stitch shows only the right, or knit, side. A list of some common symbols and their

Comparing Charts & Swatches

Notice how the stitches mimic the chart symbols in this simple lace pattern.

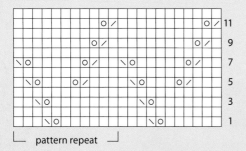

pattern repeat

The chart symbols for cables indicate the direction of the cable twists.

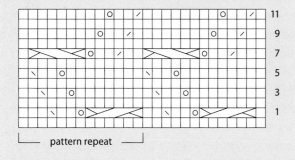

pattern repeat

rows. However, charted stockinette stitch shows only the right, or knit, side. A list of some common symbols and their right- and wrong-side definitions is provided on page 91.

No Stitch

Many stitch patterns, especially lace, involve increases or decreases that cause the stitch count to rise or fall, thereby requiring the number of boxes in a chart to vary from one row to the next. For some patterns, these variations are simply represented by uneven chart edges. For other patterns, adding or subtracting boxes at the edge of a chart may disrupt the vertical stitch alignment in the pattern. In these cases, a special symbol for "no stitch" is used within the borders of the chart so that stitches that are aligned vertically in the knitting are aligned vertically in the chart. The "no stitch" symbol accommodates a "missing" stitch while maintaining the vertical integrity of the pattern. In this book, missing stitches are represented by gray shaded boxes. When you come to a shaded box, simply skip over it and continue to the end of the row as if it doesn't exist.

Row Numbers

Rows are numbered along the side of most charts, especially long or complicated ones. Row numbers appearing along the right edge denote right-side rows to be read from right to left. Row numbers appearing along the left edge denote wrong-side rows to be read from left to right. For example, if the number 1 is on the right edge of the chart, that and all subsequent odd-numbered rows are right-side rows; all even-numbered rows are worked from the wrong side (from left to right). With few exceptions, charts in this book designate Row 1 as a right-side row. For some patterns, this necessitates a "set-up row" be worked prior to the first row of the chart to get the stitches in the necessary sequence of knits and purls before the first right-side row of the pattern.

Pattern Repeats

All charts show at least one pattern repeat. If the repeat is complex, more than one repeat is typically charted to help you see how the individual motifs look adjacent to each other.

In row-by-row instructions, pattern repeats are flanked by asterisks or square brackets. On charts, these repeats are outlined in heavy or colored boxes, or they're annotated at the lower or upper edge of the chart.

Some patterns that are worked back and forth in rows require extra stitches to balance a charted pattern. In row-by-row instructions, such patterns are reported as repeating over a multiple of a number of stitches plus extra stitches (i.e., balanced 2 x 2 ribbing worked back and forth in rows is a multiple of 4 stitches plus 2). On charts, these balancing stitches appear at the right and left margins of the chart, with the repeat clearly marked in between. On right-side rows, work from right to left, working the stitches on the right edge once, then the repeat as many times as necessary, and end by working the stitches on the left edge once. On wrong-side rows, work from left to right, working the stitches on the left edge once, the repeat box as many times as necessary, and end by working the stitches on the right edge once.

Charts for multisize garments will most likely have different numbers of edge stitches for the different sizes. Read the instructions and chart carefully and be sure to begin and end as specified for the size you are making.

TIPS for Working with Charts

✳ If a chart is so small or complicated that it causes your eyes to strain, copy it onto larger graph paper or make a photocopy enlargement. If the chart involves color work and you don't have access to a color photocopier, use colored pencils or markers to color in the appropriate boxes.

✳ Keep your place while working a chart by holding a straightedge or row finder on the chart and using a row counter on your knitting needle. You can place the straightedge either above or below the row you're working on; placing it on the row above will let you see how the stitches relate to the previous row (the one you just knitted). Once you've worked a couple of repeats from the chart, you may be able to look at your knitting rather than the chart to figure out what comes next.

✳ If you plan to design a sweater or other piece around a charted design, be sure to center the design over the center stitch of the piece. Otherwise, you will end up with a partial repeat at one edge that isn't mirrored at the other.

Common Chart Symbols & Definitions

Symbol	Definition
□	right side: knit / wrong side: purl
·	right side: purl / wrong side: knit
/	right side: k2tog / wrong side: p2tog
⊼	right side: k3tog / wrong side p3tog
\	right side: ssk / wrong side: ssp
⋀	right side: sl 2 sts individually, k1, p2sso / wrong side: p2tog and place st on left needle, pass next st over this st, return st to right needle
M	Make 1
O	yarnover
b	work through back loop of stitch
□	no stitch
⧖	Right cross: place specified number of sts onto cable needle and hold in back, knit specified number of sts, knit specified number of sts from cable needle
⧗	Left cross: place specified number of sts onto cable needle and hold in front, knit specified number of sts, knit specified number of sts from cable needle

Icarus Shawl

Miriam Felton

A lace motif from Sophia Caulfield's *Dictionary of Needlework*, first published in 1882, was the starting point for Miriam Felton's feather-light shawl. Airy columns of eyelets open up the stockinette-stitch body of the shawl and send the eye to the intricately patterned edges. Worked from the long edge to the outer ends of the shawl, the design flows downward. The softly pointed edging reminds Miriam of feathers spilling out—just as, in Greek mythology, Icarus's feathers fell away from their wax frame when he flew too close to the sun.

Finished Size
About 72" (183 cm) wide across top edge and 36" (91.5 cm) long from center of top edge to bottom point, after blocking.

Yarn
Fingering weight (#1 Super Fine).
Shown here: The Alpaca Yarn Company Suri Elegance (100% alpaca; 875 yd [800 m]/100 g): #3001 Pearl Harbor grey, 1 skein.

Needles
Size 3 (3.25 mm): 24" circular (cir). Adjust needle size if necessary to obtain the correct gauge.

Notions
Markers (m); sharp-point sewing needle; blocking wires or cotton thread for blocking.

Gauge
21 stitches and 38 rows = 4" (10 cm) in stockinette stitch, after blocking.

Notes
- Slip markers on every row as you come to them. Make sure that a marker does not accidentally slip past a yarnover next to it and migrate into the wrong position. The two center markers should always be on either side of the center stitch, and each edging marker should always be two stitches in from the end of the row.
- The triangular shape is achieved by increasing four stitches on every right side row, except when working the four edging rows. One stitch is increased at each end by working a yarnover just inside each two-stitch marked garter stitch edging, and two stitches are increased in the center of the shawl by working a yarnover on each side of the marked center stitch.
- For a larger or smaller shawl, work Rows 19–42 of Chart 1 more or fewer times before finishing Chart 1 by working Rows 19–34 once. Each 24-row repeat added or removed will increase or decrease the width across the top edge by about 8", and will increase or decrease the length of the shawl from center of top edge to bottom point by about 2½". Be aware that your stitch counts will be different from those given if you change the number of repeats. Remember to purchase more yarn if making a larger shawl than shown; our sample used 90 grams of the recommended yarn.
- If you choose to set off individual pattern repeats with markers, remove all but the four original markers (the ones on either side of the center stitch and just inside each garter stitch edge) on the last row of Chart 4 before you begin the edging.

Stitch Guide

yo4

Yo 4 times. On the foll row, drop 3 of the wraps so that you are
left with a single, extra-large yo; work this large yo as 1 st.

☐	k on RS; p on WS
•	p on RS; k on WS
O	yo
╱	k2tog
╲	ssk

⅄	sl 1 as if to knit, k2tog, pass slipped st over
▨	no stitch
☐	pattern repeat
▐	marker position

Note: Use a photocopier to enlarge these charts.

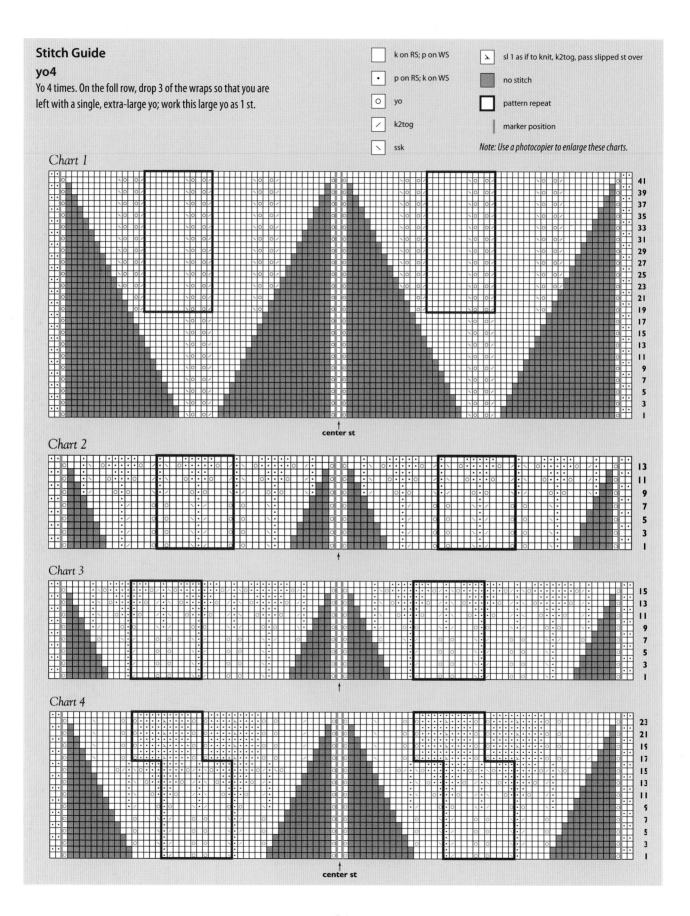

Chart 1

center st

Chart 2

Chart 3

Chart 4

center st

94

Shawl

CO 5 sts. Set up patt as foll:

Row 1: (RS) K2, yo, k1, yo, k2—7 sts.

Row 2: (WS) Knit.

Row 3: K2, yo, [k1, yo] 3 times, k2—11 sts.

Rows 4 and 6: K2, purl to last 2 sts, k2.

Row 5: K2, place marker (pm), yo, k3, yo, pm, k1 (center st), pm, yo, k3, yo, pm, k2—15 sts.

Row 7: K2, yo, k5, yo, k1 (center st), yo, k5, yo, k2—19 sts.

Row 8: Rep Row 4.

Work Rows 1–42 of Chart 1 once—103 sts. Rep Rows 19–42 only of Chart 1 five more times (see Notes for how to adjust size at this point)—343 sts. Work Rows 19–34 of Chart 1 once—375 sts; 178 rows total completed from Chart 1. Change to Chart 2, and work Rows 1–14 once—403 sts after completing Chart 2. Change to Chart 3, and work Rows 1–16 once—435 sts after completing Chart 3. Change to Chart 4, and work Rows 1–24 once—483 sts after completing Chart 4.

Edging

Row 1: (RS) K2, yo, *k5, k2tog, k4, [yo, k1f&b (see page 52), yo, p4, ssk (see page 62), p5] 18 times, yo, k1f&b, yo, k4, ssk, k5*, yo, k1 (center st), yo, rep from * to * once more, yo, k2—561 sts.

Row 2: K2, p15, [k10, p4] 18 times, p11, p1 (center st), p11, [p4, k10] 18 times, p15, k2.

Row 3: K2, yo, *k6, k2tog, k3, [k2tog, yo4 (see Stitch Guide), ssk, p10] 18 times, k2tog, yo4, ssk, k3, ssk, k6*, yo, k1 (center st), yo, rep from * to * once more, yo, k2—523 sts if counting all 4 loops of each yo4 as only 1 st; 637 sts if counting each yo4 as 4 sts.

Row 4: K2, p12, [drop 3 loops of yo4 off needle and purl into rem single loop, p1, k10, p1] 18 times, drop 3 loops of yo4 off needle and purl into rem single loop, p12, p1 (center st), p12, [drop 3 loops of yo4 off needle and purl into rem single loop, p1, k10, p1] 18 times, drop 3 loops of yo4 off needle and purl into rem single loop, p12, k2—523 sts.

BO on next row as foll: P2, *with yarn in front (wyf), sl 2 sts from right needle back to left needle, p2tog (the 2 sts just returned to left needle), p1; rep from * until all sts are bound off. *Note:* Once you are familiar with the BO, you can streamline the process by slipping the left needle into the back of the 2 sts on the right needle and behind the right needle, and working the 2 sts tog from that position, without transferring the sts and working the p2tog as two separate steps.

Finishing

With yarn threaded on a sewing needle, weave in ends by piercing the strands of the shawl on the WS to better secure the fine tails.

Blocking

Wet-block by soaking in lukewarm water or Eucalan bath for 15–20 minutes, until shawl is thoroughly saturated. Pin to finished measurements with blocking wires. As an alternative, run a strand of cotton thread along the top edge, and a second strand down the centerline. Pull the cotton guide threads straight, square them off at a 90-degree angle to each other, and pin in place. Use the guide threads to stretch the shawl straight. Pin out the BO edge into points, placing a pin in each large yo4 hole. Allow to dry thoroughly before removing blocking wires, pins, and cotton guide thread (if used).

Forest Path Stole

Faina Letoutchaia

Faina Letoutchaia drew upon the lace-knitting traditions of her Russian homeland and of the Shetland Islands, variations on stitch patterns from Barbara Walker's stitch guides, and a fascination with entrelac to create this stunningly elegant alpaca stole. Each of the three lace patterns—fern, birch leaves, and lily of the valley (all inspired by a springtime walk in the forest)—is worked inside its own entrelac unit, which means there is only one lace pattern to keep track of at a time.

Finished Size
About 30" (76 cm) wide and 85" (216 cm) long, blocked.

Yarn
Fingering weight (#1 Super Fine).
Shown here: Suri Elegance (100% Suri alpaca; 875 yd [800 m]/100 g): #0100 white house, 3 skeins (2 skeins for a shawl 71" [180 cm] long).

Needles
Size 3 (3.25 mm): 24" (60 cm) circular (cir) and set of 2 double pointed (dpn). Adjust needle size if necessary to obtain the correct gauge.

Notions
Markers (m); stitch holders; crewel embroidery needle with large eye and blunt point; tailor's wax (available at fabric stores); nylon cord for blocking.

Gauge
19 stitches and 24 rows = 4" (10 cm) in seed stitch, after blocking.

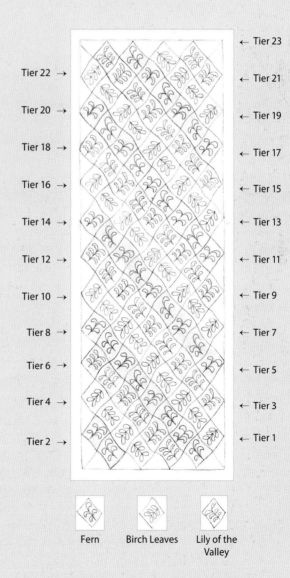

Tier 23
Tier 22 →   ← Tier 21
Tier 20 →   ← Tier 19
Tier 18 →   ← Tier 17
Tier 16 →   ← Tier 15
Tier 14 →   ← Tier 13
Tier 12 →   ← Tier 11
Tier 10 →   ← Tier 9
Tier 8 →   ← Tier 7
Tier 6 →   ← Tier 5
Tier 4 →   ← Tier 3
Tier 2 →   ← Tier 1

Fern   Birch Leaves   Lily of the Valley

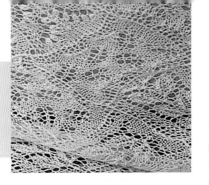

Stitch Guide
Seed Stitch: (odd number of sts)
All rows: *K1, p1; rep from *, end k1.

Notes

- To prevent excessive handling of the yarn, place stitches for sections not being worked on holders and use double-pointed needles to work only the required stitches. Transfer stitches not being worked onto holders as each unit is completed.
- Each entrelac lace unit begins and ends with a row of 20 sts, but the stitch count may change on other rows, depending on the pattern. Each chart shows the center 18 stitches of the entrelac unit. Selvedge sts are not shown on the charts; work them according to the instructions given for each tier.

Lower Border

With cir needle and using the knitted method (see page 16), CO 141 sts. Do not join. Slipping the first st of every row and knitting the last st, work seed st for 20 rows. On next row, place markers (pm) as foll: Sl 1, work 14 sts in seed st, pm, [work 22 sts in seed st, pm] 2 times, work 23 sts in seed st, pm, [work 22 sts in seed st, pm] 2 times, work 14 sts in seed st, k1. *Next row:* (RS) Sl 1, work 14 sts in seed st then place the last 15 sts worked onto a holder for right border, remove m, [k6, k2tog, k6, k2tog, k6, slip marker (sl m)] 2 times, [k6, k2tog] 2 times, k5, k2tog, sl m, [k6, k2tog, k6, k2tog, k6, sl m] 2 times, place the last 15 sts onto a holder for left border, turn work—100 sts; 20 sts each in 5 marked sections.

Base Triangles

First Triangle

Row 1: (WS) Sl 1 pwise with yarn in front (wyf), p1—2 sts on right needle, turn.

Row 2: Sl 1 kwise with yarn in back (wyb), k1, turn.

Row 3: Sl 1 pwise wyf, M1 (see page 52), p2tog—3 sts, turn.

Row 4: Sl 1 kwise wyb, k2, turn.

Row 5: Sl 1 pwise wyf, M1, k1, p2tog—4 sts, turn.

Row 6: Sl 1 kwise wyb, k1, p1, k1, turn.

Row 7: Sl 1 pwise wyf, M1, p1, k1, p2tog—5 sts, turn.

Row 8: Sl 1 kwise wyb, k1, p1, k2, turn.

Cont in this manner, working all odd-numbered (WS) rows as foll: Sl 1 pwise wyf, M1, work in seed st to last st before gap, p2tog, turn; and working all even-numbered (RS) rows as foll: Sl 1 kwise wyb, work in seed st to last st, k1, turn. When all 20 sts in this section have been worked, ending with a WS row, remove m between sections. Do not break yarn.

Second, Third, Fourth, and Fifth Triangles

With WS facing and beg with first 2 sts of next section, work second triangle same as the first. Rep for third, fourth, and fifth triangles—5 triangles of 20 sts each. If desired, place sts of first, second, third, and fourth triangles on holders. Do not break yarn. Turn.

Right Side Triangle

Row 1: (RS) Sl 1 pwise wyf, M1—2 sts on right needle for right side triangle; 19 sts on left needle for base triangle or lace unit, turn.

Rows 2 and 4: Sl 1 pwise wyf, k1, turn.

Row 3: Sl 1 pwise wyf, ssk, turn.

Row 5: Sl 1 pwise wyf, M1, ssk—3 sts on right needle for right side triangle; 17 sts on left needle for base triangle or lace unit, turn.

Row 6: Sl 1 pwise wyf, k2, turn.

Row 7: Sl 1 pwise wyf, M1, k1, ssk—4 sts on right needle for right side triangle; 16 sts on left needle for base triangle or lace unit, turn.

Row 8: Sl 1 pwise wyf, p1, k2, turn.

Row 9: Sl 1 pwise wyf, M1, k1, p1, ssk—5 sts on right needle for right side triangle; 15 sts on left needle for base triangle or lace unit, turn.

Cont in this manner, working all odd-numbered RS rows as foll: Sl 1 pwise wyf, M1, work in seed st to last st before gap, ssk, turn; and working all even-numbered WS rows as foll: Sl 1 pwise wyf, work in seed st to last st, k1, turn. Cont until all 20 sts from base triangle or lace unit have been consumed, ending with a RS row. If desired, place 20 sts for right side triangle on a holder. Do not break yarn.

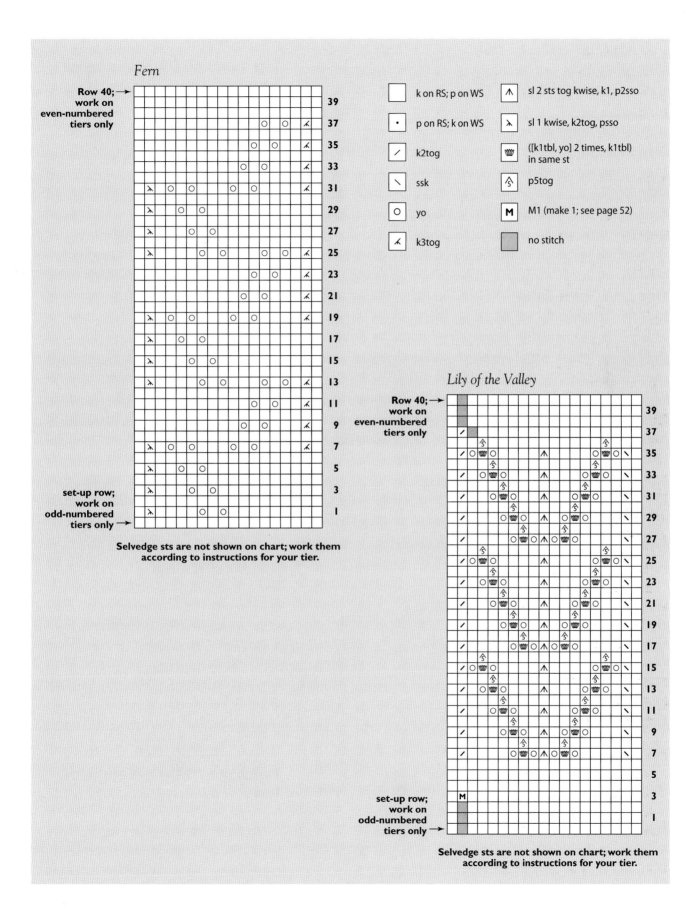

Fern

Row 40; →
work on
even-numbered
tiers only

39
37
35
33
31
29
27
25
23
21
19
17
15
13
11
9
7
5
3
1

k on RS; p on WS

p on RS; k on WS

/ k2tog

\ ssk

o yo

⅄ k3tog

∧ sl 2 sts tog kwise, k1, p2sso

⅄ sl 1 kwise, k2tog, psso

([k1tbl, yo] 2 times, k1tbl) in same st

p5tog

M M1 (make 1; see page 52)

no stitch

set-up row;
work on
odd-numbered
tiers only →

Selvedge sts are not shown on chart; work them
according to instructions for your tier.

Lily of the Valley

Row 40; →
work on
even-numbered
tiers only

39
37
35
33
31
29
27
25
23
21
19
17
15
13
11
9
7
5
3
1

set-up row;
work on
odd-numbered
tiers only →

Selvedge sts are not shown on chart; work them
according to instructions for your tier.

99

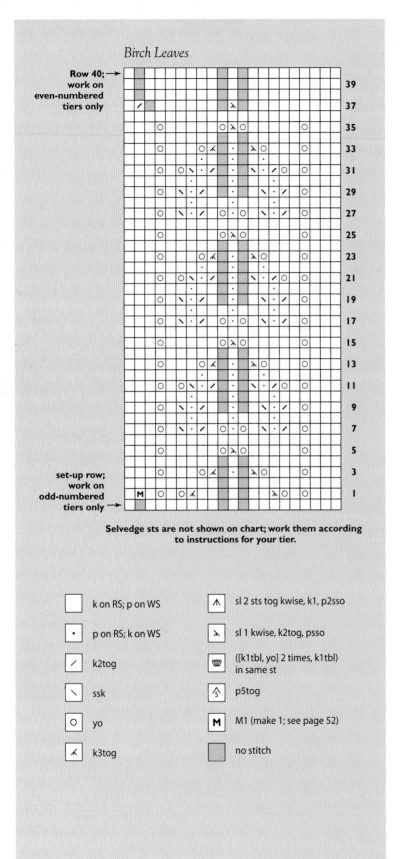

Birch Leaves

Row 40; → work on even-numbered tiers only

set-up row; work on odd-numbered tiers only →

Selvedge sts are not shown on chart; work them according to instructions for your tier.

	k on RS; p on WS
·	p on RS; k on WS
/	k2tog
\	ssk
o	yo
⋏	k3tog
∧	sl 2 sts tog kwise, k1, p2sso
⋏	sl 1 kwise, k2tog, psso
⊎	([k1tbl, yo] 2 times, k1tbl) in same st
⑤	p5tog
M	M1 (make 1; see page 52)
▨	no stitch

Tier 1 and All Odd-Numbered Tiers

(Worked from right to left) Pick up sts along selvedge of next base triangle or next lace unit as foll: With RS facing and yarn in front, insert tip of right needle from back to front under both legs of slipped selvedge st, wrap yarn around needle as if to purl, and pull up a loop. Pick up and knit 18 sts along selvedge of a base triangle, or 20 sts along selvedge of a lace unit, in this manner. *Set-up row:* (WS) Sl 1 pwise wyf, purl to end, k1, and *at the same time*, if you began with 18 sts, inc 2 sts evenly spaced—20 sts. For each lace unit, work Rows 1–39 of lace patt from chart, following illustration on page 97 for placement of lace pattern units. *At the same time*, work the lace patt selvedge sts for odd-numbered tiers as foll: *On RS:* Work first st as sl 1 pwise wyf, and work last st as ssk (to join the last st with first st of unit from previous tier); *On WS:* Work first st as sl 1 pwise wyf, and work last st as k1. If you have placed nonworking sts on holders, transfer live sts to dpn as necessary to join the units. When all units of an odd-numbered tier have been completed, end having just worked Row 39 (RS) of the last lace unit. Do not break yarn.

Left Side Triangle

With RS facing, pick up and knit 20 sts along selvedge of base triangle or lace unit according to the method used for Tier 1.
Row 1: (WS) Sl 1 pwise wyf, work seed st to last st, k1. Turn.
Row 2: Sl 1 pwise wyf, work seed st to last 2 sts, k2tog—19 sts rem.
Rep Rows 1 and 2 until 1 st rem, ending with Row 2. Turn. Do not break yarn.

Tier 2 and All Even-Numbered Tiers

(Worked from left to right) Pick up and knit 20 sts along selvedge of left side triangle or next lace unit as foll: With WS facing, insert tip of right needle from front to back under both legs of

selvedge st, wrap yarn around needle as if to knit, and pull up a loop—21 sts for first lace unit of the tier (includes 1 st left on needle from left side triangle); 20 sts for all other units in this tier, turn. For the first lace unit of tier only, dec 1 st in Row 1 of lace patt to eliminate extra st from left side triangle—20 sts. Work Rows 1–40 of each lace unit in patt according to charts, following illustration for placement of lace pattern units. *At the same time*, work the lace patt selvedge sts for even-numbered tiers as foll: *On RS:* Work first st as sl 1 kwise wyb and work the last st as k1; *on WS:* Work first st as sl 1 pwise wyf and work the last st as p2tog (to join last st with first st of unit from previous tier). Place sts for completed units on holders, if desired. When all units for an even-numbered tier have been completed, end having just worked Row 40 (WS) of the last lace unit. Do not break yarn. Work a right side triangle, then cont with next odd-numbered tier. Cont in this manner until 23 tiers have been completed. Work a left side triangle—1 st rem on needle from left side triangle. *Note:* If you would prefer a shorter shawl, work 21 or 19 tiers, making sure to end with an odd-numbered tier; every pair of tiers removed will reduce the length of the shawl by about 7" (18 cm).

Top Triangles

(Worked from left to right) With WS facing, pick up and knit 20 sts along selvedge of last left side triangle according to directions for even-numbered tiers—21 sts (includes 1 st on needle after completing the previous triangle).

Row 1: (RS) Sl 1 kwise wyb, work seed st to last st, k1, turn.

Row 2: Sl 1 pwise wyf, work seed st to last st, p2tog (to join last st with first st of unit from previous tier), turn.

Row 3: Sl 1 kwise wyb, work seed st to last 2 sts, k2tog, turn. Rep Rows 2 and 3 until 1 st rem, ending with Row 3, turn. With WS facing, pick up and knit 20 sts (as for even-numbered tiers) along selvedge of next lace unit—21 sts. Work as for previous top triangle. Cont working top triangles in this manner, joining the final top triangle to live sts of the last right side triangle. Break yarn.

Right Border

Transfer 15 held sts for right border onto a dpn. With WS facing, join new yarn, and maintaining seed st as established, work 14 sts in seed st, end k1. *Next row:* (RS) Sl 1 pwise wyf, work seed st to end. Work border while joining it to side of shawl as foll:

Row 1: (WS) Wyf, insert right needle tip from back to front under both legs of slipped selvedge st, wrap yarn around

needle as if to purl, and pull through a 12"–18" (30.5–45.5 cm) loop. Examine the loop to identify which end is anchored to the work and which end is connected to the yarn supply. Using the anchored end, work in seed st to last st, end k1, turn.

Row 2: Using the yarn from the same loop, sl 1 pwise wyf, work seed st to end. Gently pull the end of the loop connected to the yarn supply until excess yarn from loop disappears, and tighten last st.

Pulling up a new long loop every Row 1, rep Rows 1 and 2 until you reach the top of the last right side triangle, ending with Row 2. There are 20 slipped selvedge sts on the side of every triangle, so there should be about 40 rows of seed st border for every triangle. Adjust the pick-up if necessary, to make a smooth join with no gaps; the appearance of the join is more important than the actual number of rows. Place 15 sts for right border on a holder. Break off yarn.

Left Border

Transfer 15 held sts for left border onto a dpn. With RS facing, join new yarn and maintaining seed st patt as established, work 14 seed sts, end k1, turn. *Next row:* (WS) Sl 1 pwise wyf, work seed st to end of row. Work border while joining it to the side of shawl as foll:

Row 1: (RS) Wyb, insert right needle tip from front to back under both legs of slipped selvedge st, wrap yarn around needle as if to knit, and pull through a 12"–18" (30.5–40.5 cm) loop. Using the anchored end of loop as for right border, work in seed st to last st, end k1, turn.

Row 2: Using the yarn from the same loop, sl 1 pwise wyf, work seed st to end. Gently pull the end of loop connected to yarn supply until excess yarn from loop disappears, and tighten last st.

Pulling up a new long loop every Row 1, rep Rows 1 and 2 until you reach the top of the last left side triangle, ending with Row 2. Do not break yarn.

Top Border

Transfer left border sts to cir needle with WS facing. Pick up and knit 20 sts along selvedge edge of each top triangle as foll: With yarn in back, insert tip of right needle from front to back under both legs of top triangle slipped selvedge st, wrap yarn around needle as if to knit, and pull up a loop. Transfer held sts for right border to dpn and work in established seed st to last st, end k1—130 sts, turn. *Next row:* (RS) Sl 1 pwise wyf, work 14 sts of right border in seed st, k100 sts picked up bet borders, and *at the same time* inc 11 sts evenly spaced along picked-up sts, work 14 sts of left border, end k1—141 sts. Working seed st and selvedges as established, work 21 rows. Cut yarn, leaving a tail about 4 times the width of the knitting stretched to its fullest.

Finishing

To strengthen the yarn for working the sewn bind-off, pass the long tail of yarn through tailor's wax, refreshing the wax several times as you work. Thread tail on crewel embroidery needle and use the sewn method (see page 30) to loosely BO all sts. Weave in loose ends.

Blocking

Weave a fine, smooth nylon cord in and out along the side selvedges and along the top and bottom edges, leaving 20"–30" (51–76 cm) loops of cord at each corner to allow for stretching the shawl. Wash in lukewarm water with gentle shampoo and rinse in water of the same temperature. Squeeze gently to remove water and roll in a towel to further remove excess water. Stretch on a large flat surface, pulling on the nylon cord to stretch, and pin the cord in place. Allow to air-dry completely.

Beyond the Basics: KNITTED LACE

based on an article by Jackie Erickson-Schweitzer

Airy, light, and a bit mysterious—the delicate tracery of knitted lace is hard to resist. Even the simplest of lace patterns looks impressive and inspires admiration. But intricate as it may appear, knitted lace is simply a fabric punctuated with deliberate openings that can be arranged in a myriad of ways to create patterns that range from basic to complex. The wonderful thing about knitted lace is that despite its apparent intricacy, it follows a simple logic. The openings are created by special increases called yarnovers, and each yarnover is accompanied by a compensating decrease. Once you understand how yarnovers and decreases work together, you'll be on your way to mastering the vast array of lace patterns.

Traditional laceweight yarn yields beautiful lace patterns, but sport, worsted, and bulky yarns can be equally effective. A smooth, light-colored fingering or sportweight yarn worked on a needle three to four sizes larger than you'd normally use creates a fluid fabric in which the lace pattern is clearly visible. But fuzzy yarns and dark and variegated colors yield impressive results, too. Experiment with different yarns and needle sizes when you're swatching lace patterns to see the variety of effects you can create with a single pattern; you'll quickly find out what appeals to you.

Getting Started—Yarnovers and Decreases in a Simple Lace Pattern

A yarnover is a stitch made by a loop or strand of yarn placed on the right-hand needle as you work. On the return row, this loop is worked as you would any other stitch; once knitted, it leaves a small opening in the knitting. Each yarnover is counted as an increase of one stitch. To maintain a constant stitch count, every yarnover is paired with a decrease. The decrease may immediately precede or follow the yarnover, appear several stitches away from the yarnover

in the same row, or even on a later row. The decreases used in lace knitting are typically right-leaning (i.e., k2tog), left-leaning (i.e., ssk), or vertically aligned (i.e., double decrease). It is the interplay of yarnovers and right- and left-leaning decreases that produce all types of lacy patterns.

Yarnovers Worked Between Different Types of Stitches

Whether knits or purls precede or follow a yarnover determine the way it's made. It's worth reviewing the subtle differences here.

Between Two Knit Stitches

(working yarn begins in back) Bring the yarn to the front between the needle tips, over the top of the needle, and to the back, ready to knit the next stitch (Figure 1).

Figure 1

After a Knit, Before a Purl

(working yarn begins in back) Bring the yarn to the front between needle tips, over the top of the needle, and between the needles again to the front, ready to purl the next stitch (Figure 2).

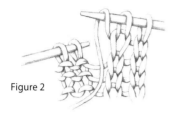

Figure 2

After a Purl, Before a Knit

(working yarn begins in front) Bring the yarn over the right-hand needle to the back ready to knit the next stitch (Figure 3).

Figure 3

Between Two Purl Stitches

(working yarn begins in front) Bring the yarn over the right-hand needle to the back, then to the front again between the tips of the needles, ready to purl the next stitch (Figure 4).

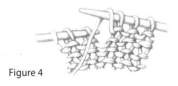

Figure 4

Decreases

Decreases can be made so that the decreased stitch slants to the right, slants to the left, or is vertically aligned.

Right-Slant Decrease (k2tog)

Knit 2 stitches together as if they were a single stitch. The second stitch lies on top of the first, causing the stitch to slant to the right.

Left-Slant Decrease (ssk)

Slip 2 stitches individually knitwise (Figure 1), insert the left needle through the front of the two slipped stitches, then knit them together through their back loops (Figure 2). The first stitch lies on top of the second, causing the stitch to slant to the left.

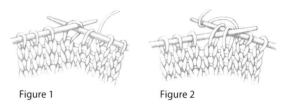

Figure 1   Figure 2

Centered Double Decrease
(Sl 2 tog knitwise, k1, pass 2 slipped sts over)

Slip 2 stitches together knitwise to the right needle (Figure 1), knit the next stitch (Figure 2), then use the tip of the left needle to lift the 2 slipped stitches up and over the knitted stitch (Figure 3) and off the needle. The center stitch lies on top of both the first and third stitch, causing the stitch to be vertically aligned.

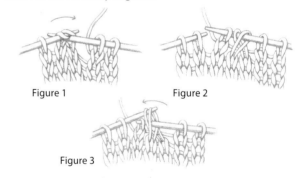

Figure 1   Figure 2

Figure 3

Balanced Lace Pattern

When a lace pattern is balanced, there are as many yarnover increases as there are decreases, and every left-slant decrease is offset by a right-slant decrease. The stitch count remains constant from row to row. Most simple lace patterns, like the one on page 105, are balanced. Two balanced lace patterns are used for the the body and sleeves of the peignoir in the Lace Peignoir and Simple Shell (page 32), and one is used in the Lotus Blossom Tank (page 82).

Note that in this pattern, all the yarnovers and decreases are worked on right-side rows. The wrong-side return rows are called "rest rows" because they are worked without any yarnovers or decreases. Although some lace patterns have patterning on every row, it is quite common for lace patterns to alternate rest rows and pattern rows. In this balanced pattern, the yarnovers are distributed in equal numbers before and after the decreases and the same number of decreases slant to the right and slant to the left in each pattern repeat.

	k on RS; p on WS
o	yo
/	k2tog
\	ssk
ʌ	sl 2 as if to k2tog, k1, p2sso

Pattern #1

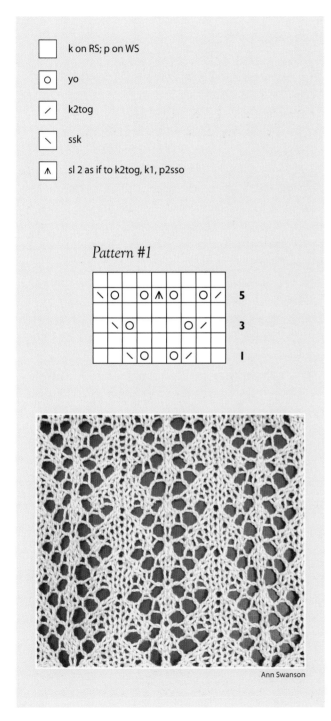

Ann Swanson

Simple Lace Pattern (multiple of 9 stitches)

Row 1: (RS) *K2, k2tog, yo, k1, yo, ssk, k2; rep from * to end of row.

Row 2: (WS) Purl.

Row 3: *K1, k2tog, yo, k3, yo, ssk, k1; rep from * to end of row.

Row 4: Purl.

Row 5: *K2tog, yo, k1, yo, sl 2 tog knitwise (as if to k2tog), k1, pass the 2 sl sts over, yo, k1, yo, ssk; rep from * to end of row.

Row 6: Purl.

Repeat Rows 1–6 for pattern.

The row-by-row instructions above can be translated graphically into a chart (see Reading Charts, page 89) that offers a visual representation of the right side of the knitted lace. As with all charts, each square represents one stitch and each row of squares represents a row of knitting. In summary, a chart is read from bottom to top; right-side rows are read from right to left, in the same direction as one normally knits. The first stitch on the left-hand needle as you're ready to begin a row corresponds to the first square in the bottom right-hand corner of the chart. The symbol key indicates what to do for each stitch; for example, a plain square represents a knitted stitch and a circle represents a yarnover. Note that in this pattern, the number of stitches stays the same in each row—for every yarnover, there is a corresponding decrease, and vice versa. On Row 1, the right-slanting k2tog decrease is paired with the yarnover that follows it, and the left-slanting ssk decrease is paired with the yarnover that precedes it. On Row 5, the double decrease (sl 2 tog knitwise, k1, pass 2 sl sts over) is paired with two yarnovers—one on each side of the decrease.

Biased Lace Pattern

Some lace patterns create biased patterns by arranging the yarnovers to fall consistently on one side of their corresponding decreases. Zigzags will form if the yarnovers alternate from being on one side of the decreases for a number of rows, then on the other side for a number of rows, as in the pattern on page 106.

Notice that the edges of this swatch are wavy and that the stitches alternate from slanting to the right and slanting to the left to create a bias look. The stitches slant

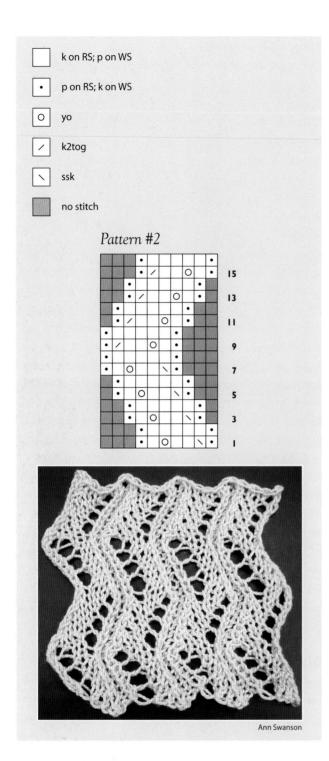

Legend:

- ☐ k on RS; p on WS
- ▪ p on RS; k on WS
- ○ yo
- ╱ k2tog
- ╲ ssk
- ▨ no stitch

Pattern #2

(chart rows labeled 1, 3, 5, 7, 9, 11, 13, 15)

Ann Swanson

are positioned to the right of their decreases, which causes fabric to angle to the right. The cast-on edge is scalloped because the increases and their compensating decreases are separated by other plain stitches. This also causes the bind-off edge to scallop, but the scallop is less pronounced because all of the stitches were knitted as they were bound off. You can increase the scalloped effect of the bind-off row by binding off in pattern, working the decreases extra tight and working the yarnovers and other stitches extra loose.

Simple Biased Lace Pattern *(multiple of 7 stitches)*

Rows 1, 3, 5, and 7: (RS) *P1, ssk, k2, yo, k1, p1; rep from * to end of row.

Even-numbered rows 2–14: (WS) *K1, p5, k1; rep from * to end of row.

Rows 9, 11, 13, and 15: *P1, k1, yo, k2, k2tog, p1; rep from * to end of row.

Row 16: *K1, p5, k1; rep from * to end of row.
Repeat Rows 1–16 for pattern.

The chart for this pattern shows how the decreases remove stitches at one edge of the piece while the yarnovers add stitches at the other edge. To maintain a consistent chart width, "no-stitch" symbols are used to denote stitches that are not present on some rows but are present on others. Each "no-stitch" is represented by a gray box, which is simply a placeholder for the stitch that isn't present on a particular row. You don't do anything when you see a no-stitch symbol; simply skip over it as if it weren't there and knit according to the symbols represented by the white squares. Notice how the "no stitch" boxes help the chart visually represent the knitted fabric. "No stitch" symbols are used to maintain straight edges in the charts for the Icarus Shawl (page 92).

Other lace patterns use "no-stitch" symbols to maintain the vertical alignment of stitches when the stitch count varies from row to row, such as when a yarnover's compensating decrease is deferred until a following row. See the Forest Path Stole (page 96) for an example.

Common Mistakes and Easy Fixes

If you discover a mistake, take a breath and stay calm. Even expert knitters make mistakes. The most common mistakes in lace knitting are fairly easy to fix.

If you forgot to make a yarnover, identify where you

to the right for the first 8 rows because the yarnovers are positioned to the left of their companion decreases, which forces the grain of the fabric to lean to the right. At the same time, the fabric angles to the left. On the following 8 rows, the stitches slant to the left because the yarnovers

omitted the yarnover and temporarily mark that spot with a removable marker or safety pin. On the return row, insert the right-hand needle from back to front under the running thread (the strand directly between and below the two needles), pick it up and place it on the left-hand needle ready to take the place of the missing yarnover.

If you make an extra yarnover, on the return row drop the extra loop and continue on. At first that area will look a bit looser, but blocking will even out any irregularities.

If the pattern design doesn't look right or the stitch count is off, and you can't identify the problem, unwork stitches one by one across the row. Recheck your stitch count until you get to a place where the pattern works properly, then proceed from there.

Using a Lifeline

A lifeline is a temporary thread inserted through a row of stitches that serves as a checkpoint if you need to rip out and redo several rows. If possible, insert the lifeline in an unpatterned "rest row" at the beginning or end of a pattern repeat (for example, Row 6 of Simple Lace Pattern on page 105. After completing this row, thread a fine, smooth thread (crochet thread works well) in a contrasting color onto a tapestry needle and run it through the bottom of each stitch on the needle (but not through any markers that may be on the needle). Gently pull the lifeline thread so that it hangs at least 6" (15 cm) down on each end of the row (Figure 1). Then resume knitting according to the pattern, being careful not to knit the lifeline into the new stitches (Figure 2).

With luck, you'll never need to use the lifeline. But if you discover a mistake, remove the knitting needle and ravel down to the stitches held by the lifeline. Transfer the stitches from the lifeline onto a knitting needle (it's easiest if you use a smaller needle for this) one stitch at a time (Figure 3), being careful to pick up the stitches in the correct orientation with the leading leg on the front of the needle, and leaving the lifeline in place as you go (in case you need to rip out again). Count the stitches to be sure that you've got them all, then resume knitting with the original size needles.

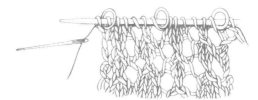

Figure 1

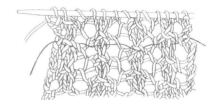

Figure 2

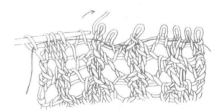

Figure 3

Tips for Knitting Lace

* Be sure that you can easily read and keep your place in the instructions. Enlarge charts and, if necessary, transcribe texts or charts into terminology or symbols that work for you.

* Place a magnetic strip, ruler, or Post-it Note just above the row you're working. This will help your eyes focus on that row and see how that row relates to the previous rows.

* Work in a place with good light and minimal distractions, and avoid knitting lace when you are tired.

* Check your work often, count stitches, use markers liberally, and visually compare your knitting against the chart(s) and sample photograph(s).

* Read the pattern out loud as you work through the pattern the first few times. Simultaneous seeing, hearing, and doing can be helpful.

Cambridge Jacket

Ann Budd

Inspired by the casual men's sweater jackets that were popular in the 1950s, this trim cardigan uses placed ribs for fit and knitterly detail. A single-crochet edging around the bottom edge of body and sleeve cuffs prevents the stockinette-stitch edge from rolling, and a zipper up the center front and tidy set-in sleeves give the sweater a clean finish. Knit it in a fiery orange, or, for a more conservative version, try it in a cool blue.

Finished Size

35 (39, 44, 48, 52)" (89 [99, 112, 122, 132] cm) bust/chest circumference, zipped. Cardigan shown measures 39" (99 cm). *Note:* Ribbed sections of garment can be blocked wider to produce a slightly larger finished chest size.

Yarn

Worsted weight (#4 Medium).
Shown here: Cascade Yarns Cascade 220 Heathers (100% wool; 220 yd [201 m]/100 g): #2425 rust, 6 (6, 7, 8, 9) skeins.

Needles

Body and sleeves—size 9 (5.5 mm). Collar—size 8 (5 mm). Adjust needle size if necessary to obtain the correct gauge.

Notions

Markers (m); removable markers or waste yarn; tapestry needle; size 7 (4.5 mm) crochet hook; 26 (26, 26, 27, 28)" (66 [66, 66, 68.5, 71] cm) separating zipper; sharp-point sewing needle and matching thread.

Gauge

19½ stitches and 27 rows = 4" (10 cm) in stockinette stitch on larger needles; 25 stitches and 27 rows = 4" (10 cm) in k3, p2 ribbing on larger needles, with ribbing patted gently to lie flat.

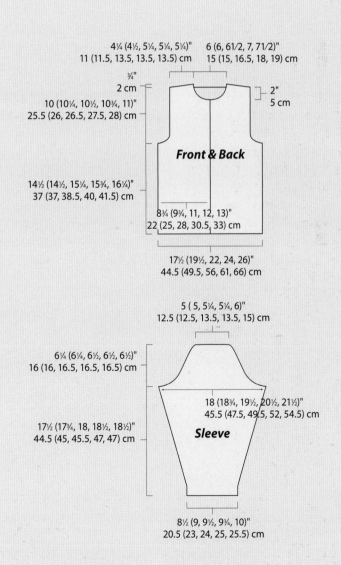

4¼ (4½, 5¼, 5¼, 5¼)"
11 (11.5, 13.5, 13.5, 13.5) cm

6 (6, 6½, 7, 7½)"
15 (15, 16.5, 18, 19) cm

¾"
2 cm

2"
5 cm

10 (10¼, 10½, 10¾, 11)"
25.5 (26, 26.5, 27.5, 28) cm

Front & Back

14½ (14½, 15¼, 15¾, 16¼)"
37 (37, 38.5, 40, 41.5) cm

8¾ (9¾, 11, 12, 13)"
22 (25, 28, 30.5, 33) cm

17½ (19½, 22, 24, 26)"
44.5 (49.5, 56, 61, 66) cm

5 (5, 5¼, 5¼, 6)"
12.5 (12.5, 13.5, 13.5, 15) cm

6¼ (6¼, 6½, 6½, 6½)"
16 (16, 16.5, 16.5, 16.5) cm

18 (18¾, 19½, 20½, 21½)"
45.5 (47.5, 49.5, 52, 54.5) cm

Sleeve

17½ (17¾, 18, 18½, 18½)"
44.5 (45, 45.5, 47, 47) cm

8½ (9, 9½, 9¾, 10)"
20.5 (23, 24, 25, 25.5) cm

Note

- When binding off for shoulders and front neck, work each p2 rib column as p2tog on right-side rows and k2tog on wrong-side rows; each 2-stitch rib column will be decreased to 1 stitch, and will count as only 1 bound-off stitch. For armholes, bind off in the usual manner.

Back

With larger needles, CO 96 (108, 122, 134, 146) sts. *Set-up row:* (WS) K1 (edge st; knit every row), p2, [k2, p3] 4 (5, 6, 7, 8) times, k2, place marker (pm), p46 (48, 52, 54, 56), pm, [k2, p3] 4 (5, 6, 7, 8) times, k2, p2, k1 (edge st; knit every row). Working edge sts in garter st, work all other sts as they appear until piece measures 14½ (14½, 15¼, 15¾, 16¼)" (37 [37, 38.5, 40, 41.5] cm) from CO, ending with a WS row.

Shape Armholes

Cont in patt, BO 4 (5, 5, 7, 8) sts at beg of next 2 rows, then BO 3 (4, 4, 6, 7) sts at beg of foll 2 rows, then BO 0 (3, 3, 4, 7) sts at beg of foll 2 rows—82 (84, 98, 100, 102) sts rem. Dec 1 st each end of needle every RS row 2 times—78 (80, 94, 96, 98) sts rem. Re-establish edge sts and cont even in patt until armholes measure 4¼ (4¼, 4½, 4½, 4¾)" (11 [11, 11.5, 11.5, 12] cm), ending with a WS row. Mark center 22 (16, 20, 22, 24) sts with waste yarn or removable markers. *Next row:* (RS) K1 (edge st), work in established rib to 12 (16, 16, 16, 16) sts before marked center sts, [k3, M1 (see page 52), p1] 3 (4, 4, 4, 4) times, k22 (16, 20, 22, 24) marked center sts, [p1, M1, k3] 3 (4, 4, 4, 4) times, work in established rib patt to last st, k1 (edge st)—84 (88, 102, 104, 106) sts. Working edge sts in garter st and inc'd sts in rev St st (purl RS rows, knit WS rows) to maintain k3, p2 rib, cont in rib until armholes measure 10 (10¼, 10½, 10¾, 11)" (25.5 [26, 26.5, 27.5, 28] cm), ending with a WS row.

Shape Shoulders

Counting bind-offs according to Note, BO 7 (8, 9, 9, 9) sts at beg of next 4 rows, then BO 7 (7, 9, 9, 9) sts at beg of foll 2 rows—32 (32, 36, 38, 40) sts rem. BO all sts for back neck, working all p2 rib columns as 2 sts in the normal manner; do not dec as you did when shaping the shoulders.

Left Front

With larger needles, CO 48 (54, 61, 67, 73) sts. *Set-up row:* (WS) K1 (edge st; knit every row), p22 (23, 25, 26, 27), pm, [k2, p3] 4 (5, 6, 7, 8) times, k2, p2, k1 (edge st; knit every row). Working

edge sts in garter st, work all other sts as they appear until piece measures 14½ (14½, 15¼, 15¾, 16¼)" (37 [37, 38.5, 40, 41.5] cm) from CO, ending with a WS row.

Shape Armhole

At armhole edge (beg of RS rows), BO 4 (5, 5, 7, 8) sts once, then BO 3 (4, 4, 6, 7) sts once, then BO 0 (3, 3, 4, 7) sts once—41 (42, 49, 50, 51) sts rem. Dec 1 st at armhole edge every RS row 2 times—39 (40, 47, 48, 49) sts rem. Re-establish edge st at armhole edge and cont even in patt until armhole measures 4¼ (4¼, 4½, 4½, 4¾)" (11 [11, 11.5, 11.5, 12] cm), ending with a WS row. With RS facing, place removable m 12 (16, 16, 16, 16) sts after the existing m for the St st section at center front. *Next row:* (RS) K1 (edge st), work in established rib to old m, [k3, M1, p1] 3 (4, 4, 4, 4) times, sl new m, knit to last st, k1 (edge st)—42 (44, 51, 52, 53) sts. Working edge sts in garter st and inc'd sts in rev St st to maintain k3, p2 rib, cont in rib until armhole measures 8 (8¼, 8½, 8¾, 9)" (10.5 [21, 21.5, 22, 23] cm), ending with a RS row.

Shape Neck

See Note on how to BO. At neck edge (beg of WS rows), BO 5 sts once, then BO 3 (3, 4, 4, 5) sts once, then BO 3 (3, 4, 4, 4) sts once, then BO 2 (2, 2, 3, 3) sts once—28 (29, 34, 34, 34) sts rem. Dec 1 st at end of next 2 (1, 1, 1, 1) RS row(s)—26 (28, 33, 33, 33) sts rem. Cont even if necessary until armhole measures same as back to shoulder, ending with a WS row.

Shape Shoulder

See Note on how to BO. At armhole edge (beg of RS rows), BO 7 (8, 9, 9, 9) sts 2 times, then BO rem 7 (7, 9, 9, 9) sts.

Right Front

With larger needles, CO 48 (54, 61, 67, 73) sts. *Set-up row:* K1 (edge st; knit every row), p2, k2, [p3, k2] 4 (5, 6, 7, 8) times, pm, p22 (23, 25, 26, 27), k1 (edge st). Working edge sts in garter st, work all other sts as they appear until piece measures 14½ (14½, 15¼, 15¾, 16¼)" (37 [27, 38.5, 40, 41.5] cm) from CO, ending with a RS row.

Shape Armhole

At armhole edge (beg of WS rows), BO 4 (5, 5, 7, 8) sts once, then BO 3 (4, 4, 6, 7) sts once, then BO 0 (3, 3, 4, 7) sts once—41 (42, 49, 50, 51) sts rem. Dec 1 st at armhole edge every RS row 2 times—39 (40, 47, 48, 49) sts rem. Re-establish edge st at armhole edge and cont even in patt until armhole measures 4¼ (4¼, 4½, 4½, 4¾)" (11 [11, 11.5, 11.5, 12] cm), ending with a WS row. With RS facing, place removable m 12 (16, 16, 16, 16) sts before the existing m for the St st section at center front. *Next row:* (RS) K1 (edge st), work in St st to the new m, [p1, M1, k3] 3 (4, 4, 4, 4) times, sl old m, work in established rib to last st, k1 (edge st)—42 (44, 51, 52, 53) sts. Working edge sts in garter st and inc'd sts in rev St st to maintain k3, p2 rib, cont in rib until armhole measures 8 (8¼, 8½, 8¾, 9)" (20.5 [21, 21.5, 22, 23] cm), ending with a WS row.

Shape Neck

See Note on how to BO. At neck edge (beg of RS rows), BO 5 sts once, then BO 3 (3, 4, 4, 5) sts once, then BO 3 (3, 4, 4, 4) sts once, then BO 2 (2, 2, 3, 3) sts once—28 (29, 34, 34, 34) sts rem. Dec 1 st at beg of next 2 (1, 1, 1, 1) RS row(s)—26 (28, 33, 33, 33) sts rem. Cont even if necessary until armhole measures same as back to shoulder, ending with a RS row.

Shape Shoulder

See Note on how to BO. At armhole edge (beg of WS rows), BO 7 (8, 9, 9, 9) sts 2 times, then BO rem 7 (7, 9, 9, 9) sts.

Sleeves

With larger needles, CO 42 (44, 46, 48, 49) sts. Knitting the first and last st of every row for edge sts, work even in St st until piece measures 1½" (3.8 cm) from CO, ending with a WS row. *Inc row:* (RS) K1 (edge st), M1, knit to last st, M1, k1 (edge st)—2 sts inc'd. Inc 1 st each end of needle in this manner every 6th row 6 (5, 4, 3, 0) more times, then every 4th row 16 (18, 20, 22, 27) times—88 (92, 96, 100, 105) sts. Cont even until piece measures 17½ (17¾, 18, 18½, 18½)" (44.5 [45, 45.5, 47, 47] cm) from CO, ending with a WS row.

Shape Cap

In the usual manner, BO 4 (5, 5, 7, 8) sts at beg of next 2 rows, then BO 3 (4, 4, 4, 4) sts at beg of foll 2 rows—74 (74, 78, 78, 81) sts rem. Dec 1 st each end of needle every RS row 16 (16, 17, 17, 17) times—42 (42, 44, 44, 47) sts rem. BO 3 sts at beg of next 6 rows—24 (24, 26, 26, 29) sts rem. BO all sts.

Finishing

Block pieces to measurements. With yarn threaded on a tapestry needle, sew shoulder seams, matching rib patt. Sew sleeves into armholes. Sew sleeve and side seams.

Collar

With smaller needle, RS facing, and beg at center front, pick up and knit 25 (27, 29, 31, 31) sts along right front neck to shoulder seam, 33 (34, 39, 39, 39) sts across back neck, and 25 (27, 29, 31, 31) sts along left front neck—83 (88, 97, 101, 101) sts total. Establish rib patt to match body of sweater as closely as possible on next WS row as foll for your size:

Size 35" only

Work across left front neck sts as k1 (edge st; knit every row), p2, [k2, p3] 4 times, k2; work across back neck sts as p3, [k2, p3] 6 times; work across right front neck sts as k2, [p3, k2] 4 times, p2, k1 (edge st).

Size 39" only

Work across left front neck sts as k1 (edge st; knit every row), p2, k2, [p3, k2] 4 times, p2; work across back neck sts as p1, [k2, p3] 6 times, k2, p1; work across right front neck sts as p2, [k2, p3] 4 times, k2, p2, k1 (edge st).

Size 44" only

Work across left front neck sts as k1 (edge st; knit every row), p3, k3, [p3, k2] 4 times, p2; work across back neck sts as p1, [k2, p3] 7 times, k2, p1; work across right front neck sts as p2, [k2, p3] 4 times, k3, p3, k1 (edge st).

Sizes 48" and 52" only

Work across left front neck sts as k1 (edge st; knit every row), p2, k1, [p3, k2] 5 times, p2; work across back neck sts as p1, [k2, p3] 7 times, k2, p1; work across right front neck sts as p2, [k2, p3] 5 times, k1, p2, k1 (edge st).

All sizes

Work 2 rows even in patt, ending with a WS row. *Dec row:* (RS) K1 (edge st), k1, ssk, work in patt to last 4 sts, k2tog, k1, k1 (edge st)—2 sts dec'd. Work 3 rows even in patt. Cont in patt, rep the last 4 rows 4 more times—73 (78, 87, 91, 91) sts rem. Work even if necessary until collar measures 3¾" (9.5 cm) from pick-up row. BO all sts loosely.

Crochet Edging

With crochet hook, RS facing and beg at lower left front edge, work 1 row of single crochet (sc; see Glossary, page 156) around lower body edge, working about 3 sc for every 4 knitted sts. Rep for each sleeve cuff and across top of collar.

Zipper

With sewing thread and sharp-point needle, sew zipper in place as described in Glossary on page 157.

Weave in loose ends. Steam-block seams carefully, if desired, to avoid stretching or flattening the ribs.

Burma Rings

Barbara Venishnick

In two far-flung corners of the world—Burma, tucked between India and Southeast Asia, and South Africa, home to the Ndebele people—women have for centuries worn brass rings around their necks. Barbara Venishnick took these rings as inspiration and knitted them into a sweater in soft merino wool. The body of this pullover is worked in the round; the sleeves are worked flat from the cuffs to the armholes, then joined to the yoke, which is also worked in the round and punctuated with reverse stockinette-stitch color bands for texture. The hemmed picot edges hang straight to give the pullover a loose, comfortable fit.

Finished Size
44 (46, 48)" (112 [117, 122] cm) bust/chest circumference. Sweater shown measures 44" (112 cm).

Yarn
Worsted weight (#4 Medium).
Shown here: Mission Falls 1824 Wool (100% merino superwash wool; 85 yd [77 m]/50 g): #004 charcoal (MC), 13 (14, 15) balls; #010 russet (A), #009 nectar (B), #014 Dijon (C), #008 earth (D), 1 ball each.

Needles
Body and sleeves—size 8 (5 mm): 24" and 16" (60 and 40 cm) circular (cir). Edging—size 6 (4 mm): 24" and 16" cir (60 and 40 cm) cir. Adjust needle size if necessary to obtain the correct gauge.

Notions
Marker (m); stitch holders; tapestry needle; size F/5 (3.75 mm) crochet hook.

Gauge
19 stitches and 27 rows = 4" (10 cm) in stockinette stitch on larger needles.

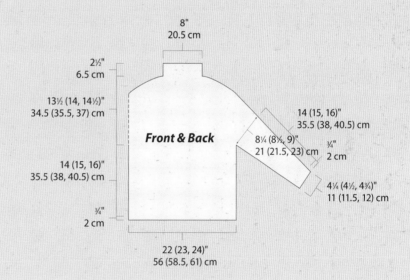

8"
20.5 cm

2½"
6.5 cm

13½ (14, 14½)"
34.5 (35.5, 37) cm

14 (15, 16)"
35.5 (38, 40.5) cm

Front & Back

14 (15, 16)"
35.5 (38, 40.5) cm

8¼ (8¼, 9)"
21 (21.5, 23) cm

¾"
2 cm

4¼ (4½, 4¾)"
11 (11.5, 12) cm

¾"
2 cm

22 (23, 24)"
56 (58.5, 61) cm

Body

With MC and smaller 24" (60 cm) needle, CO 208 (216, 224) sts. Place marker (pm) and join, being careful not to twist sts. Knit 5 rnds. Change to larger 24" (60 cm) needle and work  turning rnd as foll: *K2tog, yo; rep from *. Cont in St st until piece measures 14 (15, 16)" (35.5 [38, 40.5] cm) from turning rnd, or desired length to underarm. Do not break yarn. Set aside.

Sleeves

With MC and smaller needle, CO 41 (43, 45) sts. Do not join. Beg with a WS (purl) row, work 5 rows St st, ending with a WS row. Change to larger needle and work turning row as foll: *K2tog, yo; rep from * to last st, k1. Work 5 rows St st. Inc 1 st each end of needle on next and every foll 4 rows 15 more times—73 (75, 77) sts. Inc 1 st each end of needle every 6 rows 2 (3, 4) times—77 (81, 85) sts. Work even until piece measures 14 (15, 16)" (35.5 [38, 40.5] cm) from turning row, or desired length to underarm.

Yoke

Cont with MC, k4 body sts and place on holder for underarm, k96 (100, 104) sts for back, pm (use a different colored marker than used for beg of rnd), pm, place next 8 sts on holder for left underarm, place first 4 sts of one sleeve on holder, k69 (73, 77) sleeve sts, place last 4 sleeve sts on holder, pm, k96 (100, 104) sts for front, place last 4 body sts on holder, place first 4 sts of second sleeve on holder, pm, k69 (73, 77) sleeve sts, place last 4 sleeve sts onto holder, pm—330 (346, 362) yoke sts. Join into a rnd.
Rnd 1: [K1, k2tog, knit to 3 sts from next m, ssk, k1, sl m] 4 times—8 sts dec'd.
Rnd 2: Knit.
Rep these 2 rnds 14 (16, 18) times more—210 sts rem (all sizes).

Color Rings

Join A and knit 1 rnd, purl 3 rnds. With MC, *k8, k2tog; rep from *—189 sts rem. Knit 3 rnds. Join B and knit 1 rnd, purl 3 rnds. With MC, *k7; k2tog; rep from *—168 sts rem. Knit 3 rnds. Join C and knit 1 rnd, purl 3 rnds. With MC, *k6, k2tog; rep from *—147 sts rem. Knit 3 rnds. Join D and knit 1 rnd,

purl 3 rnds. With MC, *k5, k2tog; rep from *—126 sts rem. Knit 3 rnds. Join A and knit 1 rnd, purl 3 rnds. With MC, *k4, k2tog; rep from *—105 sts rem. Knit 3 rnds. Join B and knit 1 rnd, purl 3 rnds. With MC, *k3, k2tog; rep from *—84 sts rem. Knit 3 rnds. Join C and knit 1 rnd, purl 3 rnds. With MC, *k10, k2tog; rep from *—77 sts rem. Knit 3 rnds.

Back Neck Opening

With larger 16" (40 cm) needle, reposition sts so beg of row is at center back. Join D and turn. Beg with a RS row, work back and forth in rows (leave a 4" [10 cm] or longer tail at beg and end of each color ring; MC may be carried up the side), *purl 2 rows, knit 1 row, purl 1 row.* With MC, work 4 rows St st. Join A and rep from * to *. With MC, work 4 rows St st. Join B and rep from * to *. With MC, purl 1 row. With RS facing, work turning row as foll: *k2tog, yo; rep from *, end k1. Change to smaller needle and work St st for 2¼" (5.5 cm). BO all sts loosely.

Finishing

Buttons

Make 1 each of A, B, and D (see Glossary, page 156, for crochet instructions). With crochet hook and leaving a 6" (15 cm) tail, ch 3, join into a ring with a slip st, ch 1. Cont as foll:
Rnd 1: Work 6 sc around ring.
Rnds 2 and 3: Work 1 sc in each sc of previous rnd.
Cut yarn, leaving a 12" (30.5 cm) tail. Roll short tail and stuff inside button. Thread long tail into a tapestry needle and run through the bottom of each sc of last rnd, pulling tight to form rounded button. Sew buttons to left side of back neck opening on the rings of matching colors.

Button Loops

With matching color, join yarn to right side of back neck opening opposite buttons and work 15 sc around the tails left from color changes. Bend into loops and sew in place. With yarn threaded on a tapestry needle, use the Kitchener st (see page 152) to graft underarm sts. Sew sleeve seams. Fold all hems at turning rnds/rows and sew in place to inside of garment. Sew neck facing to inside of neck at base of color D ring. Sew sides of neck facing in place. Weave in loose ends.

Beyond the Basics: SHORT-ROWS
based on an article by Véronik Avery

Short-rows, also known as partial or turning rows, appear daunting to some knitters but in reality are very straightforward: You simply work extra rows across a portion of the stitches on the needles, thereby lengthening the fabric in that area. In garments, short-rows are most often used to shape shoulders and custom fit the bust area.

Many knitters shy away from short-rows—it isn't that they have trouble working just some of the stitches on the needle, it's the fact that doing so produces a hole in the knitting. Although in some cases the holes can be design elements, in most cases, they distract from the purpose of the short-rows—invisibly adding length to a particular area of a piece. However, there are several ways to eliminate (or hide) the holes so that the short-rows are nearly invisible.

Before beginning, you should be familiar with a few terms. The turning point is the place where the knitting changes direction between one row and the next (much like making a U-turn when driving). Unless you do something to prevent it, a hole will form at the turning point. The turning yarn is the section of working yarn that marks the turning point. The turning yarn is used to hide or mask the hole on a subsequent row. The stitch mount is the direction that the stitches lie on the needle. For the purposes of this article, we'll assume that the "correct" stitch mount has the right (leading) leg of the stitch on the front of the needle.

Wrap-and-Turn Method

In this common method, the turning yarn is wrapped around the first unworked stitch (the first stitch on the left needle that immediately follows the last worked stitch on the right needle). The way that the stitch is wrapped depends on whether the knit or purl side is facing. This type of short-row is used in her Pearl Buck Swing Jacket (page 134) and Union Square Market Pullover (page 146).

Knit Side Facing

Knit the required number of stitches to the turning point, slip the next stitch purlwise to the right needle (Figure 1), bring the yarn to the front between the needles, return the slipped stitch to the left needle (Figure 2), bring the working yarn to the back between the needles, and turn the work so that the purl side is facing—one stitch has been wrapped and the yarn is correctly positioned to purl the next stitch. Eventually, you will knit across the wrapped stitch—maybe on the next row or maybe several short-rows later. When you do, hide the wrap (the horizontal bar of yarn across the wrapped stitch) on a knit row as follows: knit to the wrapped stitch, insert the tip of the right needle into both wrap and the wrapped stitch (Figure 3), and knit them together. This forces the turning yarn (the "wrap") to the back (wrong-side) of the fabric.

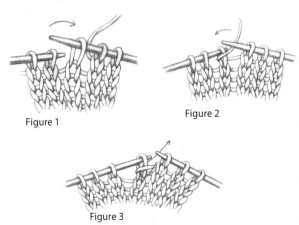

Figure 1

Figure 2

Figure 3

Purl Side Facing

Purl to the turning point, slip the next stitch purlwise to the right needle, bring the yarn to the back of the work (Figure 1), return the slipped stitch to the left needle, bring the yarn to the front between the needles (Figure 2), and turn the work so that the knit side is facing—one stitch has been wrapped and the yarn is correctly positioned to knit the next stitch.

To hide the wrap on a subsequent purl row, work to the wrapped stitch, use the tip of the right needle to pick up the turning yarn from the back, place it on the left needle (Figure 3), then purl it together with the wrapped stitch.

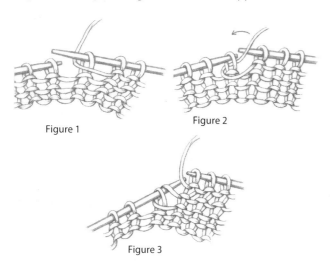

Figure 1

Figure 2

Figure 3

Yarnover Method

In the yarnover method, the turning yarn is positioned on the needle when the work is turned and is in place to work together with the next stitch (and hide the hole) on the next row. The turning yarn may be loose for some knitters, but the resulting hole is much easier to eliminate. Work the required number of stitches to the turning point (knit if a right-side row; purl if a wrong-side row), turn the work, and make a yarnover. To account for the fact that the amount of yarn required to make a yarnover depends on the type of stitch that follows it, work a typical yarnover if the knit side is facing and work a yarn forward if the purl side is facing as follows.

Knit Side Facing

Bring the yarn forward, over the top of the needle, then to the back of the work.

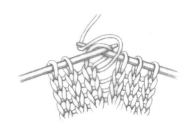

Purl Side Facing

Hold the yarn in back, insert the tip of the right needle into the next stitch, bring the yarn over the top of the right needle (yarn forward), and purl the first stitch. Note that the stitch mount of the yarn forward will be backward (leading leg in back of the needle) and will need to be corrected before it is worked on a subsequent row.

When it comes time to close the gap on a subsequent row, work the yarnover together with the nearest unworked stitch, depending on whether the knit or purl side is facing as follows.

Knit Stitch Follows

Correct the mount of the yarnover (leading leg on front of needle), then knit the yarnover together with the unworked stitch (k2tog).

Purl Stitch Follows

Slip the yarnover knitwise, slip the unworked stitch knitwise, return both stitches to the left needle (leading legs in back of the needle), and purl them together through their back loops (ssp).

Note that these instructions are for working stockinette stitch back and forth in rows. If you're working a different stitch pattern or are working in rounds, the yarnover may occur before or after the gap made at the turning point, and the nearest unworked stitch may be a knit or a purl. For a truly invisible transition, work the yarnover together with the unworked stitch as follows, depending on your particular situation.

Gap Follows Yarnover

Work to the yarnover, then proceed as follows (see page 116 for specific techniques):

Wrong (purl) side facing; knit stitch follows: K2tog.
Right (knit) side facing; knit stitch follows: Ssk.
Wrong side facing; purl stitch follows: P2tog.
Right side facing; purl stitch follows: Ssp.

Gap precedes yarnover

Work to one stitch before the gap, then proceed as follows:

Right side facing; knit stitch follows: Ssk.
Wrong side facing; knit stitch follows: K2tog.
Right Side Facing; purl stitch follows: Ssp.
Wrong side facing; purl stitch follows: P2tog.

Japanese Method—Mark the Turning Yarn

Executed in a way similar to the yarnover, this method marks the turning yarn with a removable marker such as a split-ring marker, safety pin, or waste yarn. It uses less yarn than the preceding methods, and it is ideal for working short-row heels and toes on socks. Work the required number of stitches to the turning point, then turn the work. Place a removable marker on the turning yarn (Figure 1). When it's time to close the gap on a subsequent row, slip the stitch immediately before the turning yarn, pull up on the marker and place the turning yarn on the needle, then transfer the slipped stitch back onto the left needle (Figure 2), and work the turning yarn together with the next stitch as described for the yarnover method.

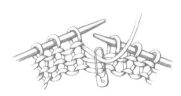

Figure 1

Figure 2

Catch Method

There are two ways to work this method. While it is easier to close the gap with the second method (because the yarn is already in position to work together with the slipped stitch), it does use more yarn. For both methods, work the required number of stitches to the turning point, then turn the work.

Method 1

If the purl side is facing, slip the first stitch purlwise with the yarn in front (Figure 1); if the knit side is facing, slip the stitch with the yarn in back. When it's time to close the gap, pick up the stand of yarn below the slipped stitch (Figure 2), and work it together with the slipped stitch as for the yarnover method.

Method 2

Slip the first stitch purlwise while holding the working yarn over the needle (instead of in front or back of the needle), effectively executing a yarnover (Figure 3). Close the gap as for the yarnover method.

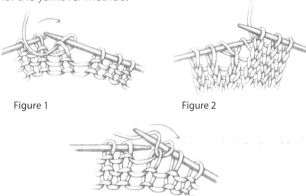

Figure 1   Figure 2

Figure 3

TIPS for Short-Rows

❋ Avoid interruptions while working short-rows and try to work all short-rows in a series at the same sitting.

❋ Remember that short-rows are worked in pairs—a right-side partial row followed by a wrong-side partial row or vice versa.

❋ When counting stitches, the "unworked" stitches are the stitches at the end(s) of the needles that are not worked; the "worked" stitches are the stitches in the center of the needle that were knitted (or purled) on the last row.

❋ If desired, use a row counter to keep track of the number of short-rows worked.

Man's Brioche Vest

Erica Alexamder

This handsome vest featuring soft brioche ribs and a button-up front is a relaxed version of the classic, conservative, man's vest. Erica Alexander chose to work it in a lightly plied Australian wool that gives the vest a soft texture. The tidy knit-and-purl ribs flow easily into the body's brioche pattern; the neck and armhole bands are worked on a larger needle and edged with a slight reverse-stockinette roll for a clean finish. With a boxy fit and not-too-deep V-neckline, it's a modern vest for work or play.

Finished Size

40 (45, 50½, 56)" (101.5 [114.5, 128.5, 142] cm) chest circumference, buttoned. Vest shown measures 45" (114.5 cm).

Yarn

Worsted weight (#4 Medium).
Shown here: Baabajoes NZ WoolPak 10-Ply (430 yd [393 m]/250 g): #02 mist, 3 (3, 4, 4) skeins. *Note:* This particular yarn has been discontinued.

Needles

Sizes 8 (5 mm) and 3 (3.25 mm). Adjust needle sizes if necessary to obtain the correct gauge.

Notions

Tapestry needle; six ¾" (2 cm) buttons.

Gauge

18 stitches and 40 rows = 4" (10 cm) in brioche rib with one size 8 (5 mm) needle and one size 3 (3.25 mm) needle, slightly stretched.

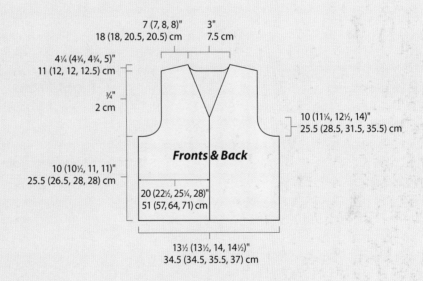

7 (7, 8, 8)"
18 (18, 20.5, 20.5) cm

3"
7.5 cm

4¼ (4¾, 4¾, 5)"
11 (12, 12, 12.5) cm

¾"
2 cm

10 (11¼, 12½, 14)"
25.5 (28.5, 31.5, 35.5) cm

10 (10½, 11, 11)"
25.5 (26.5, 28, 28) cm

Fronts & Back

20 (22½, 25¼, 28)"
51 (57, 64, 71) cm

13½ (13½, 14, 14½)"
34.5 (34.5, 35.5, 37) cm

Stitch Guide
Brioche Rib (multiple of 3 sts)

Row 1: (RS) With larger needle, knit.

Row 2: With smaller needle, k2, *p2, k1 into st below next st on larger needle (do not work st on needle); rep from *, end p2, k2.

Repeat Rows 1 and 2 for pattern.

Back

With smaller needles, CO 118 (134, 150, 166) sts. *Set-up row:* (WS) K2, *p2, k2; rep from *. Cont in rib as established until piece measures 1" (2.5 cm) from beg, ending with a RS row. *Dec row:* (WS) K2, *p2, k2tog; rep from * to last 4 sts, p2, k2—90 (102, 114, 126) sts rem. Change to one size 8 (5 mm) needle for RS rows and one size 3 (3.25 mm) needle for WS rows. Work in brioche rib (see Stitch Guide) until piece measures 13½ (13½, 14, 14½)" (34.5 [34.5, 35.5, 37] cm) from beg, ending with a WS row.

Shape Armholes

BO 5 (6, 7, 8) sts at beg of next 2 rows—80 (90, 100, 110) sts rem. BO 3 (4, 5, 6) sts at beg of foll 2 rows, then dec 1 st each end of needle every RS row 2 (4, 6, 9) times—70 (74, 78, 80) sts rem. Cont in patt (knit the last st of every row) until armholes measure 10 (10½, 11, 11)" (25.5 [26.5, 28, 28] cm).

Shape Neck and Shoulders

Cont in patt across 21 (23, 23, 24) sts, join new yarn and BO 28 (28, 32, 32) sts for neck, work to end as established—21 (23, 23, 24) sts each side. Working each side separately as established, at each neck edge BO 1 st every other row 2 times, and *at the same time* at each shoulder edge, BO 6 (7, 7, 8) sts 2 (2, 2, 1) time(s), then BO 7 sts 1 (1, 1, 2) time(s).

Left Front

With smaller needles, CO 58 (66, 74, 82) sts. *Set-up row:* (WS) K2, *p2, k2; rep from *. Cont in rib as established until piece measures 1" (2.5 cm) from beg, ending with a RS row. *Dec row:* (WS) K2, p2, *k2tog, p2; rep from *, end k2—45 (51, 57, 63) sts rem. Change to one size 8 (5 mm) needle for RS rows and one size 3 (3.25 mm) needle for WS rows. Work even in brioche rib until piece measures 13½ (13½, 14, 14½)" (34.5 [34.5, 35.5, 37] cm) from beg, ending with a WS row.

Shape Armhole

(RS) BO 5 (6, 7, 8) sts at beg of row—40 (45, 50, 55) sts rem. BO 3 (4, 5, 6) sts at beg of next RS row, then dec 1 st at armhole edge every RS row 2 (4, 6, 9) times—35 (37, 39, 40) sts rem. Cont even until armhole measures 3" (7.5 cm), ending with a WS row.

Shape V-Neck

(RS) Work in patt to last 3 sts, k2tog, k1—1 st dec'd. Work 3 rows even in patt. Rep the last 4 rows 12 (10, 13, 13) more times, then dec 1 st at end of row in this manner every 6 rows 3 (5, 4, 4) times—19 (21, 21, 22) sts rem. Cont even until armhole measures same as back to shoulder, ending with a WS row.

Shape Shoulder

At armhole edge (beg of RS rows) BO 6 (7, 7, 8) sts 2 (2, 2, 1) time(s), then BO 7 sts 1 (1, 1, 2) time(s).

Right Front

Work as left front to armhole, ending with a RS row—piece should measure 13½ (13½, 14, 14½)" (34.5 [34.5, 35.5, 37] cm).

Shape Armhole

(WS) BO 5 (6, 7, 8) sts at beg of row—40 (45, 50, 55) sts rem. BO 3 (4, 5, 6) sts at beg of next WS row, then dec 1 st at armhole edge every RS row 2 (4, 6, 9) times—35 (37, 39, 40) sts rem. Cont even until armhole measures 3" (7.5 cm), ending with a WS row.

Shape V-Neck

(RS) K1, ssk, work in patt to end—1 st dec'd. Work 3 rows even in patt. Rep the last 4 rows 12 (10, 13, 13) more times, then dec 1 st at beg of row in this manner every 6 rows 3 (5, 4, 4) times—19 (21, 21, 22) sts rem. Cont even until armhole measures same as back to shoulder, ending with a RS row.

Shape Shoulder

At armhole edge (beg of WS rows) BO 6 (7, 7, 8) sts 2 (2, 2, 1) time(s), then BO 7 sts 1 (1, 1, 2) time(s).

Finishing

Block pieces to measurements. Weave in loose ends. With yarn threaded on a tapestry needle, sew shoulder and side seams.

Buttonband

With larger needles, CO 8 sts. *Next row:* (WS) P5, k3. *Next row:* P3, k5. Rep the last 2 rows until band fits along right front edge and to middle of back neck, slightly stretched. Place sts on holder. With yarn threaded on a tapestry needle, sew band to right front and neck edge to center back neck. Mark placement of six buttons, one ½" (1.3 cm) up from lower edge, one about 1" (2.5 cm) below beg of neck shaping, and the other 4 evenly spaced in between.

Buttonhole Band

With larger needles, CO 8 sts. *Next row:* (WS) K3, p5. *Next row:* K5, p3. Rep the last 2 rows until band fits along left front edge and to middle of back neck, slightly stretched, and *at the same time* work buttonholes on RS rows opposite markers as foll: k3, yo, k2tog, p3. Sew band to left front and neck edge, so that end of band meets end of button band, ripping out rows or adding rows of knitting as necessary for a perfect fit. Use the Kitchener st (see page 152) to graft live band sts tog.

Armbands

With larger needles, CO 8 sts. Work one band as for buttonband and one band as for button-hole band (omitting buttonholes) until band fits around armhole. BO all sts. Beg and ending at underarms, sew armbands into armholes. Sew armband seams.

Sew buttons to buttonband opposite button-holes. Block again if desired.

VIP Cardigan

Charlotte Morris

Charlotte Morris transformed the classic textured Aran cardigan into something delicate and feminine by choosing a lightweight yarn and subtle textures. Instead of the traditional cables, Charlotte worked twisted ribs, traveling stitches, and a tiny smock pattern against a seed stitch background. To add to the distinctly feminine feel, she worked it all in a sportweight wool-cashmere yarn called VIP and finished it off with a pretty flared collar and pearl buttons.

Finished Size
36 (40, 44½, 48½, 52½)" (91.5
 [101.5, 113, 123, 133.5] cm). Cardigan
 shown measures 40" (101.5 cm).

Yarn
Sportweight (#2 Fine).
 Shown here: Lana Gatto VIP (80% wool/20%
 cashmere; 218 yd [200 m]/50 g): #2322
 sage green, 8 (8, 10, 12, 13) balls.

Needles
Body and sleeves—size 5 (3.75 mm).
 Ribbing—size 3 (3.25 mm). Adjust needle
 sizes if necessary to obtain the correct gauge.

Notions
Stitch holders; markers (m); tapestry needle;
 size D/3 (3.25 mm) crochet hook; nine
 (nine, nine, ten, ten) ½" (1.3 cm) buttons.

Gauge
34 sts and 38 rows = 4" (10 cm) in smocking
 stitch on larger needles; 29 sts and 34
 rows = 4" (10 cm) in twisted seed stitch
 on larger needles; 25-st diamond panel =
 3½" (9 cm) wide; 34 rows of diamond panel
 = 4" (10 cm) high on larger needles.

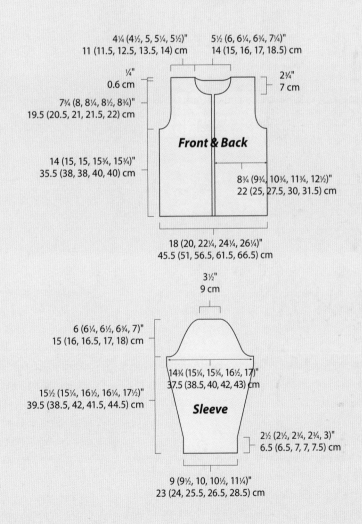

4¼ (4½, 5, 5¼, 5½)"
11 (11.5, 12.5, 13.5, 14) cm

5½ (6, 6¼, 6¾, 7¼)"
14 (15, 16, 17, 18.5) cm

¼"
0.6 cm

2¾"
7 cm

7¾ (8, 8¼, 8½, 8¾)"
19.5 (20.5, 21, 21.5, 22) cm

Front & Back

14 (15, 15, 15¾, 15¾)"
35.5 (38, 38, 40, 40) cm

8¾ (9¾, 10¾, 11¾, 12½)"
22 (25, 27.5, 30, 31.5) cm

18 (20, 22¼, 24¼, 26¼)"
45.5 (51, 56.5, 61.5, 66.5) cm

3½"
9 cm

6 (6¼, 6½, 6¾, 7)"
15 (16, 16.5, 17, 18) cm

14¾ (15¼, 15¾, 16½, 17)"
37.5 (38.5, 40, 42, 43) cm

15½ (15¼, 16½, 16¼, 17½)"
39.5 (38.5, 42, 41.5, 44.5) cm

Sleeve

2½ (2½, 2¾, 2¾, 3)"
6.5 (6.5, 7, 7, 7.5) cm

9 (9½, 10, 10½, 11¼)"
23 (24, 25.5, 26.5, 28.5) cm

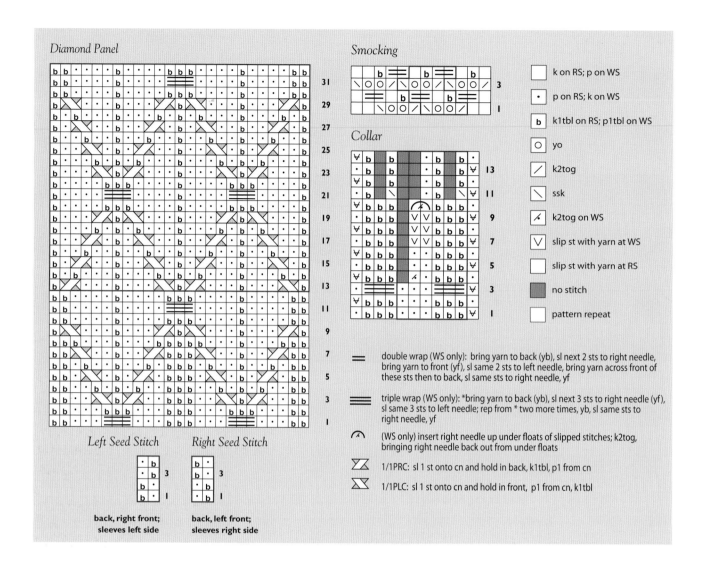

Diamond Panel

Smocking

Collar

Left Seed Stitch — back, right front; sleeves left side

Right Seed Stitch — back, left front; sleeves right side

☐	k on RS; p on WS
•	p on RS; k on WS
b	k1tbl on RS; p1tbl on WS
O	yo
/	k2tog
\	ssk
⟋	k2tog on WS
V	slip st with yarn at WS
☐	slip st with yarn at RS
■	no stitch
☐	pattern repeat

= double wrap (WS only): bring yarn to back (yb), sl next 2 sts to right needle, bring yarn to front (yf), sl same 2 sts to left needle, bring yarn across front of these sts then to back, sl same sts to right needle, yf

≡ triple wrap (WS only): *bring yarn to back (yb), sl next 3 sts to right needle (yf), sl same 3 sts to left needle; rep from * two more times, yb, sl same sts to right needle, yf

⌒ (WS only) insert right needle up under floats of slipped stitches; k2tog, bringing right needle back out from under floats

⟋⟍ 1/1PRC: sl 1 st onto cn and hold in back, k1tbl, p1 from cn

⟍⟋ 1/1PLC: sl 1 st onto cn and hold in front, p1 from cn, k1tbl

Notes

- To compensate for the slight difference in row gauges, work a pair of short-rows in the smocking stitch areas every 20 rows.
- Work neck shaping bind-offs in stockinette stitch, not in smocking stitch pattern. Work partial pattern repeats in stockinette stitch.

Back

With smaller needles, CO 138 (154, 170, 186, 202) sts. *Border set-up row:* (RS) [P1, k1 through back loop (tbl)] 8 (10, 12, 14, 16) times, p2, [k1tbl] 2 times, p3, [(k1tbl) 3 times, p3] 3 times, [k1tbl] 2 times, p2, k1tbl, [p2, (k1tbl) 2 times] 11 (13, 15, 17, 19) times, p2, k1tbl, p2, [k1tbl] 2 times, p3, [(k1tbl) 3 times, p3] 3 times, [k1tbl] 2 times, p2, k1tbl, p1] 8 (10, 12, 14, 16) times. Cont

in established rib until piece measures 2½ (2½, 2¾, 23/4, 3)" (6.5 [6.5, 7, 7, 7.5] cm) from CO, ending with a WS row. Change to larger needles. *Body set-up row:* Beg with Row 1 of charts, work 16 (20, 24, 28, 32) sts according to Right Seed Stitch chart, place marker (pm), p2, pm, work 25 sts according to Diamond Panel chart, pm, p2, pm, work 48 (56, 64, 72, 80) sts according to Smocking chart, pm, p2, pm, work 25 sts according to Diamond Panel chart, pm, p2, pm, work rem 16 (20, 24, 28, 32) sts according to Left Seed Stitch chart. Work as established through Row 32 of Diamond Panel chart, working short-rows in the smocking stitch areas every 20 rows (see Notes), then rep Rows 13–32 only of Diamond Panel chart (cont working other sts as established), until piece measures 14 (15, 15, 15¾, 15¾)" (35.5 [38, 38, 40, 40] cm) from beg, ending with a WS row.

Shape Armholes

BO 3 (4, 5, 6, 7) sts at beg of next 4 rows—126 (138, 150, 162, 174) sts rem. Dec 1 st each end of needle every other row 6 (7, 7, 8, 9) times—114 (124, 136, 146, 156) sts rem. Dec 1 st each end of needle every 4 rows 3 (4, 5, 6, 7) times—108 (116, 126, 134, 142) sts rem. Cont even until armholes measure 7¾ (8, 8¼, 8½, 8¾)" (19.5 [20.5, 21, 21.5, 22] cm), ending with Row 26 (16, 16, 26, 26) of Diamond Panel chart. *Next row:* (RS) Work 31 (33, 36, 38, 40) sts in patt, tightly BO next 46 (50, 54, 58, 62) sts for neck in St st, work in patt to end—31 (33, 36, 38, 40) sts rem each side. Working each side separately, work 2 rows even, ending with Row 29 (19, 19, 29, 29) of Diamond Panel chart. Place sts on holders for each shoulder.

Right Front

With smaller needles, CO 68 (76, 84, 92, 100) sts. *Border set-up row:* (RS) K1 (selvedge st), p2, k1tbl, [p2, (k1tbl) 2 times] 4 (5, 6, 7, 8) times, p2, k1tbl, p2, [k1tbl] 2 times, p3, [(k1tbl) 3 times, p3] 3 times, [k1tbl] 2 times, p2, [k1tbl, p1] 8 (10, 12, 14, 16) times. Working selvedge st at center front edge in garter st (knit every row), cont as established until piece measures 2½ (2½, 2¾, 2¾, 3)" (6.5 [6.5, 7, 7, 7.5] cm) from CO, ending with a WS row. Change to larger needles. *Body set-up row:* Beg with Row 1 of charts, k1 (selvedge st), p2, pm, work 20 (24, 28, 32, 36) sts according to Smocking chart, pm, p2, pm, work 25 sts according to Diamond Panel chart, pm, p2, pm, work 16 (20, 24, 28, 32) sts according to Left Seed Stitch chart. Working selvedge st in garter st, cont in patt as established until piece measures same as back to armhole, ending with a RS row.

Shape Armhole

BO 3 (4, 5, 6, 7) sts at beg of next 2 WS rows—62 (68, 74, 80, 86) sts rem. Dec 1 st at armhole edge every other row 6 (7, 7, 8, 9) times—56 (61, 67, 72, 77) sts rem. Dec 1 st at armhole edge every 4 rows 3 (4, 5, 6, 7) times—53 (57, 62, 66, 70) sts rem. Cont even until armhole measures 5¼ (5½, 5¾, 6, 6¼)" (13.5 [14, 14.5 15, 16] cm), ending with a WS row.

Shape Neck

(RS) BO 8 (8, 8, 10, 10) sts, work to end—45 (49, 54, 56, 60) rem. At neck edge, BO 3 (4, 5, 5, 6) sts 2 times (see Notes)—39 (41, 44, 46, 48) sts rem. Dec 1 st at neck edge every row 4 times, then dec 1 st every other row 4 more times—31 (33, 36, 38, 40) sts rem. Cont even until piece measures about the same length as back, but end with Row 31 (21, 21, 31, 31) of Diamond Panel chart. Place sts on holder.

Left Front

Work as for right front, reversing shaping by working armhole BO on RS rows and neck BO on WS rows, and working set-up rows as foll: *Border set-up row:* (RS) [P1, k1tbl] 8 (10, 12, 14, 16) times, p2, [k1tbl] 2 times, p3, [(k1tbl) 3 times, p3] 3 times, [k1tbl] 2 times, p2, k1tbl, [p2, (k1tbl) 2 times] 4 (5, 6, 7, 8) times, p2, k1tbl, p2, k1 (selvedge st; work in garter throughout). *Body set-up row:* Work 16 (20, 24, 28, 32) sts according to Right Seed Stitch chart, pm, p2, pm, work 25 sts according to Diamond Panel chart, pm, p2, pm, work 20 (24, 28, 32, 36) sts according to Smocking chart, pm, p2, k1 (selvedge st; work in garter throughout).

Sleeves

With smaller needles, CO 65 (69, 73, 77, 81) sts. *Border set-up row:* (RS) [P1, k1tbl] 9 (10, 11, 12, 13) times, p2, [k1tbl] 2 times, [p3, (k1tbl) 3 times] 3 times, p3, [k1tbl] 2 times, p2, [k1tbl, p1] 9 (10, 11, 12, 13) times. Cont as established until piece measures 2½ (2½, 2¾, 2¾, 3)" (6.5 [6.5, 7, 7, 7.5] cm) from CO, ending with a WS row. Change to larger needles. *Body set-up row:* (RS) Beg with Row 1 of charts, work 18 (20, 22, 24, 26) sts according to Right Seed Stitch chart, pm, p2, pm, work 25 sts according to Diamond Panel chart, pm, p2, pm, work 18 (20, 22, 24, 26) sts according to Left Seed Stitch chart. Work 1 row even. *Next row:* Work first st, M1 (see page 52), work in patt to last st, M1, work last st—2 sts inc'd; 67 (71, 75, 79, 83) sts total. Cont in patt as established, working through Row 32 of Diamond Panel chart, then rep Rows 13–32 only, and *at the same time* inc 1 st each end of needle as before every 6 rows 10 (6, 12, 12, 16) times more, then every 4 rows 10 (14, 8, 8, 4) times, working new sts in seed st—107 (111, 115, 119, 123) sts total. Cont even in patt until piece measures 15½ (15¼, 16½, 16¼, 17½)" (39.5 [38.5, 42, 41.5, 44.5] cm) from beg, ending with Row 30 (28, 16, 14, 22) of Diamond Panel chart.

Shape Cap

BO 3 (4, 5, 6, 7) sts at beg of next 4 rows—95 sts rem. Work 1 row even. Dec 1 st each end of needle on next row, then every other row 16 (18, 20, 22, 24) times more (ending with Row 28 [30, 22, 24, 16] of chart), then every row 10 (8, 6, 4, 2) times (ending with Row 18 [18, 28, 28, 18] of chart)—41

sts rem. BO 4 sts at beg of next 4 rows (ending with Row 22 [22, 32, 32, 22] of chart)—25 sts rem. BO all sts.

Collar

With smaller needles, CO 209 (227, 251, 269, 287) sts. Rep Rows 1 and 2 of Collar chart until piece measures 1¾" (4.5 cm), then work Rows 3–12 once—106 (115, 127, 136, 145) sts rem. Work Rows 13 and 14 three times (6 rows total). Place sts on waste yarn.

Finishing

Buttonband

With smaller needles, CO 163 (175, 175, 184, 184) sts. *Set-up row:* K1 (selvedge st; knit every row), k1tbl, p1, k1tbl, *p2, [k1tbl, p1] 3 times, k1tbl; rep from * 2 (1, 1, 2, 2) more time(s), **p2, [k1tbl, p1] 9 times, k1tbl; rep from ** 6 (7, 7, 7, 7) more times, p2, k1tbl, p1, k1tbl, k1 (selvedge st; knit every row). Work 8 rows as established. Place sts on waste yarn. With crochet hook and using a slip-stitch crochet seam (see page 129), join band to live sts of left front. Sew a button in the center of each p2 pair.

Buttonhole Band

CO as for buttonband. *Set-up row:* K1 (selvedge st), k1tbl, p1, k1tbl, *p2, [k1tbl, p1] 9 times, k1tbl; rep from * 6 (7, 7, 7, 7) more times, **p2, [k1tbl, p1] 3 times, k1tbl; rep from ** 2 (1, 1, 2, 2) more time(s), p2, k1tbl, p1, k1tbl, k1 (selvedge st). Work 3 rows as established. *Buttonhole row:* (RS) *Work in patt to 1 st before first p2 pair, sl 1 pwise with yarn in back (wyb), sl 1 kwise wyb, pass both slipped sts back to left needle and k2tog tbl, [yo] 2 times, sl 1 pwise wyb, sl next st as if to purl tbl, pass both slipped sts back to left needle and k2tog; rep from *. *Next row:* (WS) Work in patt as established, working each double yarnover as k1, k1tbl. Finish as for buttonband. Use slip-stitch crochet to join piece to right front edge as for buttonband.

Blocking

Pin body and sleeve pieces to measurements, spray with water, and leave to air-dry. (Blocking by immersion not recommended.) Shape collar into a gentle curve, folding it along the line formed by Rows 7–10 of Collar chart so that RS of collar will show when collar is attached to body. Spray with water.

Using the three-needle method (see page 29), join fronts to back at shoulders. Use slip-stitch crochet to join live collar sts to neck edge, centering the selvedges of the collar on the front bands and distributing sts as foll: Join 3 sts from band center to front edge, join 14 (16, 18, 20, 22) sts along front neck BO sts, 18 sts along the shaped side of front neck, 36 (41, 49, 54, 59) sts along back neck, 18 sts down other shaped side of front neck, 14 (16, 18, 20, 22) sts along front neck BO sts, 3 sts along band edge to center. With yarn threaded on tapestry needle, sew sleeve and side seams. Weave in loose ends. Sew buttons opposite buttonholes.

Beyond the Basics: SEAMS
based on an article by Charlotte Morris

Garments that are worked back and forth on straight needles must be joined together by seams—along the sides, sleeves, shoulders, and armholes. Just as there are different ways to cast on, increase, decrease, and bind off, there are different ways to work the seams. Properly worked, a seam should blend in with the garment's stitch pattern, without stretching or puckering. It should be strong and durable with minimal bulk. Different techniques are used for sewing knitted pieces together along vertical edges, horizontal edges, and a combination of the two. Just like in other aspects of knitting, you can choose from a variety of seaming techniques, each with its own characteristics.

Seaming Yarn

No matter which type of seam you choose, it will be least conspicuous if you work it with the same yarn used to knit the garment. However, there are instances when the knitting yarn is not ideal for seaming. Highly textured novelty yarns can add unnecessary bulk and catch on stitches. Extremely fuzzy yarns (such as mohair) can obscure stitches and stick to themselves. Fat yarns (such as bulky or chunky) can add bulk and pull and distort adjacent stitches. Unusually soft fibers may fray, weaken, or even break. For such yarns, substitute a smooth, even yarn of the same color (and lighter weight, if necessary).

Vertical Seams

Work vertical seams (i.e., side seams and sleeve sleeves) upward from the lower (cast-on) edge. If your working yarn is suitable for seaming, work the first part of the seam with the tail leftover from the cast-on row. Doing so will eliminate one end to weave in later and will help make a smooth seam join. If the tail left from the cast-on row is not long enough to work the seam, join a length of yarn about twice as long as the length to be sewn. Do not make a knot; instead, leave a few inches of the seaming yarn hanging—when the seam is sewn, go back and tighten the end, then work the tail into the seam. Begin by catching the cast-on stitch on each piece. If the cast-on loops are difficult to see, begin with the first row you can see clearly, and the corresponding one on the other side, then when the seam is established, go back and work the first part of the seam.

At the end of the seam, secure the working yarn by darning it into the wrong side of the seam (i.e., in the seam allowance) for a few inches. Do not tie a knot. If, despite efforts for perfect matching, there is a slight displacement between the two pieces at the end of the seam, take another stitch back through the top of the lower side to even them out.

Mattress or Ladder Stitch Seam

This seam, worked with a tapestry needle and with the right side of the knitting facing, is aptly called an invisible seam. Because it is worked from the right side, this is the best method for matching stitches from one side of the seam to the other. When worked correctly, the rows of stitches line up beautifully without distortion and the seaming yarn is concealed in the seam. Ideally, the two pieces to be seamed should have the same number of rows. If one piece is a row longer, begin and end the seam on the longer piece. This type of seam can be blocked flat.

Stockinette Stitch

Working with the right sides of the knitting facing you, use the threaded needle to pick up one bar between the first two stitches on one piece (Figure 1), then the corresponding bar plus the bar above it on the other piece (Figure 2). *Pick up the next two bars on the first piece, then the next two bars on the other (Figure 3). Repeat from * to the end of the seam, finishing by picking up the last bar (or pair of bars) at the top of the first piece. To reduce bulk, pick up the bars in the center of the edge stitches instead of between the last two stitches. To prevent a half-row displacement at the seam, be sure to start the seam by picking up just one bar on the first side, then alternate two bars on each side.

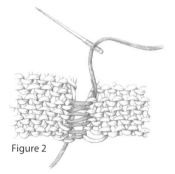

Figure 2

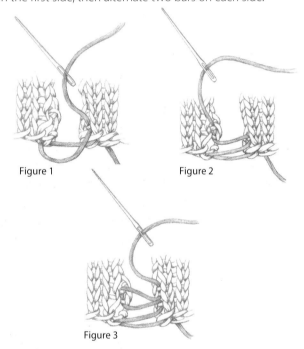

Figure 1

Figure 2

Figure 3

Repeat from *, always working in the lower purl bar on the first side and the upper bars on the other (otherwise, the purl bars will be mismatched at the seam).

Reverse Stockinette Stitch

Working with the right sides of the knitting facing you, use the threaded needle to *pick up the lower purl bar between the last two stitches on one piece (Figure 1), then the upper purl bar of the edge stitch on the other piece (Figure 2).

Figure 1

Seed Stitch

If the edge stitches on each piece match (i.e., purl stitches are opposite purl stitches and knit stitches are opposite knit stitches on each piece), work the seam as for reverse stockinette stitch. Use the threaded needle to *pick up the lower purl bar between the last two stitches on one piece (Figure 1), then the upper purl bar of the edge stitch on the other piece (Figure 2). Repeat from *. If the edge stitches don't match (i.e., knit stitches are opposite purl stitches), work the seam between the last two stitches on each side. Use the threaded needle to *pick up the lower purl bar between the last two stitches on one piece, then the lower purl bar between the last two stitches on the other (Figure 3). Because the purl bars are staggered, occurring on odd rows on one piece and even rows on the other, the seam maintains the appearance of seed stitch.

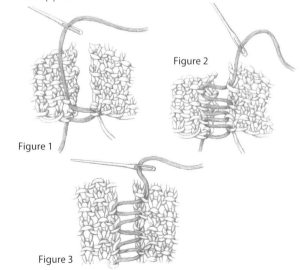

Figure 2

Figure 1

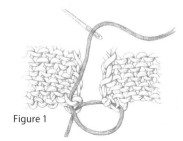

Figure 3

Garter Stitch

Working with the right sides of the knitting facing you, use the threaded tapestry needle to pick up the lower purl bar between the last two stitches on one piece (Figure 1), then the upper purl bar from

Figure 1

the stitch next to the edge stitch on same row on the other piece (Figure 2). To reduce bulk, work into the upper bar from the edge stitch (Figure 3) instead of the second-to-last stitch, but keep in mind that the seam will be less firm.

Slip-Stitch Crochet Seam

A slip-stitch crochet seam is a good choice if you're seaming with a weak yarn that may abrade or break when subjected to the repeated in-and-out motion of the other seam types. It is relatively elastic, easy to undo, and generally ensures a smooth, even seam without puckers. A slip-stitch crochet seam is worked with a crochet hook with the wrong side of the work facing you. It produces a line of stitches along one side of the seam and a crochet chain along the other. Like a backstitch seam (see at right), a slip-stitch crochet seam is

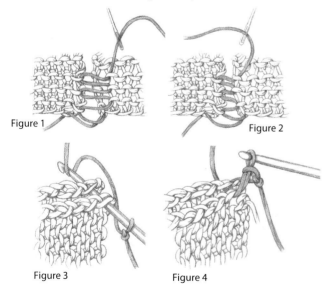

Figure 1

Figure 2

Figure 3

Figure 4

relatively bulky and not suitable for heavy yarns.

With right sides facing each other, pin together the two pieces to be seamed so that the edges are even and the fabric evenly distributed. Make a slipknot and place it on a crochet hook. *Insert hook through both pieces of fabric

one stitch in from the selvedge (Figure 1), wrap the yarn around the hook to make a loop, pull this loop back through fabric and through the loop already on the hook (Figure 2). Repeat from *, pulling the working yarn gently but firmly so that each stitch is snug but not tight.

Backstitch Seam

A backstitch seam is ideal for seams that can't be matched row for row, such as two pieces that are worked in different stitch patterns. This type of seam is worked with a tapestry needle with the wrong side of the work facing you and requires frequent flipping from wrong side to right to check the matching of stitches. Properly worked, a backstitch seam is nearly invisible, although it is relatively bulky and may be difficult to block flat.

With right sides facing each other, pin together the two pieces to be seamed so that the edges are even and the fabric is evenly distributed. Work upward from the cast-on edges between the last two stitches on each piece. Working from right to left, one stitch in from the selvedge, bring the threaded needle up through both pieces of the knitted fabric (Figure 1), then back down through both layers a short distance (about a row) to the right of the starting point (Figure 2). *Bring the needle up through both layers a row-length to the left of the backstitch just made (Figure 3), then back down to the right, in the same hole used before (Figure 4). Repeat from *, working backward one row for every two rows worked forward.

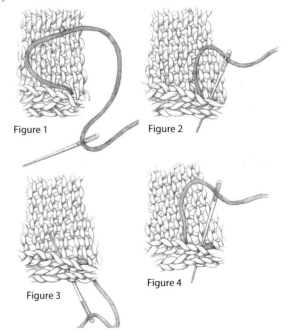

Figure 1

Figure 2

Figure 3

Figure 4

Horizontal Seams

To give a polished look to a horizontal seam, such as a shoulder seam, match the pieces to be seamed stitch for stitch. There are several ways for working the seam, each of which will give professional results.

Joining Live Stitches

If the stitches are left on the needles, rather than binding them off individually, you can join the live stitches to each other as you bind off both sets of stitches together as follows.

Three-Needle Bind-Off

This common method produces a firm seam that allows for perfect stitch-to-stitch matching. It is worked with the yarn still attached to one of the shoulder pieces. This method can be used in almost any pattern that calls for bound-off shoulders, except those where the back and front were worked in different stitch patterns and do not have the same number of stitches at the shoulder. In such cases, the shoulder stitches should be bound off separately and sewn together.

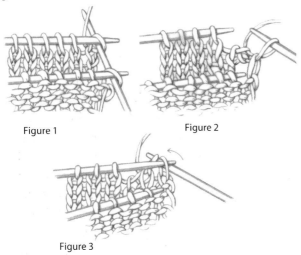

Figure 1

Figure 2

Figure 3

To work a three-needle bind-off, place the stitches to be joined on two separate needles. Hold the needles parallel to each other, with the right sides of the knitting facing together. *Insert a third needle into the first stitch on each of the other two needles (Figure 1), wrap yarn around the needle, and pull the loop through both stitches, thereby knitting the two stitches together as one (Figure 2). Knit the next stitch on each needle the same way, then use one of the left needle tips to lift the first stitch over the second

stitch (Figure 3) and off the third needle. Repeat from * until one stitch remains on the third needle. Cut yarn and pull the tail through the last stitch to secure.

Joining Bound-Off Stitches

Most sweater patterns call for the shoulder stitches to be bound off. In this type of edge, the bound-off stitches lie at right angles to the knitted stitches and thereby stabilize them by preventing them from stretching widthwise. This consideration is important along shoulder seams, which bear the weight of the entire sweater. There are three good ways to join such bound-off edges.

Invisible Weaving

Sometimes also called grafting, this method gives the same appearance as Kitchener stitch (see page 152), but because there are no live stitches involved, the seam is more stable. It is worked with yarn threaded on a tapestry needle. The following instructions are for seaming pieces worked in stockinette stitch, but the same principles apply for other stitch patterns.

Working with the bound-off edges opposite each other, right sides of the knitting facing toward you, and working into the stitches just below the bound-off edges, bring the threaded tapestry needle out at the center of the first stitch (i.e., go under half of the first stitch) on one side of seam, then bring the needle in and out under the first whole stitch on the other side (Figure 1). *Bring the needle into the center of the same stitch it came out of before, then out in the center of the adjacent stitch (Figure 2), then bring the

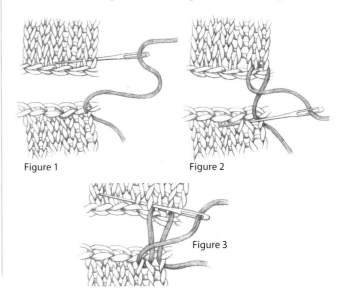

Figure 1

Figure 2

Figure 3

needle in and out under the next whole stitch on the other side (Figure 3). Repeat from *, ending with a half-stitch on the first side. Be sure to work along the same row of stitches on each side for a tidy seam. If the shoulder is sloped and if the final stitches were bound off in steps, there will be a jog or stairstep of two rows between each group of bound-off stitches. To give the seam a smooth appearance in these cases, do not follow the exact line of stitches just below the bound-off stitches—use the seaming yarn to visually even out the jogs over the distance of two or three stitches.

Backstitch

A backstitch seam is ideal for seams that can't be matched stitch for stitch, such as two pieces that are worked in different stitch patterns. This type of seam is worked with a tapestry needle with the wrong side facing outward, and it requires frequent flipping from wrong side to right to check that the stitches on each side of the seam match. Properly worked, a backstitch seam is nearly invisible, although it is relatively bulky and may be difficult to block flat.

With right sides facing each other, pin together the two pieces to be seamed so that the edges are even and the fabric is evenly distributed. Working from right to left (if

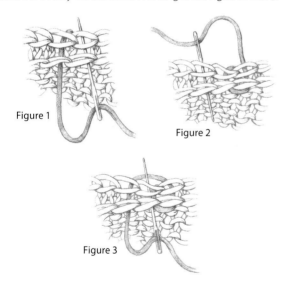

Figure 1

Figure 2

Figure 3

you're left-handed, you may prefer to work from left to right) into the stitch just below the bound-off row, bring the threaded needle up between the first two stitches on each piece of knitted fabric, then back down through both layers, one stitch to the right of the starting point (Figure 1). *Bring the needle up through both layers a stitch-length to the

left of the backstitch just made (Figure 2), then back down to the right, through the same hole used before (or the edge of the piece for the first stitch; Figure 3). Repeat from *, working backward one stitch for every two stitches worked forward.

Slip-Stitch Crochet

This method is a good choice for seaming with weak yarns that may abrade or break when subjected to the repeated in-and-out motion of other seam types. It is relatively elastic, easy to undo, and generally ensures a smooth, even seam without puckers. A slip-stitch crochet seam is worked with a crochet hook, with the wrong side of the work facing. Like a backstitch seam, a slip-stitch crochet seam is relatively bulky and therefore is not suitable for heavy yarns.

With right sides facing each other, pin together the

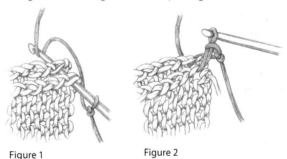

Figure 1

Figure 2

two pieces to be seamed so that the edges are even and the fabric is evenly distributed. Make a slipknot with the seaming yarn and place it on a crochet hook. *Insert the hook through both pieces of knitting under the bound-off stitches, wrap the yarn around the hook to make a loop (Figure 1), and pull this loop back through both pieces of knitting and through the loop already on the hook (Figure 2). Repeat from *, pulling the working yarn gently but firmly so that each stitch is snug but not tight. End by cutting the seaming yarn and pulling the tail through the last stitch to secure.

Mixed Seams

Knitters are faced with mixed seams (joining the tops of bound-off stitches to the sides of edge stitches) when sewing sleeves into armholes or sewing collars into neck openings. Unlike vertical or horizontal seams that involve matching two pieces of knitting stitch for stitch, mixed seams involve matching rows to stitches. Because the number of rows per inch of knitting seldom matches the number of stitches per inch, this type of seam requires careful pinning of the two pieces to ensure smooth results. The instructions that follow are for sewing sleeves into armholes, but the same principles apply for any situation where stitches are seamed to rows.

Invisible Weaving

Invisible weaving is suitable for seaming all the basic stitches in which the stitches and rows are easily identified, such as stockinette, reverse stockinette, seed, garter, and ribbing. The method you choose to follow will depend on whether the shoulder is dropped or set-in. Holding pieces to be seamed adjacent to each other with right sides facing outward, match center of sleeve bind-off edge to shoulder seam and pin in place. For either type of shoulder shaping, consider beginning the seam at the top shoulder line and working downward to the underarm in two sections—front and back. Doing so will reduce the chance of the sleeve cap slipping and thereby ensure a smooth seam at the shoulder area where it is most visible, reduce the stress on the seaming yarn by one-half, and make seaming easier because you'll be working with shorter lengths of yarn.

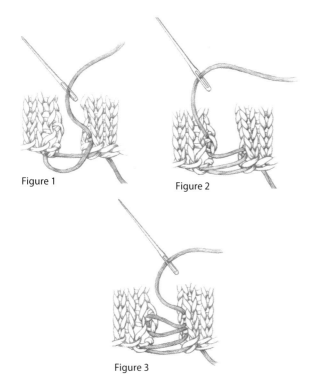

Figure 1

Figure 2

Figure 3

For Dropped Shoulders

Sweaters with dropped shoulders have no armhole or sleeve cap shaping, and therefore the seams involve sewing the stitches of the straight bind-off edge at the top of the sleeve to the rows along the straight selvedge edge of the front and back armholes. Measure the armhole depth along the side seams and pin the sleeve seam (or unseamed edges) at those points. Pin the rest of the sleeve along the armhole edge. Ideally, you'll want to distribute the fabric evenly by calculating the ratio of stitches to rows to determine how many row bars to catch per stitch. For example, if the armhole is 40 rows long on the front and back, and the sleeve top is 60 stitches wide, there will be 30 stitches to match to 40 rows, back and front. In this case you would catch one row bar per stitch for two seam stitches, then two row bars for the third seam stitch. Or you might prefer to simply balance the distribution by eye. Along the vertical edge of the armhole, work between the edge stitch and the stitch adjacent to it; along the horizontal edge of the sleeve, work along the row of stitches just below the bind-off row.

With yarn threaded on a tapestry needle, pick up one bar between the first two stitches along the vertical edge (Figure 1), then pick up one complete stitch along the horizontal edge (Figure 2). *Pick up the next one or two bars on the first piece (depending on the ratio you've calculated), then the next whole stitch on the other piece (Figure 3). Repeat from * to the end of the seam, ending by picking up one bar on the vertical edge. If you want to reduce bulk, pick up the bars in the center of the edge stitches along the vertical piece instead of between the last two stitches.

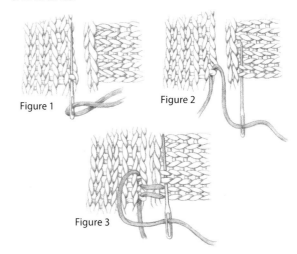

Figure 1

Figure 2

Figure 3

For Set-in Sleeves

Pin the pieces together, matching the bound-off stitches at the beginning of the sleeve cap shaping to the corresponding bound-off stitches of the front and back armhole. Pin the rest of the sleeve into the armhole, distributing the fabric as evenly as possible. Join the bound-off edges stitch for stitch as described for invisible weaving for bound-off stitches on page 130. Continue to weave along the shaped edge of the cap, taking one or two bars (rows) on the armhole side for each stitch of the cap, working between the edge stitch and the next stitch along the vertical armhole edge, and along the stitches next to the edge stitch along the shaped cap edges (Figure 1). If the sleeve cap was worked with full-fashioned shaping so that the decreases were worked one or more stitch(es) in from the edge, work between the edge stitch and the stitch next to it (Figure 2). Seam the horizontal bound-off section at the top of the cap as for dropped-shoulder shaping.

Slip-Stitch Crochet

Slip-stitch crochet is quite elastic and produces a durable seam for joining sleeves into armholes, especially when the individual stitches and/or rows of knitting are complex or too difficult to distinguish for invisible weaving.

With right sides facing together, pin the sleeve into the armhole, matching the center of the bound-off edge of the sleeve cap to the shoulder seam, and align the shaped edges of the sleeve cap with the armhole edges. Working along the row of stitches below the bind-off on the horizontal edge and between the edge stitch and the stitch next to it in other areas, use slip-stitch crochet as described for joining bound-off stitches (see page 131).

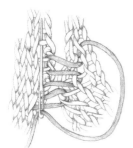

Figure 1

Figure 2

TIPS for Seaming

✳ Vertical seams look best when they are matched row for row. Therefore, it's preferable to count rows instead of inches for vertical measurements while knitting.

✳ Horizontal seams look best when they are matched stitch for stitch. Whenever possible, make sure that there is the same number of stitches on each side of the seam.

✳ For a smooth, even seam without puckers, take care to maintain as consistent a stitch length as possible. Small stitches will reduce the risk of puckering.

✳ Whenever possible, work along the same column of stitches along vertical seams and the same row of stitches along horizontal seams.

✳ Do not pull the seaming yarn too tight. Doing so will cause the seam to gather, alter the length of the seam, and distort the garment.

✳ As you work a seam, take care not to split the yarn in knitted stitches—doing so may weaken the yarn and give the seam a sloppy look.

✳ For edges that will be folded back, such as cuffs, sew the seam so that the seam allowance will not show on the public side.

✳ Be sure to begin stockinette-stitch seams by taking just one purl bar on the first side, then alternating two bars from each side. Otherwise, there will be a half-row displacement between the two sides of the seam.

Pearl Buck Spring Jacket

Kate Gilbert

The swingy A-line shaping and delicate stitch detail in Kate Gilbert's little jacket were inspired by the loose-fitting tops worn by Chinese women in Pearl S. Buck's novel, *The Good Earth*. The body of the jacket widens gently from bust to hem, and the back features a tapered box pleat, decorated with a traveling diamond-stitch motif, to provide graceful drape and gentle swing with every step. Half-diamonds edge each side of the front opening, and the bracelet-length sleeves flair slightly at the cuff.

Finished Size
36 (41, 44, 49)" (91.5 [104, 112, 124.5] cm) bust circumference, with front edges just meeting at center. Jacket shown measures 36" (91.5 cm).

Yarn
DK weight (#3 Light).
Shown here: Jaeger Extra Fine Merino Double Knitting (100% merino; 137 yd [125 m]/50 g): #944 elderberry, 9 (11, 12, 14) skeins.

Needles
Size 6 (4 mm): straight, 24" or 32" (60 or 80 cm) circular (cir), and set of 2 double-pointed (dpn). Adjust needle size if necessary to obtain the correct gauge.

Notions
Tapestry needle; stitch holders; removable stitch markers in 2 different colors; cable needle (cn).

Gauge
22 stitches and 31 rows = 4" (10 cm) in stockinette stitch; 6-stitch zigzag patt from chart measures about ⅞" (2.2 cm) wide.

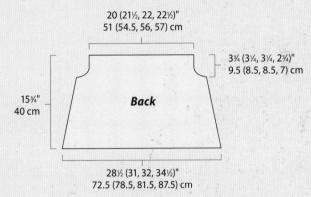

20 (21½, 22, 22½)"
51 (54.5, 56, 57) cm

3¾ (3¼, 3¼, 2¾)"
9.5 (8.5, 8.5, 7) cm

15¾"
40 cm

Back

28½ (31, 32, 34½)"
72.5 (78.5, 81.5, 87.5) cm

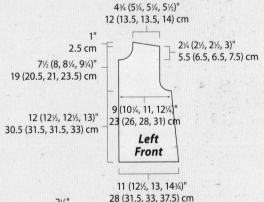

4¾ (5¼, 5¼, 5½)"
12 (13.5, 13.5, 14) cm

1"
2.5 cm

2¼ (2½, 2½, 3)"
5.5 (6.5, 6.5, 7.5) cm

7½ (8, 8¼, 9¼)"
19 (20.5, 21, 23.5) cm

12 (12½, 12½, 13)"
30.5 (31.5, 31.5, 33) cm

9 (10¼, 11, 12¼)"
23 (26, 28, 31) cm

Left Front

11 (12½, 13, 14¾)"
28 (31.5, 33, 37.5) cm

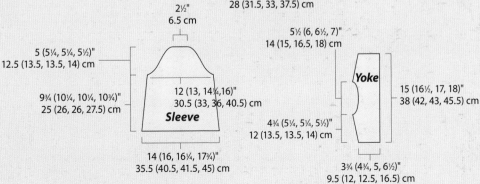

2½"
6.5 cm

5 (5¼, 5¼, 5½)"
12.5 (13.5, 13.5, 14) cm

5½ (6, 6½, 7)"
14 (15, 16.5, 18) cm

9¾ (10¼, 10¼, 10¾)"
25 (26, 26, 27.5) cm

12 (13, 14¼, 16)"
30.5 (33, 36, 40.5) cm

Sleeve

14 (16, 16¼, 17¾)"
35.5 (40.5, 41.5, 45) cm

Yoke

15 (16½, 17, 18)"
38 (42, 43, 45.5) cm

4¾ (5¼, 5¼, 5½)"
12 (13.5, 13.5, 14) cm

3¾ (4¾, 5, 6½)"
9.5 (12, 12.5, 16.5) cm

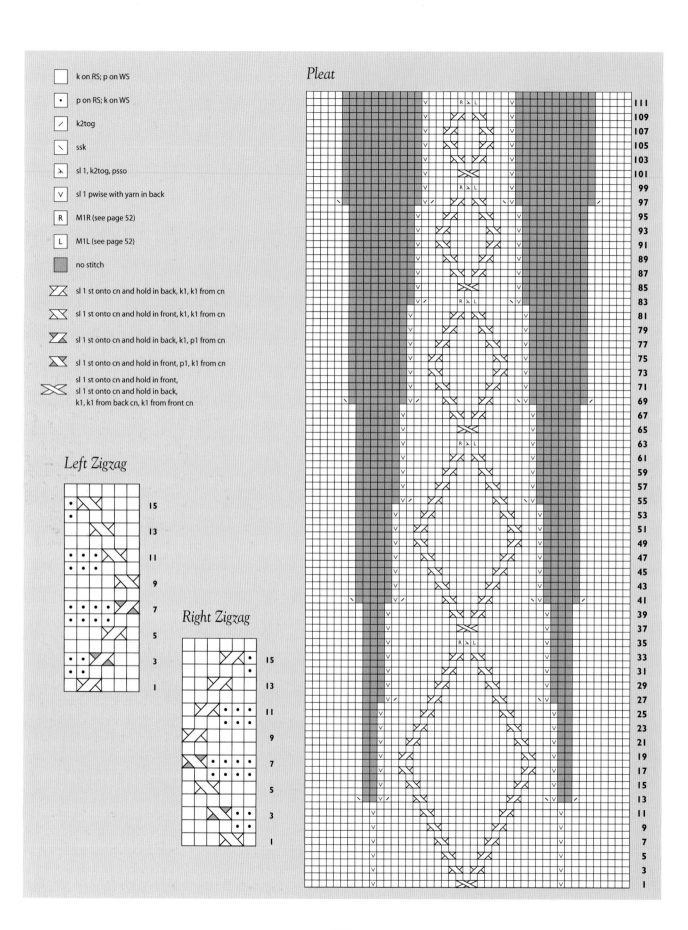

Pleat

Left Zigzag

Right Zigzag

Legend:

☐	k on RS; p on WS
•	p on RS; k on WS
/	k2tog
\	ssk
⋏	sl 1, k2tog, psso
V	sl 1 pwise with yarn in back
R	M1R (see page 52)
L	M1L (see page 52)
▨	no stitch
⤬	sl 1 st onto cn and hold in back, k1, k1 from cn
⤬	sl 1 st onto cn and hold in front, k1, k1 from cn
⤬	sl 1 st onto cn and hold in back, k1, p1 from cn
⤬	sl 1 st onto cn and hold in front, p1, k1 from cn
⤬	sl 1 st onto cn and hold in front, sl 1 st onto cn and hold in back, k1, k1 from back cn, k1 from front cn

Notes

- The fold lines for back pleat are worked in columns of purled or slipped stitches, depending on the direction of the fold.
- Use two different-colored removable stitch markers to remind you when to work either a purl or slipped-stitch fold line. Mark the individual stitches, instead of placing markers on the needle, and move these markers up as the work progresses.
- For slip-stitch fold lines, slip the stitch as if to purl with the yarn held in back.

Back

With cir needle and using the long-tail method (see page 15), CO 157 (171, 177, 189) sts. Work lower edging and establish fold line positions as foll:

Row 1: (RS) P65 (72, 75, 81), sl 1 pwise with yarn in back (wyb) and mark this st, p25, sl 1 pwise wyb and mark this st with the same color marker, p65 (72, 75, 81)—1 marked slip st on each side of center 25 sts.

Row 2: Using different-colored markers from the ones used in Row 1, p55 (62, 65, 71), k1 and mark this st, p45, k1 and mark this st, p55 (62, 65, 71)—4 marked sts total; 9 sts between different-colored markers at each side.

Row 3: Knit to first marked st, p1, k9, sl 1 pwise wyb, k25, sl 1 pwise wyb, k9, p1, knit to end.

Row 4: Knit to second marker, p1, k25, p1, knit to end.

Row 5: Purl to second marker, sl 1 pwise wyb, p25, sl 1 pwise wyb, purl to end.

Row 6: Purl to first marker, k1, p45, k1, purl to end.

Rows 7–14: Rep Rows 3–6 two more times—piece measures about 1¼" (3.2 cm) from CO.

Establish patt from Pleat chart beg with Row 1 as foll: (RS) Knit to first marker, p1, work center 45 sts according to Pleat chart, p1, knit to end. *Next row:* (WS) Purl to first marker, k1, work center 45 sts according to Pleat chart, k1, purl to end. Cont in this manner, working center 45 sts according to chart, maintaining purled fold line sts as established, and *at the same time* shape sides by dec 1 st each end of needle (side edges) on chart Rows 25, 49, and 73 as foll: K1, ssk (side dec), work in patt to last 3 sts, k2tog (side dec), k1—2 sts dec'd outside chart. Cont without further side decs until Row 82 (86, 86, 90) of chart has been completed—135 (147, 153, 165) sts rem; 29 (27, 27, 27) sts between marked purl

pleat sts; piece measures about 12 (12½, 12½, 13)" (30.5 [31.5, 31.5, 33] cm) from CO.

Shape Armholes

Cont in patt as established, BO 4 (5, 5, 7) sts at beg of next 2 rows, then BO 3 (3, 4, 6) sts at beg of foll 2 rows. Dec 1 st at beg of next 6 (8, 10, 12) rows. Work even until Row 112 of chart has been completed—109 (119, 121, 123) sts rem; 23 chart sts between marked purl columns; piece measures about 15¾" (40 cm) from CO; armholes measure about 3¾ (3¼, 3¼, 2¾)" (9.5 [8.5, 8.5, 7] cm).

Fold Pleat

With RS facing, BO sts until 6 sts rem before first marked purl column st, sl next 6 sts onto dpn, slip foll 6 sts pwise onto second dpn, fold fabric along slip-stitch column so that the right sides of the fabric on the 2 dpns are touching, hold left-hand needle in front of both dpns with RS of pleat patt facing you. BO the next 6 sts of all 3 layers tog as foll: *Insert right-hand needle tip into first st on left-hand needle and both dpns, k3tog (first st from all 3 needles)—2 sts on right-hand needle. BO 1 st. Rep from * 5 more times to empty both dpns. Knit the center pleat st, and BO 1 st. Sl next 6 sts onto dpn, slip foll 6 sts pwise onto second dpn, fold fabric along slip-stitch column so that WS of the fabric on the 2 dpns are touching, hold left-hand needle behind both dpns with RS of pleat patt facing you. BO the next 6 sts of all 3 layers tog as before. BO rem sts to end.

Yoke

With straight needles and using the long-tail method, CO 20 (26, 28, 36) sts. Beg and ending with a WS row, work 5 rows St st. *Inc row:* (RS) Knit to last 2 sts, M1 (see Glossary, page 52), k2—1 st inc'd. Work 5 rows even in St st, ending with a WS row. Rep the last 6 rows 3 (4, 4, 5) more times—24 (31, 33, 42) sts. Rep inc row 1 (0, 0, 0) time(s), then work 3 (0, 0, 0) rows even. Rep the last 4 (0, 0, 0) rows 1 (0, 0, 0) more time(s)—26 (31, 33, 42) sts. Work 0 (6, 6, 2) rows even, ending with a WS row—piece measures about 4¾ (5¼, 5¼, 5½)" (12 [13.5, 13.5, 14] cm) from CO.

Shape Neck

(RS) Work to last 3 sts, k2tog, k1—1 st dec'd. Work 1 row even. Rep the last 2 rows once more—24 (29, 31, 40) sts rem. Rep dec row, then work 3 rows even—1 st dec'd. Rep the last 4 rows 2 more times—21 (26, 28, 37) sts rem; piece measures about 2" (5 cm) from beg of neck shaping. Work even until piece measures 3¾ (4¼, 4¾, 5¼)" (9.5 [11, 12, 13.5] cm) from beg of neck shaping, ending with a WS row. *Next row:* (RS) Work to last 2 sts, M1, k2—1 st inc'd. Work 3 rows even. Rep the last 4 rows once more—23 (28, 30, 39) sts. Rep inc row, then work 1 row even—1 st inc'd. Rep the last 2 rows 1 more time, then work RS inc row once more—26 (31, 33, 42) sts—piece measures about 5½ (6, 6½, 7)" (14 [15, 16.5, 18] cm) from beg of neck shaping, and about 10¼ (11¼, 11¾, 12½)" (26 [28.5, 30, 31.5] cm) from CO. Work 3 (11, 11, 7) rows even, ending with a WS row. *Next row:* (RS) Work to last 3 sts, k2tog, k1—25 (30, 32, 41) sts.

Size 36" only

Work 3 rows even, then rep dec row once more—1 (0, 0, 0) st(s) dec'd.

All sizes

Work 5 rows even, then rep dec row—1 st dec'd. Rep the last 6 rows 3 (3, 3, 4) more times—20 (26, 28, 36) sts rem. Work 5 rows even; piece measures about 15 (16½, 17, 18)" (38 [42, 43, 45.5] cm) from CO. BO all sts.

Left Front

With straight needles and using the long-tail method, CO 61 (68, 72, 81) sts. Beg with a RS row, work as foll: [purl 2 rows, knit 2 rows] 3 times, then purl 2 rows—14 rows total; piece measures about 1¼" (3.2 cm) from CO. *Next row:* (RS) K1, ssk (side dec), knit to last 6 sts, work Row 1 of Left Zigzag chart over 6 sts (center front edge)—1 st dec'd. Cont as established, working 6 sts at front edge according to chart and rem sts in St st, and work 7 rows even. Cont in established patt, rep the shaping of the last 8 rows 9 (7, 7, 7) more times—51 (60, 64, 73) sts rem. Cont in established patt, work side dec row 0 (1, 1, 1) more time(s), then work 0 (5, 5, 5) rows even—0 (1, 1, 1) st(s) dec'd. Cont in established patt, rep the shaping of the last 0 (6, 6, 6) rows 0 (2, 2, 3) more times—51 (57, 61, 69) sts rem. Cont even in patt until piece measures 12 (12½, 12½, 13)" (30.5 [31.5, 31.5, 33] cm) from CO, ending with a WS row.

Shape Armhole

Cont in patt as established, BO 4 (5, 5, 7) sts at beg of next RS row, then BO 3 (3, 4, 6) sts at beg of foll RS row, then dec 1 st at beg of next 3 (4, 5, 6) RS rows—41 (45, 47, 50) sts rem. Work even until armhole measures 5¼ (5½, 5¾, 6¼)" (13.5 [14, 14.5, 16] cm), ending with a RS row.

Shape Neck

At neck edge (beg of WS rows), BO 4 (4, 5, 6) sts once, then BO 3 (4, 5, 6) sts once, then BO 2 sts 3 times, then BO 1 st 2 times—26 (29, 29, 30) sts rem; piece measures about 2" (5 cm) from beg of neck shaping. Work even until armhole measures 7½ (8, 8¼, 9¼)" (19 [20.5, 21, 23.5] cm), ending with a RS row.

Shape Shoulders

Work short-rows (see page 115) as foll:
Short-row 1: (WS) Purl to last 6 sts, wrap next st, turn.
Short-rows 2, 4, and 6: Knit to end.

Short-row 3: Purl to 5 (6, 6, 6) sts before previous wrapped st, wrap next st, turn.

Short-rows 5 and 7: Rep Short-row 3.

Short-row 8: Knit to end.

On the next WS row, BO all sts as if to purl, purling all wrapped sts tog with their wraps for the BO.

Right Front

With straight needles and using the long-tail method, CO 61 (68, 72, 81) sts. Beg with a RS row, work as foll: [purl 2 rows, knit 2 rows] 3 times, purl 2 rows—14 rows total; piece measures about 1¼" (3.2 cm) from CO. *Next row:* (RS) Work Row 1 of Right Zigzag chart over first 6 sts, knit to last 3 sts, k2tog (side dec), k1—1 st dec'd. Cont as established, working 6 sts at front edge according to chart and rem sts in St st, and work 7 rows even. Cont in established patt, rep the shaping of the last 8 rows 9 (7, 7, 7) more times—51 (60, 64, 73) sts rem. Cont in established patt, work side dec row 0 (1, 1, 1) more time(s), then work 0 (5, 5, 5) rows even—0 (1, 1, 1) st(s) dec'd. Cont in established patt, rep the shaping of the last 0 (6, 6, 6) rows 0 (2, 2, 3) more times—51 (57, 61, 69) sts rem. Cont even in patt until piece measures 12 (12½, 12½, 13)" (30.5 [31.5, 31.5, 33] cm) from CO, ending with a RS row.

Shape Armhole

Cont in patt as established, BO 4 (5, 5, 7) sts at beg of next WS row, then BO 3 (3, 4, 6) sts at beg of foll WS row, then dec 1 st at beg of next 3 (4, 5, 6) WS rows—41 (45, 47, 50) sts rem. Work even until armhole measures 5¼ (5½, 5¾, 6¼)" (13.5 [14, 14.5, 16] cm), ending with a WS row.

Shape Neck

At neck edge (beg of RS rows), BO 4 (4, 5, 6) sts once, then BO 3 (4, 5, 6) sts once, then BO 2 sts 3 times, then BO 1 st 2 times—26 (29, 29, 30) sts rem; piece measures about 2" (5 cm) from beg of neck shaping. Work even until armhole measures 7½ (8, 8¼, 9¼)" (19 [20.5, 21, 23.5] cm), ending with a WS row.

Shape Shoulders

Work short-rows as foll:

Short-row 1: (RS) Knit to last 6 sts, wrap next st, turn.

Short-rows 2, 4, and 6: Purl to end.

Short-row 3: Knit to 5 (6, 6, 6) sts before previous wrapped

st, wrap next st, turn.

Short-rows 5 and 7: Rep Short-row 3.

Short-row 8: Purl to end.

On the next RS row, BO all sts as if to knit, knitting all wrapped sts tog with their wraps for the BO.

Sleeves

With straight needles and using the long-tail method, CO 76 (82, 88, 98) sts. Beg with a RS row, work as foll: [purl 2 rows, knit 2 rows] 3 times, purl 2 rows—14 rows total; piece measures about 1¼" (3.2 cm) from CO. Work 2 rows even in St st, ending with a WS row. *Dec row:* (RS) K1, ssk, knit to last 3 sts, k2tog, k1—2 sts dec'd. Work 11 rows even. Cont in St st, rep the shaping of the last 12 rows 4 more times—66 (72, 78, 88) sts rem. Cont even until piece measures 9¾ (10¼, 10¼, 10¾)" (25 [26, 26, 27.5] cm) from beg, ending with a WS row.

Shape Cap

BO 4 (5, 5, 7) sts at beg of next 2 rows, then BO 3 (3, 4, 6) sts at beg of foll 2 rows—52 (56, 60, 62) sts rem. BO 1 st at beg of next 6 (8, 12, 12) rows—46 (48, 48, 50) sts rem. *Work 2 rows even, then BO 1 st at beg of next 2 rows; rep from * 3 (2, 0, 0) more times—38 (42, 46, 48) sts rem. BO 1 st at beg of next 10 (14, 18, 20) rows—28 sts rem for all sizes. BO 3 sts at beg of next 2 rows, then BO 4 sts at beg of foll 2 rows—14 sts rem; cap measures about 5 (5¼, 5¼, 5½)" (12.5 [13.5, 13.5, 14] cm). BO all sts.

Finishing

Block pieces to measurements. With yarn threaded on a tapestry needle, sew yoke to back, easing in any back fullness. Sew shoulder and side seams.

Collar

With straight needles, RS facing, and beg at right front neck edge, pick up and knit 89 (97, 97, 114) sts evenly spaced around neck edge. *Beg with a WS row, purl 2 rows, then knit 1 row, ending with a WS row. *Dec row:* (RS) K1, ssk, knit to last 3 sts, k2tog, k1—2 sts dec'd. Rep from * once more—85 (93, 93, 110) sts rem. Purl 1 WS row. *Next row:* (RS) P1, ssp (see page 62), purl to last 3 sts, p2tog, p1—83 (91, 91, 108) sts rem. BO all sts kwise on next WS row. With yarn threaded on a tapestry needle, sew sleeve seams. Sew sleeve caps into armholes. Weave in loose ends. Lightly steam-block seams.

Weekend Getaway Satchel

Marta McCall

Bright, bold colors make Marta McCall's felted satchel a lively twenty-first-century version of the nineteenth-century carpetbag. To add more detail to the color intarsia patterns, Marta embellishes her motifs with simple embroidery stitches after completing the knitting. A trip through the washing machine softens the boundaries between the knitting and embroidery, and imparts a uniform look. Special touches like silver buckles and tiny handbag feet add satchel authenticity. Knit one up, pack a few essentials, and take off for a weekend—but don't expect to travel incognito.

Finished Size
After felting, 18" (45.5 cm) wide at top (with satchel closed), 24" (61 cm) wide at base, 8" (20.5 cm) deep from front to back at base, and 16" (40.5 cm) tall, not including handles.

Yarn
Worsted weight (#4 Medium).

Shown here: Reynolds Lite-Lopi (100% wool; 109 yd [100 m]/50 g): #0005 black heather (MC), 15 skeins; #0434 crimson, 5 skeins; #0439 cherry red, #0414 burnt red, #0444 dark grass green, #0240 golden green, #0435 goldenrod, #0443 bright blue, #0438 light fuchsia, #0436 pumpkin, #0442 royal blue, #0264 mustard, #0441 leaf (light green), and #0440 bright purple, 1 skein each. All colors are used double throughout for knitting and embroidery.

Needles
Size 15 (10 mm): 24" (60 cm) circular (cir). Adjust needle size if necessary to obtain the correct gauge.

Notions
Tapestry needle; milliner's needle (available at quilting and craft stores); sewing thread to match #0434 crimson yarn; 1 skein dark gray embroidery floss to match #0005 black heather yarn; long quilting pins; disposable razor; 18" (45.5 cm) straight hex-open frame for top opening (available online from Ghee's at www.ghees.com); set of 4 silver handbag feet (also available from Ghees); two 1" (2.5-cm) nickel halter buckles for straps (style #132, available from Oregon Leather Company in Portland, Oregon); ⅛" (3 mm) masonite board cut to 7" x 24" (18 x 61 cm) for base of satchel; optional fabric to cover masonite board.

Gauge
12 stitches and 16 rows = 4" (10 cm) in stockinette stitch with yarn doubled, before felting.

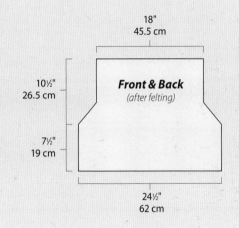

18"
45.5 cm

Front & Back
(after felting)

10½"
26.5 cm

7½"
19 cm

24½"
62 cm

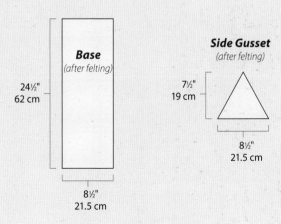

24½"
62 cm

Base
(after felting)

8½"
21.5 cm

Side Gusset
(after felting)

7½"
19 cm

8½"
21.5 cm

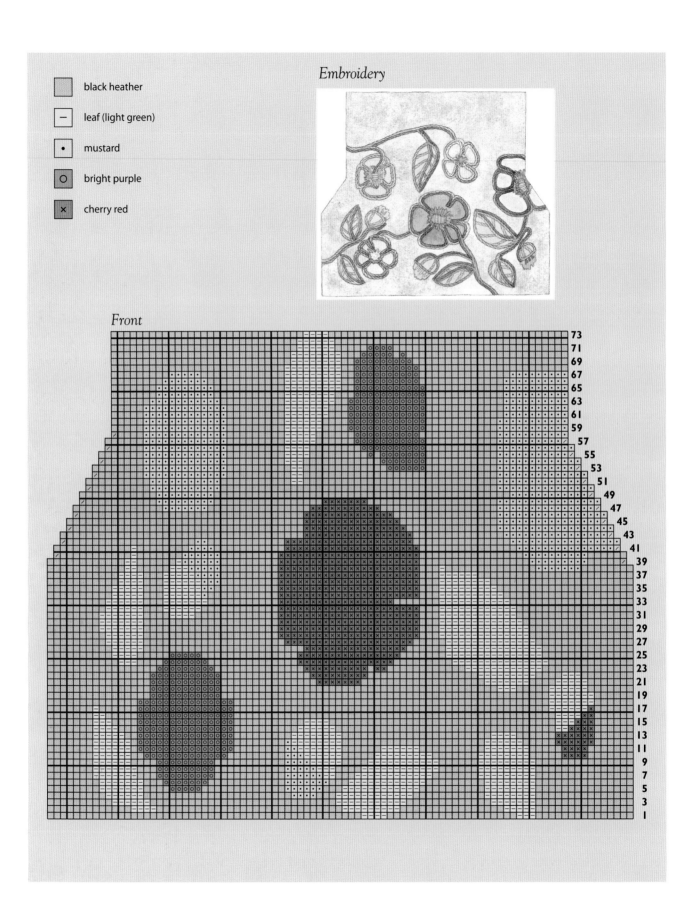

Embroidery

Front

black heather

leaf (light green)

mustard

bright purple

cherry red

73
71
69
67
65
63
61
59
57
55
53
51
49
47
45
43
41
39
37
35
33
31
29
27
25
23
21
19
17
15
13
11
9
7
5
3
1

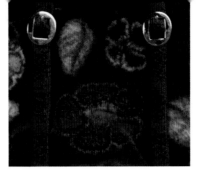

Notes

- A circular needle is used to accommodate the weight of the pieces in progress, but all pieces are worked back and forth in rows.
- The Front chart is worked in stockinette-stitch intarsia. Use a different length of yarn for each color section and cross yarns at the color changes to prevent holes from forming. Embroidered details are added after the knitting has been completed.
- Work embroidery with double strand of yarn threaded on a tapestry needle; see Glossary, pages 156–157, for embroidery stitches. Take care not to pucker the knitted fabric as you stitch. Working according to the directions below and following the diagram on page 142, use backstitches ¾" (2 cm) long for outlining motifs and stems, satin stitches for the center of each flower, and individual straight stitches of varying lengths radiating out from the flower centers.
- Depending on your individual felting results, the pieces may be slightly larger than shown on the schematic, but they will be trimmed exactly to the schematic measurements before being sewn together.

Back

With two strands of MC held tog, CO 81 sts. Work St st until piece measures 10½" (26.5 cm) from CO. Cont in St st, work k2tog at beg of next 20 rows—61 sts rem. Work even in St st until piece measures 26½" (67.5 cm) from CO. Loosely BO all sts.

Base

With two strands of MC held tog, CO 27 sts. Work St st until piece measures 33½" (85 cm) from CO. Loosely BO all sts.

Side Gussets (make 2)

With two strands of MC held tog, CO 27 sts. Work St st for 3 rows. Cont in St st, work k2tog at beg of next 2 rows—25 sts rem. Work 4 rows even. Rep the last 6 rows once more—23 sts rem. Work k2tog at beg of next 7 rows, then work 2 rows even—16 sts rem. Work k2tog at beg of next 6 rows, then work 2 rows even—10 sts rem. Work k2tog at beg of next 8 rows, then work 2 rows even—2 sts rem; 42 St st rows total; piece measures about 10½" (26.5 cm) from CO. Loosely BO all sts.

Straps (make 2)

With two strands of crimson held tog (use one strand each from two different skeins), CO 8 sts. Work in St st until piece measures about 8' 2" (249 cm), or until about 24" (61 cm) of yarn remains from whichever skein ends first. Loosely BO all sts.

Front

(*Note:* The front is intentionally worked slightly larger than the back to allow for any variation in the color-work gauge. After felting, it will be trimmed to the same size as the back.) With two strands of MC held tog, CO 91 sts. Work St st for 5 rows, beg and ending with a WS row. *Next row:* (RS) Beg with Row 1, and using the intarsia method, work Rows 1–73 of Front chart, decreasing where indicated—71 sts rem after completing Row 58; piece should measure about 19½" (49.5 cm) from CO after completing Row 73. When chart is finished, cont even with MC only until piece measures 33" (84 cm) from CO. Loosely BO all sts.

Finishing
Embroidery

Following illustration on page 142, outline the leaves and base of each flower bud using stem stitches (see Glossary, pages 156–157, for embroidery techniques) and dark grass green. Next to the dark grass green outlines, embroider a second line of stem stitches using crimson as shown. Work stem stitches in golden green for the veins in the leaves and the base of each flower bud. Outline the lower left purple flower twice with stem stitches; once with royal blue, once with light fuchsia. Work the flower center in satin stitches using bright blue and add radiating straight stitches in light fuchsia. Outline the mustard bud above the lower left purple flower twice with stem stitches, once with bright purple, and once with goldenrod; work straight stitches of varying lengths in goldenrod and pumpkin for the bud. Outline the upper left mustard flower twice with stem stitches, again with bright purple and goldenrod; work the flower center in dark grass green with radiating straight stitches in bright purple and goldenrod. Decorate the mustard bud at lower center with straight stitches of varying lengths in goldenrod. Outline the center cherry red flower with stem stitches in burnt red and light fuchsia; work the flower center in satin stitches with dark grass green, with radiating straight stitches in burnt red and pumpkin. Outline the purple flower at upper center twice in stem stitches with royal blue and leaf green; work the flower center in satin stitches with burnt red, with radiating straight stitches in leaf green. Decorate the cherry red bud at lower right with straight stitches of varying lengths in burnt red. Outline the mustard flower at upper right twice with stem stitches in burnt red and pumpkin; work the flower center in satin stitches with dark grass green, with radiating straight stitches in cherry red and pumpkin.

Felting

In preparation for felting, weave in all loose ends. To maintain color brightness, felt in three groups. First felt back, base, and gussets; then felt front. Felt the red straps in a pillowcase or mesh bag to prevent tangling around the agitator. Set the washing machine for a low water level and a normal cycle of hot-water wash followed by a cold-water rinse and spin cycle. Add 1 teaspoon of detergent and run

through one complete cycle. Repeat the wash-rinse cycle, but do not add detergent the second time, and remove the pieces before the final spin cycle. Pat and stretch as necessary to achieve the correct shape. You may need to work a little to get the strap edges straight—place each strap on an ironing board and use your hands to stretch it to a uniform width; if it is too wide in one area, place a damp cotton cloth over the wide portion and use a hot iron to coax it to shrink to the desired width. Lay all pieces flat on towels and allow to air-dry thoroughly; the pieces will continue to shrink as they dry.

Assembly

Cut each piece exactly to the dimensions shown on the schematic. The three sides of the side gusset pieces are not all exactly the same length; mark the top point of each triangle with a quilting pin so you can assemble the side gussets the correct way up. If necessary, use a disposable razor to lightly shave the fuzz off the front panel so that the design is clearer. You may also shave the right side of each

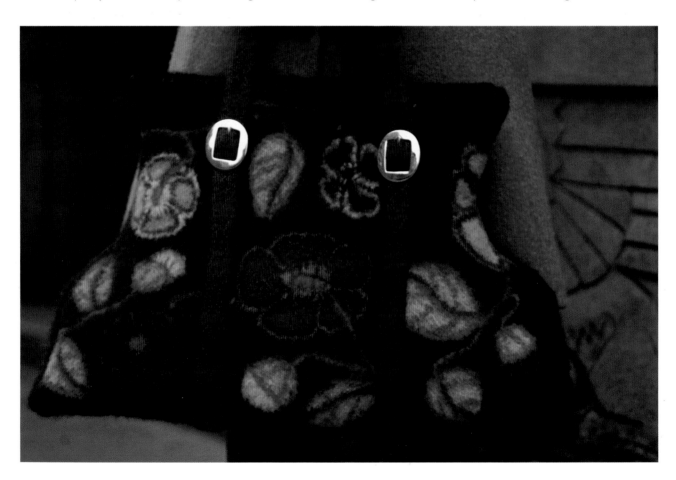

strap to create a smoother appearance; it is not necessary to shave the other pieces.

Seams

Sew pieces tog by hand or machine using ¼" (6 mm) seams all around, holding pieces with right sides facing so the seam allowances are on the wrong side of the finished satchel. Sew the bottom edge of each side gusset to short end of the base, taking care that the marked gusset points are pointing upwards. Sew the bottom edge of the back to one long side of the base, then sew the bottom edge of the front to the other long side of the base. Sew the lower straight selvedges of the back and front to the sides of the gussets. Sew the back and front tog at each side above gusset points to the top edge. Turn satchel right side out.

Frame

Assemble the hex-open frame according to manufacturer's instructions. Place assembled frame at the inside top of the satchel, turn the top edge down evenly over it about 1"–2" (2.5–5 cm) to enclose the frame, and pin in place. With embroidery floss threaded on a tapestry needle, sew all the way around the top opening to secure the frame.

Straps

Measure 8½" (21.5 cm) in from each side gusset seam along the seam joining the front and back to the base, and mark these four positions with pins. Measure 5¼" (13.5 cm) in from each side seam along the top edge and mark these four positions with pins. Center the first strap over one of the marked positions on the seam between the back and the base, leaving a 4" (10 cm) tail of strap extending beyond the bottom seam. Pinning the strap in place as you go, bring the strap straight across the base and center it over the marked position on the seam between the front and the base. Bring the strap straight up the front, center it over the marked position at the top edge, and stop pinning about 4½" (11.5 cm) down from the top. Avoid covering the main flower motifs with the strap; readjust the marked positions slightly and re-pin, if necessary. Slip one buckle onto the strap from the free end, oriented so the tongue of the buckle is pointing up and the right side of the buckle is facing out. Slide the buckle into place as shown in photograph, and continue pinning strap until you reach the top edge. Leaving about 12" (30.5 cm) free at top edge to form handle, center the strap over the other marked position at the top

edge and pin in place. Slip the second buckle onto the strap from the free end, oriented so the tongue is pointed up and right side is facing out as before. Bring the strap straight down the front and center it over the marked position at the bottom seam. Again, avoid covering any flower motifs and reposition if necessary. Bring the strap straight across the base and center it on the remaining marked position on the seam between the back and the base, leaving at least a 4" (10 cm) tail extending beyond the bottom seam. With red thread and a milliner's needle, use tiny running sts about 1⁄16" (2 mm) from the edge of the strap to sew strap to satchel, making sure to sew through all layers with each st. Center the second strap over one of the marked positions on the seam between the back and the base, leaving a 4" (10 cm) tail of strap extending beyond the bottom seam; these tails will be trimmed and joined later. Pinning the strap in place as you go, bring the strap straight up the back, and center it over the marked position at the top edge. Leaving the same amount of strap free at top edge to form a matching handle, center the strap over the other marked position at the top edge and pin in place. Bring the strap straight down the back and center it over the marked position at the bottom seam, leaving a 4" (10 cm) tail extending beyond the bottom seam. Stitch the second strap in place the same as the first. Carefully trim the tails of the front strap so the cut edges align exactly with the bottom seam. Trim the tails of the back strap to butt up against the cut ends of the front strap. With red thread and milliner's needle, use small stitches to sew the cut ends of straps tog. With crimson yarn threaded on a tapestry needle, work chain stitch embroidery over the whipstitches to cover them. Felt the chain stitching by steaming it with a hot iron held over a damp pressing cloth.

Feet

Following manufacturer's directions, attach 4 silver handbag feet to base of bag, placing 2 feet centered on each strap, and positioning each foot about 1½" (3.8 cm) in from the bottom seam.

If desired, cover the masonite board with fabric and place in bottom of satchel.

Union Square Market Pullover

Kate Gilbert

This flirty, yet comfortable sweater will take you from Saturday morning at the market to an afternoon coffee date. Worked in the softest alpaca, the contoured bodice gently follows your curves. The body is worked in the round from the bottom up, then the back and front are worked separately from the armholes to the neck. The sleeves are also worked in the round to the armholes and short-rows are used to shape the belled, slightly medieval sleeves along the way. A touch of contrasting color adds a fresh note at the neck and hem and highlights the sleeve points.

Finished Size

33½ (35½, 37, 40, 44)" (85 [90, 94, 101.5, 112] cm) bust circumference. Sweater shown measures 35½" (90 cm).

Yarn

Sportweight (#2 Fine).

Shown here: Plassard Alpaga (100% alpaca; 198 yd [181 m]/50 g): #202 wine red (MC), 7 (7, 7, 8, 9) skeins; #201 pink (CC), 2 skeins (all sizes).

Needles

Body and sleeves—size 3 (3 mm): 24" and 32" (60 and 80 cm) circular (cir) and set of 4 double-pointed (dpn). Bind-off—size 9 (5.5 mm): 1 straight. Adjust needle size if necessary to obtain the correct gauge.

Notions

Waste yarn for provisional cast-on; markers (m); removable markers or safety pins; tapestry needle; six ½" (1.3 cm) buttons for shoulders; one ⅞" (2.2 cm) button for front neck.

Gauge

27 stitches and 38 rows = 4" (10 cm) in stockinette stitch, worked in the round.

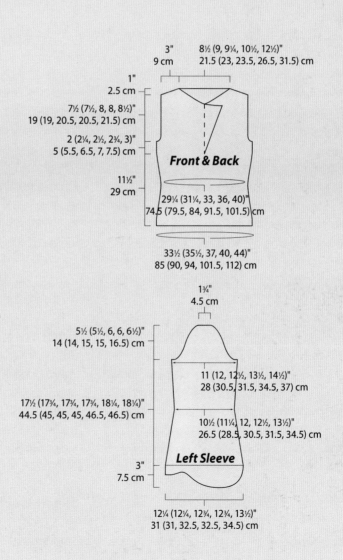

3"
9 cm

8½ (9, 9¼, 10½, 12½)"
21.5 (23, 23.5, 26.5, 31.5) cm

1"
2.5 cm

7½ (7½, 8, 8, 8½)"
19 (19, 20.5, 20.5, 21.5) cm

2 (2¼, 2½, 2¾, 3)"
5 (5.5, 6.5, 7, 7.5) cm

Front & Back

11½"
29 cm

29¼ (31¼, 33, 36, 40)"
74.5 (79.5, 84, 91.5, 101.5) cm

33½ (35½, 37, 40, 44)"
85 (90, 94, 101.5, 112) cm

1¾"
4.5 cm

5½ (5½, 6, 6, 6½)"
14 (14, 15, 15, 16.5) cm

11 (12, 12½, 13½, 14½)"
28 (30.5, 31.5, 34.5, 37) cm

17½ (17¾, 17¾, 17¾, 18¼, 18¼)"
44.5 (45, 45, 45, 46.5, 46.5) cm

10½ (11¼, 12, 12½, 13½)"
26.5 (28.5, 30.5, 31.5, 34.5) cm

Left Sleeve

3"
7.5 cm

12¼ (12¼, 12¾, 12¾, 13½)"
31 (31, 32.5, 32.5, 34.5) cm

Notes

- You may find it helpful to use a different-colored marker to indicate the beginning of the round.
- Measure length straight up along a single column of stitches; do not measure along the curved shaping lines.
- For the sleeve cuffs, each round begins at the center of the thumb edge of the hand so that the shallowest part of the cuff will fall toward the front of the sweater and the deepest part will fall at the back. After each cuff has been completed, the end-of-round marker for the sleeve is moved to its customary location, in line with the center of the underarm.

Lower Body

With CC, waste yarn, shorter cir needle, and using the invisible method (see page 17), CO 226 (238, 250, 270, 298) sts. Join for working in the rnd, being careful not to twist sts, and place marker (pm) for beg of rnd. Place a second marker in the first rnd after working 113 (119, 125, 135, 149) sts to mark other side "seam."

Hem

Knit until there are 9 rnds total in CC. Cut off CC. Carefully remove waste yarn and place sts from CO on smaller spare needle. Fold facing with WS of fabric touching. With MC and longer cir needle, close top edge of hem by working k2tog (1 st from main needle and 1 st from needle holding CO sts) to end of rnd—finished hem will measure about ½" (1.3 cm) high.

Cont with MC, work 4 rnds even. *Dec rnd:* *K1, ssk, knit to 3 sts before marker (m), k2tog, k1; rep from * once more—4 sts dec'd. Knit 5 rnds. Rep the last 6 rnds 6 more times—198 (210, 222, 242, 270) sts rem. Knit 16 rnds even—piece should measure about 7" (18 cm) from finished lower edge (fold line of hem). *Inc rnd:* *K2, M1L (see page 53), knit to 2 sts before m, M1R (see page 53) k2, slip marker (sl m); rep from * once more—4 sts inc'd. Knit 5 rnds. Rep the last 6 rnds 6 more times—226 (238, 250, 270, 298) sts; piece should measure about 11½" (29 cm) from finished lower edge.

Front Flap

Front Inc Rnd 1: K56 (59, 62, 67, 74), M1L, k1 at center front and mark this st with a removable marker or safety pin, M1R, knit to end—115 (121, 127, 137, 151) front sts; 113 (119, 125, 135, 149) back sts.

Work 3 rnds even.

Front Inc Rnd 2: Knit to 2 sts before marked center st, M1L, k5, M1R, knit to end—2 sts inc'd on front.

Work 3 rnds even.

Front Inc Rnd 3: Knit to 4 sts before marked center st, M1L, k9, M1R, knit to end—2 sts inc'd on front.

Work 3 rnds even—17 rnds completed above last waist shaping inc rnd. *Note:* Front flap shaping continues at the same time as other shaping; read the next section all the way through before proceeding. Cont in this manner, working incs on front every 4th rnd, working 2 more sts before marked center st, and knitting 4 more sts bet incs on each successive inc rnd. Work 2 (4, 6, 8, 10) more rnds—19 (21, 23, 25, 27) rnds completed above last waist inc rnd; 4 (4, 5, 5, 6) total front inc rnds completed; 121 (127, 135, 145, 161) front sts; piece measures 13½ (13¾, 14, 14¼, 14½)" (34.5 [35, 35.5, 36, 37] cm) from finished lower edge. Work a front inc rnd for sizes 35½" and 40" only in foll dividing rnd.

Divide for Front and Back

Work to 4 (5, 5, 5, 5) sts before side m, BO 8 (10, 10, 10, 10) sts for armhole, work in patt to 4 (5, 5, 5, 5) sts before end-of-rnd m, BO 8 (10, 10, 10, 10) sts for other armhole, removing end-of-rnd m when you come to it—113 (119, 125, 137, 151) front sts; 105 (109, 115, 125, 139) back sts; 13 (17, 17, 21, 21) knit sts bet incs on last front inc rnd completed.

Back

Rejoin yarn to 105 (109, 115, 125, 139) back sts with RS facing. Work St st back and forth in rows as foll: BO 2 sts at beg of next 2 (2, 4, 4, 4) rows, then BO 1 st at beg of foll 4 (4, 4, 6, 6) rows—97 (101, 103, 111, 125) sts rem. Work 2 rows even. BO 1 st at beg of next 2 rows—95 (99, 101, 109, 123) sts rem. Work even until armholes measure 7 (7, 7½, 7½, 8)" (18 [18, 19, 19, 20.5] cm) from dividing rnd, ending with a RS row.

Shape Shoulders

Work short-rows (see page 115) as foll:

Short-rows 1 and 2: Work to last 4 sts, wrap next st, turn.

Short-rows 3–8: Work to 5 sts before previous wrapped st, wrap next st, turn.

Top Edging

Break yarn. Sl all sts so next row will be a WS row, and join CC with WS facing. Work 9 rows St st across all sts, beg and ending with a WS row, and working all wraps tog with their wrapped sts on first row. With smaller spare needle, and WS facing, pick up a loop in each of the purl "bumps" along the color change; do not pick up and knit these sts; simply slip the smaller needle into each st. Fold hem with WS of fabric touching. With CC and larger straight needle, close top edging and bind off at the same time as foll: K2tog (1 st from main needle and 1 st from needle with picked-up sts), *k2tog (next st from each needle), pass first st on larger needle over the second st to BO 1 st loosely; rep from * to end, fasten off last st—finished top edging should measure about ½" (1.3 cm) high; armholes should measure about 7½ (7½, 8, 8, 8½)" (19 [19, 20.5, 20.5, 21.5] cm) above dividing rnd.

Front

Join yarn to 113 (119, 125, 137, 151) front sts with WS facing. *Note:* Center front shaping continues at same time as armhole shaping; read the next section all the way through before proceeding. Cont center front shaping as established, working inc row every other RS row (every 4th row). *At the same time* work armhole shaping as foll: BO 2 sts at beg of next 2 (2, 4, 4, 4) rows, then BO 1 st at beg of foll 4 (4, 4, 6, 6) rows, work 2 rows even, then BO 1 st at beg of next 2 rows, ending with a RS row—109 (113, 117, 127, 143) sts rem; 10 (10, 14, 16, 16) sts BO for armhole shaping; 6 (4, 6, 6, 8) sts inc'd at front; 7 (7, 8, 9, 10) total inc rnds/rows worked at front; 25 (25, 29, 33, 37) knit sts bet incs on last front inc row completed. Cont to shape front neck, work 39 (39, 41, 39, 43) more rows, ending with a WS row—armholes measure about 5 (5, 5½, 5½, 6)" (12.5 [12.5, 14, 14, 15] cm)—127 (133, 137, 147, 163) sts; 16 (17, 18, 19, 20) total inc rnds/rows worked at front; 61 (65, 69, 73, 77) knit sts bet incs on last front inc row completed. Last row completed is 3rd (1st, 3rd, 1st, 3rd) row worked even foll last front inc row.

Shape Left Front V-Neck

Cont working front incs as established and *at the same time* shape left front neck as foll:

Short-row 1: (RS) Work in patt to 2 sts before marked center st, wrap next st, turn.

Short-row 2: Purl to end.

Short-row 3: Work in patt to 3 (3, 4, 4, 4) sts before previous wrapped st, wrap next st, turn.

Short-row 4: Purl to end.

Short-row 5: Work in patt to 3 (4, 4, 4, 5) sts before previous wrapped st, wrap next st, turn.

Short-row 6: Purl to end.

Short-rows 7–18: Rep Short-rows 3–6 three more times.

Short-row 19: Work in patt to 3 (3, 4, 4, 4) sts before previous wrapped st, wrap next st, turn—19 rows completed at left front armhole edge from beg of neck shaping; armhole measures about 7 (7, 7½, 7½, 8)" (18 [18, 19, 19, 20.5] cm) from dividing rnd; 137 (143, 147, 157, 173) sts; 21 (22, 23, 24, 25) total inc rnds/rows worked at front; 81 (85, 89, 93, 97) knit sts bet incs on last front inc row completed; 2 (0, 2, 0, 2) rows worked even after last front inc row. Do not work any more front inc rows.

Short-row 20: Purl to last 4 sts before armhole edge, wrap next st, turn.

Short-row 21: Knit to 3 (3, 4, 4, 4) sts before previous wrapped st at center front, turn.

Short-rows 22 and 24: Purl to 5 sts before previous wrapped st at armhole edge, wrap next st, turn.

Short-row 23: Knit to 3 (4, 4, 4, 5) sts before previous wrapped st at center front, wrap next st, turn.

Short-row 25: Knit to 3 (3, 4, 4, 4) sts before previous wrapped st at center front, wrap next st, turn.

Short-row 26: Purl to 5 sts before previous wrapped st at armhole edge, wrap next st, break yarn.

Shape Right Front V-Neck

With RS facing, sl sts to 2 sts past marked st at center front, and join yarn. Cont working front incs as established until there are a total of 21 (22, 23, 24, 25) front inc rnds/rows as for left front neck and *at the same time* shape right front neck using short-rows as foll:

Short-row 1: (RS) Work in patt to end, turn.

Short-row 2: Purl to 3 (3, 4, 4, 4) sts before st where yarn was joined at center front, wrap next st, turn.

Short-row 3: Work in patt to end.

Short-row 4: Purl to 3 (4, 4, 4, 5) sts before previous wrapped st, wrap next st, turn.

armhole edge, wrap next st, break yarn.

Sl all sts so next row will be a WS row, and join CC with WS facing. Work hemmed top edging as for back.

Left Sleeve

With CC, waste yarn, shorter cir or dpn, and using the invisible method, CO 92 (92, 96, 96, 100) sts. Join for working in the rnd, being careful not to twist sts, and place marker (pm) for beg of rnd. Place a second marker in the first rnd after working 46 (46, 48, 48, 50) sts to mark center of rnd.

Hem

Knit until there are 9 rnds total in CC. Using CC, close hem as for lower hemmed edge of back—finished cuff hem should measure about ½" (1.3 cm) high. Cont in short-rows with CC to shape curved edge of cuff as foll:

Short-row 1: (RS) Knit to 4 sts before end-of-rnd m, wrap next st, turn.

Short-row 2: Purl to 4 sts before end-of rnd m, wrap next st, turn.

Short-row 3: Knit to 4 sts before previous wrapped st, wrap next st, turn.

Short-row 4: Purl to 4 sts before previous wrapped st, wrap next st, turn.

Short-row 5: Knit to 3 sts before center m, k2tog, k2, ssk, knit to 3 sts before previous wrapped st, wrap next st, turn—90 (90, 94, 94, 98) sts rem.

Short-row 6: Purl to 3 sts before previous wrapped st, wrap next st, turn.

Short-row 7: Knit to 3 sts before center m, k2tog, k2, ssk, knit to 2 sts before previous wrapped st, wrap next st, turn—88 (88, 92, 92, 96) sts rem.

Short-rows 8 and 10: Purl to 2 sts before wrapped st, wrap next st, turn.

Short-row 9: Knit to 2 sts before wrapped st, wrap next st, turn.

Short-row 11: Knit to 3 sts before center m, k2tog, k2, ssk, knit to 2 sts before previous wrapped st, wrap next st, turn—86 (86, 90, 90, 94) sts rem.

Short-rows 12 and 14: Purl to 2 sts before previous wrapped st, wrap next st, turn.

Short-row 13: Knit to 2 sts before previous wrapped st, wrap next st, turn.

Short-row 15: Knit to 3 sts before center m, k2tog, k2, ssk,

Short-row 5: Work in patt to end.

Short-rows 6–17: Rep Short-rows 2–5 three more times.

Short-row 18: Purl to 3 (3, 4, 4, 4) sts before previous wrapped st, wrap next st, turn.

Short-row 19: Work in patt to end—19 rows completed at right front armhole edge from beg of neck shaping; armhole measures about 7 (7, 7½, 7½, 8)" (18 [18, 19, 19, 20.5] cm) from dividing rnd; 137 (143, 147, 157, 173) sts; 21 (22, 23, 24, 25) total inc rnds/rows worked at front; 81 (85, 89, 93, 97) knit sts bet incs on last front inc row completed; 2 (0, 2, 0, 2) rows worked even after last front inc row. Do not work any more front inc rows.

Short-row 20: Purl to 3 (3, 4, 4, 4) sts before previous wrapped st at center front, wrap next st, turn.

Short-row 21: Knit to 4 sts before armhole edge, wrap next st, turn.

Short-row 22: Purl to 3 (4, 4, 4, 5) sts before previous wrapped st at center front, wrap next st, turn.

Short-rows 23 and 25: Knit to 5 sts before previous wrapped st at armhole edge, wrap next st, turn.

Short-row 24: Purl to 3 (3, 4, 4, 4) sts before previous wrapped st at center front, wrap next st, turn.

Short-row 25: Knit to 5 sts before previous wrapped st at

knit to 3 sts before wrapped st, wrap next st, turn—84 (84, 88, 88, 92) sts rem.

Short-rows 16, 18, and 20: Purl to 3 sts before wrapped st, wrap next st, turn.

Short-row 17: Knit to 3 sts before wrapped st, wrap next st, turn.

Short-row 19: Knit to 3 sts before center m, k2tog, k2, ssk, knit to 3 sts before previous wrapped st, wrap next st, turn—82 (82, 86, 86, 90) sts rem.

Short-row 21: Knit to 4 sts before previous wrapped st, wrap next st, turn.

Short-row 22: Purl to 4 sts before previous wrapped st, wrap next st, turn—cuff should measure about ½" (1.3 cm) from finished lower edge at each end of rnd, and about 3" (7.5 cm) from finished lower edge in the center, measured along the center dec line.

Cut off CC. Join MC and knit 1 rnd across all sts, working wrapped sts tog with their wraps, and removing center m as you come to it. Remove end-of-rnd m, k21 (21, 22, 22, 23), replace m for new end-of-rnd aligned with center of underarm. *Work even in St st with MC for 2 (3½, 3½, 11, 11)" (5 [9, 9, 28, 28] cm). *Next rnd:* Dec 1 (dec 1, dec 1, dec 1, inc 1) st at each end of rnd—2 sts dec'd for 4 smallest sizes; 2 sts inc'd for largest size. Rep from * 4 (2, 2, 0, 0) more times—72 (76, 80, 84, 92) sts; sleeve measures about 10½ (11, 11, 11, 11)" (26.5 [28, 28, 28, 28] cm) from color change at top of cuff. **Work even in St st with MC for 6¼ (3, 3, 2, 2)" (16 [7.5, 7.5, 5, 5] cm). *Next rnd:* Inc 1 st at each end of rnd—2 sts inc'd. Rep from ** 0 (1, 1, 2, 2) more time(s)—74 (80, 84, 90, 98) sts; sleeve measures about 16¾ (17, 17, 17, 17)" (42.5 [43, 43, 43, 43] cm) from color change at top of cuff. Work even until piece measures 17 (17¼, 17¼, 17¾, 17¾)" (43 [44, 44, 45, 45] cm) from color change at top of cuff, ending 4 (5, 5, 5, 5) sts before end-of-rnd m on last rnd.

Shape Cap

BO 8 (10, 10, 10, 10) sts, removing m as you come to it, work to end—66 (70, 74, 80, 88) sts rem. Working back and forth in rows, BO 2 sts at beg of next 2 (2, 4, 4, 4) rows, then BO 1 st at beg of foll 4 (4, 4, 6, 6) rows—58 (62, 62, 66, 74) sts rem. Work 4 (2, 4, 2, 2) rows even. *BO 1 st at beg of next 2 rows, work 2 rows even; rep from * 4 (6, 4, 3, 3) more times—48 (48, 52, 58, 66) sts rem. BO 1 st at beg of next 14 (4, 14, 16, 18) rows, then BO 2 sts at beg of next 4 (6, 6, 8, 8) rows, then BO

3 sts at beg of next 2 (4, 2, 2, 4) rows, then BO 4 sts at beg of next 2 rows—12 sts rem; cap measures about 5½ (5½, 6, 6, 6½)" (14 [14, 15, 15, 16.5] cm). BO all sts.

Right Sleeve

Work as for left sleeve until all short-rows of cuff have been completed—82 (82, 86, 86, 90) sts rem. Cut off CC. Join MC and knit 1 rnd across all sts, working wrapped sts tog with their wraps, and removing center m as you come to it. Remove end-of-rnd m, k61 (61, 64, 64, 67), replace m for new end of rnd aligned with center of underarm. Complete as for left sleeve.

Finishing

Block to measurements, arranging front flap by folding it exactly along the centerline, then carefully folding it toward the left shoulder as shown in photograph. Identify the left and right sleeves by checking that the longest part of the cuff falls to the back of the garment. With yarn threaded on a tapestry needle, sew sleeves into armholes, matching first BO row of sleeve cap to center of underarm shaping, and with folded edges of front and back just touching (not overlapping). Do not sew shoulder seams. Weave in loose ends. Mark positions for 3 buttons on each front shoulder, 1" (2.5), 2" (5 cm), and 3" (7.5 cm) in from armhole seam. Sew small buttons to front shoulders at marked positions.

Button Loops

Mark positions for 3 button loops on each back shoulder opposite front buttons. Make button loops at edge of back shoulders as foll: Thread about 30" (76 cm) of CC on tapestry needle. Bring needle through the fold line 1 st to the side of marked position, remove needle, and pull the two yarn ends even. With a book or other heavy weight to hold the garment still, make a twisted cord (see Glossary, page 157) with the two ends. Thread the cord on tapestry needle and bring needle through the fold line 1 st on the other side of marked position (2 sts away from where you started). Adjust the length of the button loop cord to accommodate button, tie a knot to secure button loop, weave in ends. Rep for rem 5 button loops. Make a larger loop on WS exactly at center front, anchored in the hem BO row of top edging. Try on sweater, arrange front flap for best effect, and mark position for large front button. Sew on large button.

Beyond the Basics: GRAFTING

based on an article by Charlotte Morris

Grafting, often called Kitchener stitch, is a technique for invisibly joining together the live stitches of two separate pieces of knitting. It is worked with the knitting yarn threaded on a tapestry needle. The threaded needle is worked back and forth between the two sets of live stitches to join them in a way that mimics the sinuous path—like old-fashioned ribbon candy—of a row of knitting, connecting the loops (stitches) of the two knitted pieces. A grafted seam is as soft and flexible as a row of knitting; there is no seam allowance to add bulk. However, grafted joins are not as strong as traditional seams because the sinuous path of the grafted stitches has the same amount of give as a row of knitting.

Grafting is commonly used to join the top loops of one piece to the top loops of another piece, which we'll call "top-to-top" grafting. Top-to-top grafting is used to close off the fingertips of mittens or the toes of socks. It is also traditionally used to join the shoulders of Fair Isle sweaters and the underarms of sweaters worked in the round from the bottom up. It is important to note that there is a half-stitch displacement at each end of the grafted seam because one set of stitches is "upside down" in relationship to the other. However, in most cases, this displacement can be concealed in a seam. This is the technique used join the underarm seams on Stripes Go Round (page 48) and Burma Rings (page 112), and to join the front bands on the Man's Brioche Vest (page 118).

Many knitters also rely on grafting when they lengthen or shorten the body or sleeves of a garment that has already been knitted. They cut off the edging or border, add or subtract the desired number of rows of knitting, then graft the edging or border back in place, joining the top loops of the stitches on one piece to the bottom loops of the stitches on the other. This technique, which we'll call "top-to-bottom" grafting, maintains the integrity of the direction of knitting (all of the stitches are worked in the same direction) and makes use of the edging or border already knitted. There is no stitch displacement in this type of grafting because the stitches on both pieces have the same orientation. When joining pieces top to bottom, grafting can be invisible in many knit/purl patterns; however when joining pieces top to top, its uses are much more limited and it is invisible only in stockinette, reverse stockinette, and garter stitch patterns.

Getting Started

Place each group of stitches to be grafted onto a separate knitting needle. The knitting needles may be held parallel in one hand while the grafting is done with the other hand, or the two pieces can be laid flat on a table, one above the other, with the knitting needles between them and facing in the same direction.

Use the yarn attached to one of the pieces, if possible, or cut a piece of working yarn about four times the length of the row to be joined, and thread this yarn on a tapestry needle. (The following illustrations show grafting from right to left, but if you're left-handed, you may prefer to work from left to right; just ignore the illustrations and follow the text—the instructions are the same for working either direction.) Follow the steps below for the type of stitch pattern you want to imitate in the grafting.

Stockinette Stitch
Joining Pieces Top to Top

Step 1: Bring the threaded needle up (from back to front) through the first stitch on the lower needle, then up (from back to front) through the first stitch on the upper needle (Figure 1).

Step 2: Bring the threaded needle down (front to back) through the first stitch on the lower needle (the stitch entered in Step 1), then up (back to front) through the next stitch (Figure 2).

Step 3: Bring the threaded needle down (front to back) through the first stitch on the upper needle (the stitch entered in Step 1), then up (back to front) through the next stitch (Figure 3).

Repeat Steps 2 and 3, ending by bringing the threaded needle down (front to back) through the last stitch on the lower needle, then down (front to back) through the last stitch on the upper needle (Figure 4).

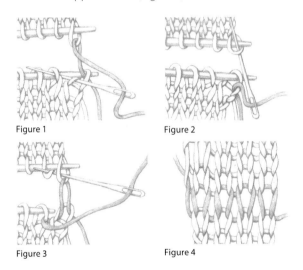

Figure 1

Figure 2

Figure 3

Figure 4

Joining Pieces Top to Bottom

Step 1: Bring the threaded needle up (from back to front) through the first stitch on the lower needle (Figure 1).

Step 2: Bring the threaded needle down (from front to back) through the first loop (or behind the cut yarn end if it's at this end of the row) on the upper needle, then up (back to front) through the next loop on the upper needle (Figure 2).

Step 3: Bring the threaded needle down (front to back) through the first stitch on the lower needle (the stitch entered in Step 1), then up (back to front) through the next stitch (Figure 3).

Step 4: Bring the threaded needle down (front to back) through the first loop on the upper needle (the loop entered in Step 2), then up (back to front) through the next loop (Figure 4). (*Note:* For the last loop on the upper needle, be sure loop stays twisted, or if the working yarn connected to the stitches is at this end of row, take grafting yarn around it from back to front.)

Repeat Steps 3 and 4, ending by bringing the threaded needle down (front to back) through the last stitch on the lower needle (Figure 5).

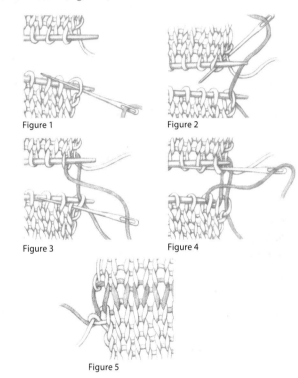

Figure 1

Figure 2

Figure 3

Figure 4

Figure 5

Reverse Stockinette Stitch

To graft two reverse stockinette-stitch pieces (i.e., to mimic purl stitches), simply turn the pieces to their wrong (knit) sides and follow the instructions for grafting stockinette stitch.

Garter Stitch
Joining Pieces Top to Top

This example has the lower piece ending with a RS row (knit loops nearest needle) and the upper piece ending with a WS row (purl bumps nearest needle).

Step 1: Bring the threaded needle down (from front to back) through the first stitch on the lower needle, then up (back to front) through the first stitch on the upper needle (Figure 1).

Step 2: Bring the threaded needle up (back to front) through the first stitch on the lower needle (the stitch entered in Step 1), then down (front to back) through the next stitch (Figure 2).

Step 3: Bring the threaded needle down (front to back) through the first stitch on the upper needle (the stitch entered in Step 1), then up (back to front) through the next stitch (Figure 3).

Repeat Steps 2 and 3, ending by bringing the threaded needle up (back to front) through the last stitch on the lower needle, then down (front to back) through the last stitch on the upper needle (Figure 4).

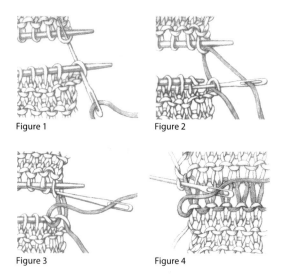

Figure 1 Figure 2

Figure 3 Figure 4

Joining Pieces Top to Bottom

This example has the lower piece ending with a WS row (purl bumps nearest the needle) and the upper piece ending with a RS row (knit loops nearest the needle).

Step 1: Bring the threaded needle up (back to front) through the first stitch on the lower needle (Figure 1).

Step 2: Bring the threaded needle up (back to front) through the first loop on the upper needle (or in front of the cut yarn end, if it's at this end of the needle), then down (front to back) through the next loop (Figure 2).

Step 3: Bring the threaded needle down (front to back) into the first stitch on the lower needle (the stitch entered in Step 1), then up (back to front) through the next stitch (Figure 3).

Step 4: Bring the threaded needle up (back to front) through the first loop on the upper needle (the loop entered

in Step 2), then down (front to back) through the next loop (Figure 4).

Repeat Steps 3 and 4, ending by bringing the threaded needle down (front to back) through the last stitch on the lower needle (Figure 5).

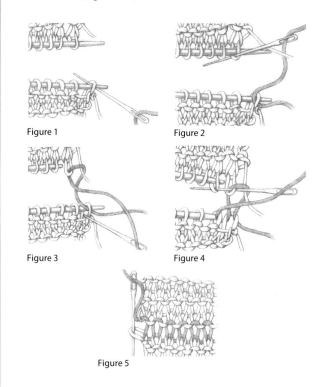

Figure 1 Figure 2

Figure 3 Figure 4

Figure 5

Ribbing

The directions here are given for k1, p1 ribbing, but the method can be applied to any ribbing and many knit/purl pattern stitches, such as moss or seed stitch.

Joining Pieces Top to Top

Simply divide the stitches on each piece between two needles—the knit stitches on one needle and the purl stitches on the other. Graft the sets of knit stitches together as described for stockinette stitch on page 153, then turn the work over so the purl stitches appear as knit stitches and do the same for them. This technique reduces the elasticity of the ribbing because the grafting yarn makes two passes across the piece, each pass connecting every other stitch, in the case of k1, p1 ribbing, instead of one pass connecting every stitch. Also, a zigzag line will form at the join, due to the half-stitch displacement on pieces worked in opposite directions.

Joining Pieces Top to Bottom

Notice that each loop on the upper needle is actually two halves of two different stitches—half of a purl stitch and half of a knit stitch. The knit side of each loop will tend to turn out and away from the knit stitch it belongs to (Figure 1) and will need to be forced back inward toward the knit stitch (Figure 2) before grafting as illustrated below—you may find it helpful to take the loops off the needle to do this.

Figure 1   Figure 2

The example here begins with a knit stitch.

Step 1: Bring the threaded needle up (back to front) through the first stitch on the lower needle (Figure 1).

Step 2: Bring the threaded needle down (front to back) through the first loop (or behind cut yarn end) on the upper needle, then up (back to front) through the second loop (Figure 2).

Step 3: Bring the threaded needle down (front to back) through the first stitch on the lower needle (the stitch entered in Step 1), then down (front to back) through the next stitch (Figure 3).

Step 4: Bring the threaded needle up (back to front) through the first loop on the upper needle (the stitch entered in Step 2), then down (front to back) through the next loop (Figure 4).

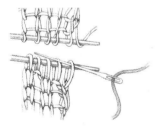

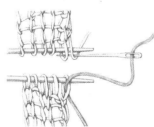

Figure 1   Figure 2

Step 5: Bring the threaded needle up (back to front) through the first stitch on the lower needle, then up (back to front) through the next stitch (Figure 5).

Step 6: Bring the threaded needle down (front to back) through the first loop on the upper needle, then up (back to front) through the next loop (Figure 6).

Repeat Steps 3–6. If the last stitch is a purl stitch, end after Step 4 by bringing the seaming yarn up (back to front) through this stitch. If the last stitch is a knit stitch, end after Step 6 by bringing the seaming yarn down (front to back) through this stitch.

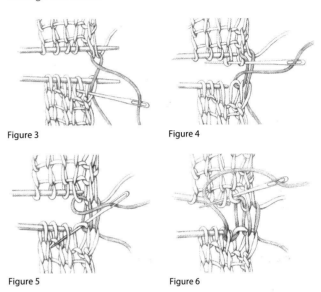

Figure 3   Figure 4

Figure 5   Figure 6

TIPS for Grafting

✳ When grafting a color-work pattern, choose a single-color row for the grafting, if possible.

✳ When grafting a textured stitch pattern, choose a stockinette-stitch row for the grafting, if possible.

✳ As you graft, you can either slip each live stitch from the needle as the grafting needle first enters it or wait until after the grafted stitch is complete. You may find it easier to drop the stitch from the knitting needle first, then use the tip of the grafting needle to adjust the tension if necessary.

✳ When grafting a border to the body or sleeve of a garment, where possible, work the grafted row close to the border where there is a visual change in pattern anyway. A slight difference in tension will not be as noticeable.

✳ Do not graft large areas with hairy yarns like mohair, as the fuzzy fibers tangle together; or novelty yarns like gimp, bouclé, or knop, whose nubs do not travel smoothly when pulled through stitch after stitch across a row. For small joins such as mitten and sock tops, or underarms, though, it may be possible to nurse such yarn through with care.

Glossary of Terms and Techniques

Abbreviations

beg	begin(s); beginning
BO	bind off
CC	contrast color
cm	centimeter(s)
cn	cable needle
CO	cast on
cont	continue(s); continuing
dec(s)	decrease(s); decreasing
dpn	double-pointed needles
foll	follow(s); following
g	gram(s)
inc(s)	increase(s); increasing
k	knit
k1f&b	knit into the front and back of same st
kwise	knitwise, as if to knit
m	marker(s)
MC	main color
mm	millimeter(s)
M1	make one (increase)
p	purl
p1f&b	purl into front and back of same st
patt(s)	pattern(s)
psso	pass slipped st over
pwise	purlwise, as if to purl
rem	remain(s); remaining
rep	repeat(s); repeating
rev St st	reverse stockinette stitch
rnd(s)	round(s)
RS	right side
sl	slip
sl st	slip st (slip 1 st pwise unless otherwise indicated)
ssk	slip, slip, knit (decrease)
St st	stockinette stitch
tbl	through back loop
tog	together
WS	wrong side
wyb	with yarn in back
wyf	with yarn in front
yd	yard(s)
yo	yarnover
*	repeat starting point
* *	repeat all instructions between asterisks
( )	alternate measurements and/or instructions
[ ]	work instructions as a group a specified number of times

Bind-Offs
(see pages 29–31)

Blocking
(see pages 38–39)

Cast-Ons
(see pages 15–17)

Crochet
Crochet Chain (ch)
Make a slipknot and place it on crochet hook if there isn't a loop already on the hook. *Yarn over hook and draw through loop on hook. Repeat from * for the desired number of stitches. To fasten off, cut yarn and draw end through last loop formed.

Single Crochet (sc)
*Insert hook into the second chain from the hook or the next stitch, yarn over hook and draw through a loop, yarn over hook (Figure 1), and draw it through both loops on hook (Figure 2). Repeat from * for the desired number of stitches.

Figure 1   Figure 2

Slip Stitch Crochet
*Insert hook into stitch, yarn over hook and draw a loop through both the stitch and the loop already on hook. Repeat from * for the desired number of stitches.

Decreases
(see pages 61–63)

Embroidery
Backstitch
Bring threaded needle out from back to front between the

first two knitted stitches you want to cover. *Insert the needle at the right edge of the right stitch to be covered, then bring it back out at the left edge of the second stitch. Insert the needle again between these two stitches and bring it out between the next two to be covered. Repeat from *.

Duplicate Stitch

Bring the threaded needle out from back to front at the base of the V of the knitted stitch you want to cover. Working right to left, *pass needle in and out under the stitch in the row above it and back into the base of the same stitch. Bring needle back out at the base of the V in the next stitch to be covered. Repeat from * for the desired number of stitches.

Satin Stitch

Work straight stitches (below) closely spaced and in graduated lengths as desired to completely cover the background.

Stem Stitch

*Bring threaded needle out of knitted background from back to front at the center of a knitted stitch. Insert the needle into the upper right edge of the next stitch to the right, then out again at the center of the stitch below. Repeat from * as desired.

Straight Stitch

*Bring threaded needle out of knitted background from back to front at the base of the stitches to be covered, then in from front to back at the tip of the stitches to be covered (Figure 1). Repeat from *, working in straight lines (Figure 2) or radiating from a point as desired.

Figure 1

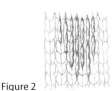

Figure 2

Grafting
(see pages 152–155)

Increases
(see pages 51–53)

Seams
(see pages 127–133)

Short-Rows
(see pages 115–117)

Twisted Cord

Cut several lengths of yarn about five times the desired finished cord length. Fold the strands in half to form two equal groups. Anchor the strands at the fold by looping them over a doorknob. Holding one group in each hand, twist each group tightly in a clockwise direction until they begin

to kink. Put both groups in one hand, then release them, allowing them to twist around each other counterclockwise. Smooth out the twists so that they are uniform along the length of the cord. Knot the ends.

Zipper

With right side facing and zipper closed, pin zipper to fronts so front edges cover the zipper teeth. With contrasting thread and right side facing, baste zipper in place close to teeth (Figure 1). Turn work over and with matching sewing thread and needle, stitch outer edges of zipper to wrong side of fronts

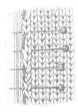

Figure 1

(Figure 2), being careful to follow a single column of stitches in the knitting to keep zipper straight. Turn work back to right side facing, and with matching sewing thread, sew knitted fabric close to teeth (Figure 3). Remove basting.

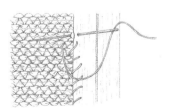

Figure 2

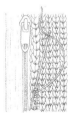

Figure 3

Sources

Alpaca Yarn Company
144 Roosevelt Ave., Bay 1
York, PA 07401
www.thealpacayarnco.com
  Suri Elegance

**B. Brookman Imports Inc./
Plassard**
105 Dixon Dr.
Chestertown, MD 21620
www.plassdyarnusa.com
  Plassard Alpaga

Baabajoes Wool
(this company is no longer in
business)
NZ WoolPak 10-Ply (discontinued)

Cascade Yarns
PO Box 58168
1224 Andover Park East
Tukwila, WA 98188
www.cascadeyarns.com
  Cascade 220

Classic Elite Yarns
122 Western Ave.
Lowell, MA 01851
www.classiceliteyarns.com
  Montera

CNS Yarns/Mission Falls
100 Walnut, Door 4
Champlain, NY 12919
www.missionfalls.com
In Canada:
1050 8th St.
Grand-Mère, QC G9T 4L4
  Mission Falls 1824 Wool

Diamond Yarn
9697 St. Laurent, Ste. 101
Montreal, QC H3L 2N1
and
115 Martin Ross, Unit #3
Toronto, ON Canada M3J 2L9
www.diamondyarn.com

Goddess Yarns
2911 Kavanaugh Blvd.
Little Rock, AR 72205
www.goddessyarns.com
  Phoebe

JCA Inc./Jo Sharp/Reynolds
35 Scales Ln.
Townsend, MA 01469
www.jacrafts.com
  Jo Sharp Classic DK Wool
  Reynolds Cabaret (discontinued)
  Reynolds Lite Lopi

Knit One, Crochet Too Inc.
91 Tandberg Tr., Unit 6,
Windham, ME 04062
www.knitonecrochettoo.com
  Douceur et Soie

**Knitting Fever Inc.
Debbie Bliss**
35 Debevoise Ave.
Roosevelt, NY 11575
www.knittingfever.com
In Canada: Diamond Yarn
  Debbie Bliss Cashmerino
  Super Chunky

**LanaKnits Designs Hemp
For Knitting**
320 Vernon St. Ste. 3B
Nelson, BC, Canada V1L 4V4
www.lanaknits.com
  All Hemp Hemp3

Louet North America
808 Commerce Park Dr.
Ogdensburg, NY 13669
www.louet.com
In Canada:
RR #4
Prescott, ON K0E 1T0
  Euroflax Sport Weight
  Gems Sport Weight

Muench Yarns Inc./GGH
1323 Scott St.
Petaluma CA 94954-1135
www.muenchyarns.com
In Canada: Oberlyn Yarns
  GGH Mystik
  Muench Bergamo (discontinued)
  Muench Sir Galli

Needful Yarns/Lana Gatto
4476 Chesswood Dr.,
Unit 10–11
Toronto, ON
Canada M3J 2B9
www.needfulyarnsinc.com
  Lana Gatto VIP

Oberlyn Yarns
5640 Rue Valcourt
Brossard, QC
Canada J4W 1C5
www.muenchyarns.com

Patons/Spinrite
320 Livingstone Ave. South
Listowel, ON
Canada N4W 3H3
  Classic Wool (discontinued)

South West Trading Company
918 S. Park Ln., Ste. 102
Tempe, AZ 85281
www.soysilk.com
  Bamboo

Westminster Fibers/Jaeger
165 Ledge St.
Nashua, NH 03060
www.westminsterfibers.com
In Canada:
Diamond Yarn
  Jaeger Extra Fine Merino
  Double Knitting

Yarns International
PO Box 467
Cabin John, MD 20818-0467
www.yarnsinternational.com
  Shetland 2000

Index

Join the Best of Interweave Knits Knitalong!

Share your finished objects, helpful tips, and ideas for variations on the patterns from the book at **bestofknits.com**

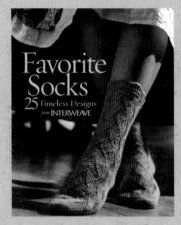